# Sonoita Seasons

## Recipes from Karen's Wine Country Café

*This book is dedicated to Mary, whose help was appreciated more than she will ever know, and to the physicians and staff at University Medical Center, Arizona Cancer Center, whose kindness and caring meant so much during a very difficult time. Thank you!*

Published by Karen and Harold Callaghan.

ISBN: 0-615-11660-4
Library of Congress: 00-105820

Sonoita Seasons by Karen Callaghan
Food Photography by Thomas Veneklasen
Scenic Photography by Jay W. Smith
Art Direction & Graphic Design by Paula Schaper of WestWordVision
Printed and bound in Korea

# Our Sincere Thanks To The Following:

How to thank all those wonderful people who have contributed to this project? Such a difficult task because there are so many to whom we feel a great debt of gratitude.

Our guests. We always felt our restaurant was an extension of our home and the guests who visited...our friends. They truly were the joy and delight we felt while we were part of Karen's. Thank you!

Paula Schaper of WestWordVision who brought it all together.....a wizard, at least!

Tom Veneklasen and Allen Russ, his assistant, for their expertise in the food photography. We laughed and said we dreaded the food photog- raphy sessions but when it was over we felt it had been a great big party. What fun!

Jay and Sandy Smith, two dear friends, who supported us so much while we had the restaurant and provided the beautiful scenic photography we needed for this endeavor. Our many and heartfelt thanks!

And to our family...always the most important part of our lives!

Mom, aka Ev, for her example in showing us the beauty of food presented in an artistic manner. Kevin and Tami and our grandsons Patrick and Ryan, Kent and Lisa and our granddaughters Caitlin and Claire. Their love and support kept us going through all the ups and downs. We love you!

Mom and Dad

*Karen and Harold*

# *Contents*

# *Our Humble Beginnings*

*Diners at the original Karen's Wine Country Café in Elgin, AZ.*
Photo: Lawrence Cheek

The idea to start a restaurant of light. We (our son Kent, front porch one balmy evening featuring pork tenderloin medalfinished with a port wine sauce, came to us with almost the speed Harold and I) were sitting on our having a candlelight dinner, lions crusted with hazelnuts, drinking a marvelous red wine when Kent said, "Gee, mom, you ought to do a restaurant." We looked at each other and said, "Let's do it!"

We already owned a building, which had been an Italian restaurant that had a 1950's dated look. All we had to do was remodel it and join the ranks of other martyrs who are willing to work extremely long, hard hours for the joy of feeding people.

Our philosophy regarding each course and each item of a course was that each one should be able to stand on its own merit. That meant that our guests should enjoy each as if it was the entrée and would be judged on its own. This philosophy has carried through all of our endeavors. We were never satisfied and were always striving to bring the highest quality to our guests.

There was another consideration for opening a restaurant. We had already planted a small, experimental, wine grape vineyard and were preparing to plant another, larger one. What better relationship than a winery to a restaurant. Thus began our odyssey of eight years into a world we knew virtually nothing about. We have often laughed and said maybe that was the appeal of our cafés. They were not like anything anyone had ever seen. We decided to do what we liked most about restaurants we visited and would hope that it would appeal to others. It did!

This cookbook is an attempt to share with readers some of the recipes that evolved during those first eight years. As Sonoita is a very picturesque and unique part of Arizona, we felt we would like to share the charm and beauty that contributed to the success of our Café. We hope you enjoy the photographs and historical vignettes, which illustrate life in the "Wine Country of Arizona."

# The Staff

Photographers, Sandy and Jay Smith, have been dear friends of ours for years. Jay, while officially a physician and professor of medicine, is a talented photographer. He's been photographing for his entire adult life and has captured countless volumes of gorgeous scenics from across the United States (he graciously contributed his scenic photographic works to this cook book). Sandy's photography deals more with portraits of people and communities. Her book, *Portraits of Clay*, was recently published by the University of Arizona Press and combines photographs with dialogue to give an intimate glimpse of the potters in Mata Ortiz, Chihuahua. Her photography exhibit by the same name has been shown at The Field Museum in Chicago and the Southwest Museum in Los Angeles.

We had previously met with Paula Schaper, a marketing communications specialist, regarding other projects but nothing had come to fruition as yet. When it came time to put our ideas to paper, we contacted Paula to create the initial designs for *Sonoita Seasons*. We had seen her work before and knew that she had experience with print collateral, food service and marketing in general. She resides in the beautiful Arizona High Country and has a deep appreciation for the area. It just seemed like a natural fit to work with her on this project.

Harold has done the computer work. His patience in prying recipes that had been in my head for years and committing this information to a page was phenomenal. My attention span, as Harold knows, has never been lengthy. I can't stand to sit still for very long!

And then me...I had to get all those recipes together and finally complete the project I had been talking about all those years! It's been hard work but it has been rewarding to see the idea become reality.

I hope these recipes will bring with them many good memories as they have for us.

Enjoy!

*Karen Callaghan*

*Karen in front of the original Karen's Wine Country Café.*
Photo: Lawrence Cheek

# How We Became Involved In The Restaurant Business

People always ask us how we became involved in the restaurant business. It is a long, rather convoluted story.

I am a home economist by profession and I always loved preparing interesting and unusual dishes. My husband gained 10 pounds at one point from the homemade breads I was experimenting with.

We bought a summer home on Galiano Island in British Columbia in 1979. It was here that we first realized how much good, fresh ingredients added to the flavor and quality of a meal. Fresh fruit and vegetables, fresh herbs, and natural grains were all very much a part of life among the residents of Galiano Island.

*A view of the bay and ferry from Galiano Island*
Photo: Harold Callaghan

We also became friends with Huguette Benger of "La Berengerie," the Country French restaurant on Galiano and spent many memorable evenings enjoying and exploring different tastes and unusual foods.

Then, one year as we were leaving Galiano to return to Sonoita, we heard that another island friend of ours, Jim McDonald, was offering a class in home winemaking. Specifically, blackberry wine. As we knew that wine grapes had been planted in the Sonoita-Elgin area Harold decided to enroll in the class. The fruit, blackberries, used in the wine grew wild all over the island. We had a wonderful patch just outside our entrance gate. Those fresh berries not only made excellent wine but wonderful jams, jellies, and delicious apple-blackberry cakes and pies as well. What a wonderful place to live.

*Karen and Huguette Benger in the yard of "La Berengerie," the Country French restaurant on Galiano Island in British Columbia.*
Photo: Harold Callaghan

When we left in October we decided to return to Sonoita via the Napa-Sonoma Valleys. We were hooked. The wines were excellent, the restaurants innovative, and the food was superb. We felt our son, Kent, who had graduated in philosophy from Pomona College, would probably love the area as well.

*Kent in front of Callaghan Vineyards, Elgin, AZ.*
Photo: Harold Callaghan

We took a trip back to the California Wine Country with Kent the following February. The die was cast. We — mother, father, son — decided to plant a small experimental vineyard on some acreage close to our house and purchase an additional 80 acres on the Upper Elgin Road not far from our house to plant a larger vineyard and build, ultimately, a winery. Then in a moment of irrational thought we decided to do a restaurant in a building we owned in a town about 50 miles from our home in Sonoita. We thought this would be a good way to launch Callaghan Vineyards while demonstrating the use of wine with food. In the meantime we negotiated a lease to use the first building that had been a winery in the area, the former home of Sonoita Vineyards.

That summer when we went to Galiano Island our friend Huguette offered to let me intern in her restaurant and, since we planned to create a restaurant very similar to hers, I accepted enthusiastically. I am extremely grateful to her to this day for the generosity on her part.

Upon our return to Sonoita we began the remodeling of the first restaurant, a 1950's vintage building that had formerly housed an Italian Restaurant complete with red velvet curtains, red flocked wallpaper, and red carpet. It resembled what one would imagine a bordello to look like. It was a job that Harold, in retrospect, does not remember with fondness. What appeared to be somewhat straightforward evolved into a complete overhaul of the interior and exterior of the building. This project took six full months and completely eclipsed our budget. It did get done after the predictable confrontations with the building inspector, health inspector, and other agencies.

We planned a pre-opening dinner for friends and business associates about a week before our scheduled opening date. Our hope was to work out any glitches prior to opening. Total chaos in the kitchen! Total chaos in the dinning room! The arrival of the guests for the second seating, at the correct time, while we were still trying to catch up with serving the first seating. A fork dropped in the hair of a friend while clearing the table, it was a night to remember or, should that be to forget. Fortunately we did not charge anyone so they couldn't ask for their money back! Whew!

We decided that if we were ever going to succeed we needed to delay our opening a week in order to get ourselves straightened out. It was a wise decision.

On March 7, 1990 we opened Karen's. It was a six-course, prix-fixe menu for which we charged $21.00. Sounds too good to be true? We actually had people complain that we were too expensive! We developed some wonderful customers and met some of the most delightful people we have been fortunate to know. They have remained patrons of Karen's throughout its history and we count them as friends to this day.

We spent two years in Sierra Vista and grew weary of the late night driving and early morning drive back. Because the meal was prepared from scratch each day we would leave our house by 6:00 am and not leave the restaurant to return to Sonoita until between 12:00 am and 1:00 am. In December of 1991 we decided we had to move closer to home and negotiated to lease a building, circa 1904, in Elgin. It was a building that presented challenges we were not expecting, and another extensive remodel. We did get it finished and opened in April, 1992.

We never expected the response we got. The Arizona Wine Country was beginning to be publicized a bit and, as we called our restaurant Karen's Wine Country Café, we were included in much of the publicity. The following January we closed for a month and the first week we re-opened we received positive reviews in the Arizona Daily Star, the Scottsdale Progress, and the Mesa Tribune. We were bombarded! We survived and went on to spend a total of four years at that location.

In the summer of 1995 we learned that a new building was being built in Sonoita. Since we were having some difficulties with personalities in Elgin, we decided to talk to the owner of the new building and felt the time had come to make a move. Harold did all of the work on the cabinets, fixtures, window enclosures in the dining room, installed all counter tops, stainless steel wall covering, and equipment installation.

Because the work was done with no labor costs the move was not as costly as it might have been. This was however, our biggest cash investment in a restaurant to date. We did have to pay for the extension necessary in order to have a dining room. I would recommend to anyone that they be in really good health. It's a killer!

In April, 1996 we opened in Sonoita with the vow that the only way we would leave this location was if we sold Karen's, or, feet first!

*The entrance of Karen's Wine Country Café in Sonoita, AZ*
Photo: Harold Callaghan

# Winter

With an elevation close to 5,000 feet, Sonoita gets occasional snow. The snow can be wet and heavy or dry, light and fluffy. The landscape can be beautiful. If the conditions are right and the skies clear at night the temperature drops into the teens. Water droplets in the snow freeze into tiny crystals that sparkle like thousands of diamonds when illuminated by our headlights when we leave before morning light. The snow normally only lasts a day or two, but the snowman population increases dramatically.

We are happy to see the change of season to winter, but are just as happy to see winter leave.

# Five Onion Tart

*We served this as an appetizer at several wine tastings –*
*it works really well with dry Riesling!*

| | |
|---|---|
| ½ Cup Butter, chilled | 1 Leek, thinly sliced |
| 1⅓ Cups All-Purpose Flour | 1 Small Spanish Onion, thinly sliced |
| ½ Teaspoon Salt | 2 Shallots, diced |
| 4 Tablespoons Ice Water | 4 Scallions, thinly sliced |
| ½ Cup Margarine | 1 Teaspoon All-Purpose Flour |
| 1 Medium Bermuda Onion, thinly sliced | 1 Teaspoon Dijon Mustard |

Process the first 3 ingredients in a food processor until it resembles meal.  Add the water, little by little, until a ball is formed.  Roll out the dough to 12 inches around and press into a 9-inch pie pan.  Pierce the dough with a fork and chill for 1 hour.

Cover dough with foil and bake at 375⁰F for 15 minutes.  Remove foil and let cool.  Meanwhile, melt butter and sauté all the onions until soft and translucent.  Stir in flour and sauté 2 minutes longer.

Spread mustard on crust.  Top with sautéed onions.  Bake in a 350⁰F oven for 15 minutes.  Serve warm, sliced into wedges. SERVES 6.

# Artichoke Croustades

1 Loaf White Bread, each slice rolled thin

With a cookie cutter, cut  a round from each slice of bread and place in a muffin tin, lightly pressing down into cavities.  Bake at 350⁰F until lightly browned.  When cool and no more than ½ hour before serving, fill each baked cavity with artichoke filling.

## ARTICHOKE  FILLING
2 Cups Marinated Artichoke Hearts, finely chopped
3 Tablespoons Chives, chopped
½ Cup Shredded Parmesan Cheese
Salt & Pepper
2 Tablespoons Liquid From Artichokes

Mix all ingredients well and fill toast cups.  Broil till lightly browned.  Serve hot.  SERVES 15-20.

# Savory Cheesecake

*From top left counter clockwise: Zippy Potato Puffs, Bacon & Roasted Red Pepper Spirals and Savory Cheesecake*

6  Ounces Crackers

½ Cup Butter, melted

1  Pound Goat Cheese, at room temperature

2  Pounds Cream Cheese, at room temperature

3  Eggs

1  Teaspoon Crushed Rosemary

Salt & Pepper, to taste

½ Cup Minced Sun Dried Tomatoes, marinated in olive oil

Grease a 9-inch spring form pan.  Cover bottom and sides (½ way up) with a piece of aluminum foil.  Preheat oven to 325ºF.  Process crackers in a food processor until finely crumbed.  Add butter and process until combined.  Press all but 2 tablespoons of crumbs into bottom of spring form pan.  Chill.  Process remaining ingredients in food processor until well combined.  Spoon into springform pan and sprinkle reserved crumbs on top.

Set pan in larger pan and fill with water to ½ way up sides of springform pan.  Bake approximately 45 minutes until puffed and lightly browned.  Cool and refrigerate overnight.  Serve with crackers.  SERVES 10-12.

# Spicy Sausage In Pastry

## SAUSAGE FILLING
1 Small Onion
1 Clove Garlic
½ Cup Fresh Parsley Leaves, minced
½ Pound Fresh Mushrooms, stemmed & cleaned
1 Teaspoon Dried Mint
1 Tablespoon Butter
½ Pound Andouille Sausage Or Chorizo Sausage
1 Teaspoon Ground Cumin
¼ Teaspoon Ground Allspice
2 Ounces Softened Cream Cheese
Salt

## PASTRY
¼ Pound Butter
4 Sheets Of Phyllo (16" x 12")
1 Tablespoons Fine Fresh Bread Crumbs

FILLING: Mince the onion, garlic, and parsley. Chop the mushrooms. Melt 1 tablespoon butter in large frying pan over medium heat and sauté the onion and garlic until onion is soft, about 4 minutes. Add the mushrooms and cook, stirring, until liquid has evaporated, about 5 minutes. Remove the sausage meat from its casing and chop. Add sausage to the pan and heat through. Add the cumin, allspice, and mint and cook, stirring, for 2 minutes. Transfer the mixture to a bowl. Stir in the parsley and cream cheese and season to taste with salt. (Filling can be made a day ahead.)

Melt ¼ pound of butter. Lay one sheet of phyllo on a work surface, brush it lightly with butter, and sprinkle with ½ tablespoon of the breadcrumbs. Fold the phyllo in half like a book with the breadcrumbs inside. Cut folded sheets into thirds crosswise and then in half lengthwise. Cut off the folded edge to make six squares. Center a rounded teaspoon of the filling on top of each square. Gather up corners of phyllo and gently twist to seal. Repeat with remaining phyllo, butter, breadcrumbs, and filling.

Heat oven to 400ºF. Cook phyllo twists in preheated oven until phyllo is golden brown, about 10 minutes. Serve warm.
MAKES ABOUT 24.

Wine Recommendations:
Alsatian Pinot Gris or Gewurtztraminer (Weinbach)

# Wild Mushroom Strudel With Arugula Pesto

| | |
|---|---|
| 5 Tablespoons Butter | 3 Teaspoons Fresh Thyme, chopped |
| ¼ Cup Shallots, chopped | 1 Teaspoon Fresh Rosemary, minced |
| 2 Tablespoons Oil Packed Sun-Dried Tomatoes, drained & chopped | 28 Ounces Assorted Wild Mushrooms (oyster, button, crimini, portabello), sliced |
| 2 Large Garlic Cloves, minced | 5 Sheets Fresh Phyllo Pastry Or Frozen, thawed |
| 1 Tablespoon Fresh Basil, chopped | Arugula Pesto (see recipe below) |

Melt 2 tablespoons butter in a heavy skillet over medium heat. Add shallots, tomatoes, garlic, basil, 2 teaspoons thyme and the rosemary; sauté 2 minutes. Add mushrooms; sauté until very tender, about 15 minutes. Remove from heat. Season with salt and pepper. Cool.

Preheat oven to 400°F. Spray baking sheet with pan release (for example, Pam). Melt 3 tablespoons butter in small saucepan. Place kitchen towel on work surface. Top with 1 phyllo sheet (keep remaining phyllo sheets covered with plastic wrap and damp towel). Brush with melted butter. Top with phyllo sheet; brush with butter. Sprinkle with ½ teaspoon thyme. Repeat layering with 2 more phyllo sheets, brushing with butter and sprinkling with remaining ½ teaspoon thyme. Top with another phyllo sheet; brush with butter.

Starting 1½ inches from one long side and 2 inches from each short side, spoon mushroom mixture onto phyllo in 2½-inch diameter log parallel to long sides. Fold short sides over filling; brush folded edges with butter. Using towel as an aid and starting on the long side nearer filling, roll up strudel jelly roll style. Using spatula, transfer strudel to prepared baking sheet, seam side down. Brush strudel with butter. Freeze 5 minutes.

Bake strudel until golden brown, about 15 minutes. Cut strudel into slices. Serve with Arugula Pesto. SERVES 6.

## ARUGULA PESTO
¼ Cup Blanched Almonds, toasted
2 Cups Packed Arugula Leaves, rinsed & dried
½ Teaspoon Salt
½ Teaspoon Freshly Ground Pepper
3 Garlic Cloves
⅓ Cup Extra-Virgin Olive Oil
3 Tablespoons Freshly Grated Parmesan Cheese

In a food processor, mince the garlic. Add the arugula and nuts and process until minced. With the machine on, add the oil in a thin stream and process until well blended. Add the Parmesan and the salt and pepper and process to mix. MAKES 1 CUP.

# Cannelloni With Chicken & Four Cheeses

*We used this as an entrée as well as an appetizer.*
*At home I usually freeze some for serving at a later time.*

1 Package Wonton Skins

### FILLING

2 Cups Cooked Chicken, finely diced
2 Tablespoons Onion, finely chopped
1 Tablespoon Parsley, finely chopped
Salt & Pepper, to taste

Mix chicken, onions, and parsley together and set aside until needed.

### SAUCE

¼ Pound Butter
1 Cup Flour
3 Cups Milk
2½ Cups Jarlsberg Cheese, grated
1 Cup Plus 1 Tablespoon Grated Parmesan Cheese
¼ Teaspoon Nutmeg
1 Egg
1 Cup White Cheddar Cheese, grated
1 Cup Gouda Cheese, grated

In medium saucepan, melt the butter, add the flour, and stir over medium heat for 2 minutes. Pour in milk, slowly, stirring constantly. Bring to a boil. When sauce boils, lower heat, add 1½ cups Jarlsberg, 1 teaspoon Parmesan, nutmeg, egg, and salt and pepper to taste. Continue cooking and stirring until cheese is melted. Mix remainder of cheeses together and keep chilled till ready to assemble cannellonis.

TO ASSEMBLE CANNELLONIS: Butter well a 9 x 9-inch baking dish. Flour lightly a large cutting board. Lay wonton skins out individually on board. Place approximately 2 tablespoons of chicken filling down the center of each skin. Roll and place seam side down in the buttered baking dish. When all cannellonis are in the dish, pour sauce over and sprinkle with remaining cheese mixture. (At this point they can be refrigerated or frozen until ready to bake.)

TO BAKE: Preheat oven to 350°F. Place baking dish in oven and bake for approximately 30 minutes or until the cheese is bubbly. Add approximately 15 to 20 minutes if the cannelloni are frozen.
MAKES APPROXIMATELY 16 CANNELLONI.

# Cream Of Caramelized Onion & Roasted Shallot Soup

| | |
|---|---|
| 16 Large Shallots, peeled | 2 Cups Chicken Broth |
| 1 Tablespoon Olive Oil | 1 Cup Beef Broth |
| ¾ Cup Butter (1½ sticks) | 3 Cups Cream |
| 3½ Pounds Yellow Onions, peeled & thinly sliced | 3 Tablespoons Fresh Thyme, minced |
| 2 Tablespoons Brown Sugar | 2 Tablespoons Fresh Parsley, Chopped |
| ¾ Cup Cream Sherry | ½ Teaspoon Tabasco |
| 1 Tablespoon Dried Thyme, crumbled | Salt & Pepper |
| 1 Tablespoon Dried Sage, crumbled | 8 Fresh Sage Leaves |

Preheat oven to 375⁰F.  Toss shallots with olive oil in a bowl.  Arrange shallots on a heavy baking sheet, spacing evenly.  Bake until golden brown, turning occasionally, about 30 minutes.  Melt butter in a large pot over medium-high heat.  Add onions and sugar and cook until onions caramelize, stirring frequently to prevent any sticking, about 50 minutes.  Add whole shallots, ½ cup sherry, and dried herbs to onions.  Cook until almost no liquid remains in the pot, stirring occasionally, about 5 minutes.  Add both stocks and simmer 25 minutes.  Puree with an immersion blender.  Add cream and simmer until thickened, about 10 minutes.  (Can be prepared 1 day ahead to this point.  Cover and refrigerate.  Bring to simmer before continuing.)  Add remaining ¼ cup sherry, fresh thyme, fresh parsley, and Tabasco to soup.  Mix well and season to taste with salt and pepper.  Ladle soup into bowls and garnish with fresh sage or fresh rosemary.  SERVES 10.

# Caldo Verde

*Our favorite Portuguese dish.  We served this a lot at the restaurant.*

¾ Pound Kielbasa, sliced in thin rounds
4 Cups Diced Onions
2 Garlic Cloves, finely minced
12 Small New Red Potatoes, scrubbed & cut into small cubes
8 Cups Chicken Stock
8 Cups Chiffonade Of Fresh Spinach (leaves sliced in thin "ribbons")
Freshly Ground Pepper & Salt

Sauté Kielbasa, garlic, and onions until the onions are limp.  Add potatoes and chicken stock.  Heat to boiling, reduce heat, and simmer until potatoes are tender.  Add most of the spinach and simmer for another 5 minutes.  Adjust seasoning to taste.  To serve, use remaining spinach chiffonade as a garnish on top of the soup.  SERVES 10.

# Brie En Croute

1 Round Of Brie
1 Piece Of Puff Pastry, rolled out to ⅛" thickness, approximately 12" x 12"

Preheat oven to 375ºF. Place Brie in center of pastry square and fold corners up and over in envelope fashion, pressing lightly on top so that edges stay down during baking (you can brush with egg white also). Place on a baking sheet covered with parchment and place in oven. Bake until well browned. Allow to cool 10 minutes before serving. Place on a platter and surround with fresh fruit of your choice. SERVES 8-10.

*Brie En Croute*

# Tuscan Bean Soup

*With most of the broth poured off, this works well as a side dish for lamb or veal.*

| | | | |
|---|---|---|---|
| ½ | Pound Great Northern Beans, sorted & rinsed | 1 | 4½-Ounce Can Diced Green Chiles |
| 2 | Tablespoons Olive Oil | 3 | Tablespoons Fresh Parsley, chopped |
| 1 | Cup Yellow Onion, diced | 2 | Tablespoons Fresh Rosemary Leaves, chopped |
| 2 | Garlic Cloves, minced | ¼ | Teaspoon Pepper |
| ½ | Cup Celery, diced | | Fresh Spinach Leaves, cleaned & rinsed |
| ¼ | Cup Carrots, diced | ½ | Cup Red Peppers, diced |
| 8 | Cups Chicken Broth | | Shredded Parmesan Cheese |

Place rinsed beans in large pot and add enough cold water to cover beans by 2 inches. Bring the beans to boil over high heat. Cover with tight fitting lid, reduce heat, and simmer 10 minutes. Remove beans from heat, let sit in the water, covered, for 1 hour. Drain beans, discard the soaking liquid. Set aside.

In the now empty pot, sauté onion and garlic in the olive oil until soft, about 5 minutes. Add the celery and carrots, and sauté 5 more minutes. Add the chicken broth, chiles, herbs, pepper, and the drained beans. Stir to combine and bring the soup to a boil. Cover the soup with a lid and reduce the heat to a simmer. Cook, stirring occasionally, for 2 hours. Check beans for doneness.

To serve, place some spinach leaves into each bowl and ladle hot soup over the spinach. It will wilt almost immediately. Gently swirl the wilted spinach with a spoon to make sure the spinach is heated through.

Garnish the soup by sprinkling some diced red pepper over the top. Finish by sprinkling shredded Parmesan cheese lightly over top. SERVES 8-10.

# Karen's Black Bean Soup

*The most requested recipe we prepared at the restaurant.*

| | | | |
|---|---|---|---|
| 12 | Cups Dried Black Beans | ½ | Cup Chile Flakes |
| 2 | Cups Dry Onion Flakes | ½ | Cup Cumin Seed |
| 2 | Cups Kielbasa, coarsely chopped | 1½ | Cups Brown Sugar |

By hand, clean black beans of small stones and debris. Rinse, cover with water, and soak over night.

The next day over medium-high heat, bring to a boil, reduce heat, and add remaining ingredients. Cook until the beans are tender. Add salt to taste. Serve hot with sour cream and salsa fresca. SERVES 10-12.

*appetizers, small dishes, soups*

# Creamy Potato — Cilantro Bisque

4 Cups Chicken Broth

2 Large Thin-Skinned Potatoes, peeled & coarsely chopped

¼ Teaspoon White Pepper

½ Teaspoon Ground Cumin

1 Small Can Diced Green Chiles

1 Cup Fresh Cilantro

3 Green Onions (ends trimmed) thinly sliced, including tops

1 Cup Sour Cream

Salt

Additional Fresh Cilantro Sprigs

In a 4-quart pan, combine broth, potatoes, pepper, and cumin. Bring to a boil over high heat; reduce heat, cover, and simmer until potatoes are very tender when pierced 15 to 20 minutes.

In a food processor, combine half the potato mixture, chiles, 1 cup cilantro, and green onions; whirl until smooth. Transfer to a large bowl. Then puree remaining potato mixture and sour cream. Add to the first mixture; season to taste with salt. Cover and refrigerate until cold, at least 2 hours or up to 1 day. Stir well before serving. Garnish each serving with a cilantro sprig. SERVES 6-8.

# Creamy Potato — Leek Soup

*Another recipe that can be made into a souffle!*

2 Tablespoons Butter

3-4 Medium Sized Leeks, white part only, trimmed, split, washed & finely sliced

4 Cups Chicken Broth

3-4 Medium Sized Potatoes, peeled, quartered & thinly sliced

1 Teaspoon Coarse Salt

4 White Peppercorns, finely crushed

1 Cup Whole Milk, heated to scalding point

3 Tablespoons Flat-Leaf Parsley, finely chopped

Heat a heavy kettle over low heat and gently melt butter. Sauté the leeks very slowly, stirring them from time to time, until they become transparent without browning. This step must be done with attention so as not to destroy the fresh, sweet taste that leeks and butter will impart to the soup.

Add the broth and allow the leeks to simmer for 5 minutes. Add the potatoes and allow to simmer for 1 hour or until the potatoes are very soft. Puree the soup in a food processor or by putting it through a food mill or a sieve. Add the salt, peppercorns, and hot milk to the puree and heat the soup to the boiling point, but remove it from the heat right away.

Pour the soup into a tureen, sprinkle the surface with parsley, and serve immediately. SERVES 4-6.

# French Onion Soup

*Our favorite!  Be sure to caramelize the onions well – that's what makes the great color and taste!*

2  Tablespoons Unsalted Butter
3  Teaspoons Olive Oil
1  Pound Onions, thinly sliced
½  Pound Leeks (white part only), thinly sliced
2  Garlic Cloves, finely chopped
½  Teaspoon Salt
8  Cups Beef Broth, heated

½  Cup Dry Vermouth
Dash Of Tabasco
Freshly Ground Pepper
Salt
Toasted French Bread Slices
Gruyere Cheese, thinly sliced

Melt butter and oil in heavy pot over low heat.  Add onions, leeks, and garlic; cook until onions are softened, stirring occasionally, about 15 minutes.  Increase heat to medium-low.  Add sugar and cook until onions are deep golden brown, stirring frequently, about 30 minutes.  Add stock, vermouth, Tabasco, and pepper.  Simmer 40 minutes. Season with salt.  *(Can be prepared 1 day ahead.  Cool, cover, and refrigerate before continuing.)*  Preheat broiler. Divide soup between four 8-ounce soup crocks.  Top each with toasted bread and several cheese slices.  Broil until cheese melts and top is golden.  SERVES 4.

# Winter Beefy Vegetable Soup

3½  Pounds Beef Shortribs
9  Cups Beef Broth
2  Cups Water
1  Cup Dry White Wine
1  15-Ounce Can Stewed Tomatoes
1  Large Onion, chopped
¾  Pound Carrots, chopped

2  Celery Stalks, chopped
½  Cup Parsley Sprigs, firmly packed
4  Garlic Cloves
1  Dry Bay Leaf
½  Teaspoon Each; Dried Leaves Of Basil, Rosemary & Thyme
Salt & Freshly Ground Pepper
Grated Parmesan Cheese

Place shortribs in an 8 to 10-quart pan over medium-high heat; brown well on all sides.  Add broth, water, wine, tomatoes, onion, carrots, celery, parsley, garlic, bay, basil, rosemary, and thyme.  Bring to a boil; reduce heat, then cover and simmer until meat is very tender when pierced, about 3 hours.  Cool slightly and lift out shortribs;  when cool enough to handle, discard bones and fat.  Tear meat into small pieces and reserve to add back to soup.

Pour broth through a fine strainer into a bowl; skim off and discard fat.  Whirl vegetables in a food processor until coarsely pureed.  Return vegetables, broth, and reserved meat to pan.  Bring to a boil over high heat, stir often.  Ladle into bowls.  Serve sprinkled with shredded Parmesan cheese.  SERVES 8.

# Curried Carrot Soup

*A recipe from La Berengerie. If you have*
*leftovers, add eggs and bake a souffle!*

*Curried Carrot Soup*

3  Large Spanish Onions, peeled coarsely & chopped
2  Tablespoons Fresh Garlic, minced
3  Tablespoons Olive Oil
6  Pounds Carrots, washed, scraped & cut in 2" pieces
9  Cups Chicken Broth
3  Tablespoons Curry Powder
1½  Quarts Half & Half

Sauté onions and garlic in olive oil in a large soup pot Add carrots and sauté approximately 10 minutes.  Add Chicken broth and curry powder and simmer for 2-3 hours.  Remove from heat and puree until smooth and creamy. Add approximately 1 to 1½ quarts of half & half.  Heat over medium heat.  Adjust seasonings to taste. Serve garnished with chopped chives or thinly sliced green onions.  SERVES 10-12.

# Potatoes Dauphinoise

*Our best scalloped potato. You won't want to stop eating them!*

| | |
|---|---|
| 3 Large Baking Potatoes | 2 Tablespoons Scallions, white part only, finely chopped |
| 2 Cloves Garlic | 1 Teaspoon Kosher Salt |
| 1 Cup Half & Half | ½ Teaspoon White Pepper |
| 1 Tablespoon Butter | ½ Teaspoon Nutmeg |
| | 1 Cup Shredded Parmesan Cheese |

Peel potatoes, wash and dry them, and halve them lengthwise. Lay them cut side down and cut into ⅛-inch slices. Place in a container and cover with water. Put in refrigerator for at least 2 hours.

Remove potatoes from refrigerator, drain and dry them. Peel one of the garlic cloves and chop it fine. Put potatoes in a large sauté pan; add the chopped garlic and the milk. Place on a burner and bring the milk to the scalding point, turning the potato slices so that each one is coated with the hot milk. Simmer the potatoes in the milk very slowly for 15 minutes. Preheat the oven to 350ºF. Select a 13 x 9-inch baking dish with a cover. Cut the other clove of garlic in half and rub the interior of the baking dish with the cut edges. Discard the garlic. Butter the baking dish.

Layer the potatoes (5 to 6 layers), covering each layer with a sprinkling of scallion, pepper, nutmeg, and some cream. Pour whatever is left of the cream over the top.

Cover the dish and place in a shallow pan or another, larger baking dish containing 1 inch of water. Place the setup in the center of the oven and bake for 1½ to 2 hours, or until the cream is absorbed.

Remove the cover, sprinkle with shredded Parmesan Cheese, and brown under the broiler for a few minutes until the surface is dark and crusty. Allow cooling for a few minutes before serving. SERVES 9-12.

# Sizzling Carrots

*These can also be made with whole baby carrots or carrot "pennies."*

| | |
|---|---|
| 3 Tablespoons Butter | ½ Teaspoon Crushed Red Pepper Flakes |
| 6 Cups Grated Carrots | Salt & Freshly Ground Pepper, to taste |
| Pinch Of Sugar | 1 Tablespoon Whole Cumin Seeds, crushed |

In a large skillet, melt the butter over medium heat. Add the carrots, sugar, red pepper flakes, and cumin and sauté for 10 minutes or, until crisp tender and slightly golden. Season with salt and pepper to taste. Garnish with the chopped parsley. SERVES 4-6.

# Spanakopita
## (Spinach Pie)

*A little easier than the appetizer. This variation is wonderful for a light entrée.*

2½ Pounds Fresh Spinach, blanched in salted boiling water, chopped fine
¾ Pounds Feta Cheese, mashed
½ Cup Olive Oil
1 Cup Parsley, chopped fine
1 Cup Dill Weed, chopped fine
3 Green Onions, chopped fine
¼ Teaspoon Salt
8 Sheets Phyllo (purchased frozen & thawed)
Butter, melted

Combine spinach, cheese, and olive oil and mix well. Season with the herbs and spices. In a greased baking pan about 3 inches deep, place 4 pastry sheets, one at a time, brushing each with melted butter. Place the spinach mixture over this, spreading it evenly. Place the remaining pastry sheets over the spinach mixture to form the top of the pie, treating each sheet with melted butter. Brush the top with melted butter and sprinkle with a little water. Bake in a 375°F oven until the top is golden brown, about 40 minutes. Cool slightly before cutting into squares to serve. If preferred, chill thoroughly, for this dish is delicious cold. Only a little salt is necessary, as the cheese provides enough saltiness. SERVES 6-8.

# Roasted Potatoes With Sage & Thyme

*Another recipe that can be varied with many different herbs.*

2 Pounds Russet Potatoes, peeled & cut into bite-sized chunks
1 Clove Garlic
1 Cup Olive Oil
1 Teaspoon Dried Sage Leaves, crumbled
½ Teaspoon Dried Thyme Leaves, crumbled
Salt & Pepper

Place potatoes in a 9 x 13-inch pan. Peel and chop garlic. In small bowl, combine the garlic and the remaining ingredients, mixing thoroughly. Pour over potatoes and toss to coat all. Bake at 350°F for 1 hour, stirring occasionally until the potatoes are tender and golden. SERVES 4-6.

# Sage Glazed Carrots

*The fried sage leaves are delicious!*

6  Medium Sized Carrots, sliced thin on the diagonal
6-8  Large Fresh Sage Leaves
2  Tablespoons Butter

Steam or microwave carrots until tender.  Drain into colander and rinse under cold water.  Set aside.  In 1-quart saucepan, melt butter.  Using scissors cut sage into thin ribbons and add to butter.  Add carrots and toss while heating thoroughly, approximately 3-5 minutes.  Serve immediately garnished with fried sage leaves.

FRIED SAGE LEAVES: Melt 2 tablespoons of butter in small sauté pan.  Add 10 to 12 whole sage leaves washed and patted dry and toss till crispy, over medium heat.  Remove; drain on paper toweling, and store in refrigerator until ready to use.  SERVES 4-6.

# Parsley Rice Timbales

| | |
|---|---|
| 3 Tablespoons Unsalted Butter | ¼ Teaspoon Salt |
| 1 Small Onion, minced | ½ Cup Fresh Parsley, minced |
| ¾ Cup Rice | 2 Eggs |
| 3 Cups Chicken Broth | 1 Cup Milk |

Preheat oven to 350ºF.  Spray individual soufflé dishes, or a 2-quart dish, with a pan release spray.  In a medium saucepan, melt the butter over moderate heat.  Add the onion and cook until it is softened and translucent, about 5 minutes.  Add the rice and stir to coat.  Add the chicken broth and salt and bring to a boil.  Cover, reduce the heat to low, and cook until the rice is very tender, about 20 minutes.  Stir the parsley into the rice.  Let cool for 5 minutes.  Beat in the eggs, one at a time, then stir in the milk, and mix until well blended.  Pour the parslied rice into the buttered dish(es) and bake for about 50 minutes for the 2-quart dish, or 30 minutes for the individual soufflé dishes; or until set and lightly browned.  SERVES 4-6.

# Mashed Potato Soufflé

*These are so good!*

| | |
|---|---|
| 4-6  Russet Potatoes, peeled | 1 Cup Light Cream |
| 1 Package Dry Hidden Valley® Buttermilk Dressing | Pepper, to taste |
| 1  8-Ounce Cream Cheese | ¼ Cup Chopped Scallions |
| 4  Eggs | |

Boil potatoes until tender.  Drain.  While still hot, whip potatoes with Hidden Valley Dressing, cream cheese, eggs, and cream.  Season to taste with salt and pepper.  Fold in scallions.  Pour into buttered casserole or soufflé dish, leaving 2 to 3 inches at the top.  Bake at 350ºF for 45 minutes.  SERVES 6.

# Maple Buttered Acorn Squash Rings

*These are especially pretty if served with julienned carrots in the center.*

4  Acorn Squash, top & bottom removed & cut crosswise into ½" slices
2  Tablespoons Butter (¼ stick)
3  Tablespoons Pure Maple Syrup
Ground Nutmeg

Using sharp knife or round cookie cutter, slightly larger than seeded center, cut seeds from each squash ring. Overlap squash rings slightly in buttered 13 x 9-inch microwave safe dish. Sprinkle with salt and pepper. Cover with plastic wrap and cook in microwave on high until tender, rearranging squash rings once, about 8 minutes. Let stand 5 minutes. Drain off any liquid from pan. Melt 2 tablespoons of butter with 3 tablespoons maple syrup in small saucepan, whisking to combine. Brush squash rings generously with maple butter. Preheat broiler and broil squash rings about 3 inches from heat source until glazed, about 2 minutes. Sprinkle with ground nutmeg. Serve directly from dish or arrange on a platter and serve warm. SERVES 10.

# Baked New Potatoes & Apples

2  Pounds New Red Potatoes, scrubbed
2  Medium Size Onions, cut into 1" wedges
2  Tablespoons Olive Oil
1  Pound Red Apples (Jonathan, Winesap, etc.)

1¼  Cups Beef Broth
¾  Cup Apple Juice
2  Tablespoons Cornstarch
¾  Teaspoon Ground Allspice

Place potatoes in 9 x 13-inch baking dish. Break apart onion wedges and sprinkle over potatoes. Add oil and mix well. Bake, uncovered, in a 400°F oven for 25 minutes; stir occasionally.

Rinse apples; quarter, core, and cut into ¾-inch wedges. Mix together broth, apple juice, cornstarch, and allspice. When potatoes have cooked 25 minutes, mix in apple and juice mixture. Return to oven, spooning juices occasionally over apples and potatoes. Bake until potatoes are very tender when pierced and juices begin to form thick bubbles, about 25 minutes longer. SERVES 8.

# Roasted Tomatoes

*Huguette introduced us to this dish – we love to serve it when tomatoes are at their peak!*

4  Medium Size Tomatoes
2  Teaspoons Fresh Oregano

¼  Cup Parmesan Cheese, shredded
Freshly Ground Pepper

Clean tomatoes and cut out stem. Remove top ⅓ of tomato, reserving the top for another use. Hollow tomatoes out slightly and sprinkle with oregano, Parmesan, and pepper. Roast in a 375°F oven until hot and the cheese is melted. Serve immediately. SERVES 4.

# Santa Cruz County "Cowbelles" Salad

*The Santa Cruz county "Cowbelles" are a group of ladies who help promote the use of beef in our menus and provide many scholarships to deserving students. We created this recipe for a special luncheon. It is one of our personal favorites.*

16 Ounces Mixed Greens
24 Pieces Sliced Grilled Oriental Flank Steak (see recipe on page 128)
2 Large Portabello Mushrooms, grilled & brushed with Soy-Ginger Vinaigrette
2 Roasted Red Bell Peppers, sliced in fine strips
Red Onions, thinly sliced
1 Cup Pistachio Nuts, chopped

Arrange greens on each of 4 plates. Arrange remainder of ingredients on top of greens paying close attention to your presentation. Sprinkle with pistachio nuts. Dress with Soy-Ginger Vinaigrette (see recipe on page 210). SERVES 4.

# Curried Chicken Salad

4 Chicken Breasts, cooked & cubed
2 Cups Green Seedless Grapes, rinsed & halved
2 Cups Red Seedless Grapes, rinsed & halved
2 Cups Chopped Celery
1 Cup Slivered Almonds
1 Cup Dried Cranberries

Mix all ingredients well in a large bowl along with the Curried Mayonnaise Dressing (see recipe below). Serve with apple and orange slices. SERVES 4.

### CURRIED MAYONNAISE DRESSING
1 Cup Mayonnaise
1 Cup Plain Yogurt
3-5 Teaspoons Curry Powder, to taste

Mix dressing ingredients together well. Pour over chicken and fruit shown above.

Wine Recommendation:
Austrian Riesling (Weingartner)
Rosé (Bonny Doon)

*vegetables, salads and grains*

Once a large volume cattle shipping point in the United States, Sonoita and the surrounding rangelands ruled the state's economy a century ago. Spanish missionary Father Eusebio Francisco Kino introduced beef cattle to the region in the late 1600s.

# Hazelnut Pork

## (In A Port Wine Sauce)

*The recipe that launched the restaurant!*

*Hazelnut Pork In A Port Wine Sauce served with Asparagus and Oven Roasted Potatoes*

2   Eggs
½   Cup Milk
2   Cups Hazelnuts, finely ground
1   Cup All-Purpose Flour
8   Boneless Pork Loin Medallions, about ½" thick

In a medium bowl, blend the eggs and milk.  Place the ground nuts in a second bowl and the flour in a third bowl.  Dredge the pork in flour then dip in the egg mixture.  Bread the pork in the nuts, pressing them on to the meat firmly.  In a large sauté pan, melt a little butter.  Place the pork in the pan and brown on one side.  Turn the pork over and put the pan in a 375$^0$F oven for 5 to 10 minutes.  SERVES 4.

### PORT WINE SAUCE
1   Cup Port Wine
1   Shallot, minced
¼   Cup Red Wine Vinegar
1   Cup Heavy Cream
1   Cup Butter (2 sticks)

In a small saucepan, place the port wine, shallot, and wine vinegar.  Bring to a boil and reduce by ¾.  Add the heavy cream and reduce by ¾ again.  Cut the cup (2 sticks) of butter into small chips.  Reduce the heat to the lowest possible setting.  Slowly add the butter chips, blending with a whisk as they melt.  Be careful to start slowly with only 1 or 2 chips and gradually build up until all of the butter has been blended into the sauce.  To protect against separation of the butter from the sauce, remove from heat and serve with pork.

# Karen's Herbed Pasta Cannellonis

5-6 Pieces Of Fresh Pasta Approximately 4" x 6" (using recipe below or purchased frozen sheets cut to these dimensions)

## PASTA

| | | | |
|---|---|---|---|
| 1½ | Cups All-Purpose Flour | 1 | Tablespoon Warm Water |
| ¾ | Cup Semolina Flour | 1 | Tablespoon Parsley, finely chopped |
| 3 | Eggs | 1 | Tablespoon Thyme, finely chopped |
| 1 | Tablespoon Olive Oil | ½ | Teaspoon Granulated Garlic |

In the bowl of your food processor, place the flours, eggs, herbs, and garlic. Pulse the food processor until the ingredients are well combined. Add the water and olive oil and pulse until the dough leaves the sides of the processor bowl and makes a large ball. Remove the dough, wrap in plastic, and chill overnight.

When ready to finish, remove the pasta from the refrigerator and knead slightly before using, adding flour as necessary. Use a hand pasta machine to roll out sheets. The final setting should be #6. Cut to size indicated above.

## FILLING

| | | | |
|---|---|---|---|
| 5-6 | Mild Italian Sausages, casings removed | 1 | Egg |
| 1 | Small Onion, finely chopped | ½ | Cup Shredded Parmesan Cheese |
| 2 | Garlic Cloves, finely chopped | ½ | Cup Shredded Fontina Cheese |
| 1 | Cup Fresh Bread Crumbs, finely chopped | ½ | Cup Shredded Provolone Cheese |
| ¼ | Cup Parsley, finely chopped | | Salt & Pepper, to taste |
| 1 | Teaspoon Dry Basil Leaves | | |

Sauté Italian Sausages until almost done, breaking up into small pieces. Add onions and garlic and sauté until limp. Remove from heat and drain off any fat. In large bowl mix together the cooked sausage, onion, garlic, bread crumbs, parsley, basil, and egg. Mix well and add salt and pepper to taste. Add cheeses and mix well again. Lay pasta sheets out on a flat surface. Place approximately ¼ cup of filling down the center of each sheet. Bring the ends of the pasta sheets together and overlap slightly. Pat gently to make sure the roll is tight. Place the cannelloni rolls in a well-greased baking dish (approximately 9 x 13-inch) side by side. Chill while preparing sauce.

## SAUCE

| | | | |
|---|---|---|---|
| 2 | Tablespoons Butter | ¼ | Cup Shredded Parmesan Cheese |
| 4 | Tablespoons Flour | ¼ | Cup Shredded Provolone Cheese |
| 2 | Cups Milk Or Light Cream | ¼ | Cup Shredded Fontina Cheese |
| | Salt & Pepper, to taste | | |

In a large fry pan melt butter, add flour, mixing continuously, and cook until they begin to bubble. Add milk, whisking continually, and allow to thicken. When thickened, add remaining ingredients and allow cheeses to melt. Stir until well combined. Pour over cannellonis and place in a 350°F oven and bake approximately 45 to 50 minutes or, cover and chill approximately 1 hour before service. When ready, remove the cannellonis from the refrigerator and place in a preheated oven at 350°F oven and bake uncovered for approximately 1 hour. SERVES 6-8.

# Osso Bucco

*Our favorite veal dish. It is wonderful with Tuscan beans or garlicky mashed potatoes.*

| | | | |
|---|---|---|---|
| 8 | 1¼"-Thick Veal Shank Slices | 2 | Cups Chicken Stock |
| | All-Purpose Flour | 2 | Cups Beef Stock |
| 1 | Large Onion, diced | 1 | Can Italian Plum Tomatoes (14½-16 ounces), drained & chopped |
| 1 | Celery Stalk, diced | 2 | Tablespoons Orange Zest, finely chopped |
| 2 | Large Carrots, peeled & diced | 2 | Tablespoons Lemon Zest, finely chopped |
| 2½ | Cups Dry White Wine | ¼ | Cup Fresh Italian Parsley, chopped |

Season veal with salt and pepper. Dredge in flour. Heat oil in heavy large Dutch oven over high heat. Add veal in batches and brown on all sides, about 10 minutes. Transfer veal to plate. Reduce heat to medium. Add onion, celery, and carrots to Dutch oven and cook until vegetables are soft, about 8 minutes. Add wine and both stocks and boil until half, stirring occasionally (about 30 minutes reduces liquid). Return veal shanks to pot. Add tomatoes. Cover and simmer until veal is tender, turning occasionally, about 1 hour 45 minutes. Mix in half of orange and lemon zest. Cover and simmer 15 minutes. Season to taste with salt and pepper. Divide shanks among plates. Spoon sauce over. Sprinkle with remaining orange and lemon zest's and parsley. *Wonderful served with Garlicky Mashed Potatoes.* SERVES 8.

# Baked Breast Of Chicken In Parmesan Cream

6 Boneless, Skinless Chicken Breast Halves, about 6 ounces each

2 Tablespoons Olive Oil

1 Small Onion, finely minced

3 Tablespoons Flour

1 Cup Freshly Grated Parmesan

2 Cups Milk

2 Egg Yolks

Lightly brown chicken in hot oil but do not cook through. Remove from oil with a slotted spoon, draining as much as possible. Place in a baking dish just large enough to hold all the breasts. Cook onions in drippings from chicken, scraping up any browned bits. Add flour and stir well. Add ¾ cup Parmesan, and then gradually stir in milk and cook over low heat, stirring constantly, until sauce is thick, using a wire whisk to free the sauce of any lumps, if needed. Beat egg yolks lightly and add a little of the sauce to the yolks, whisking briskly. Whisk this mixture back into the sauce gradually. Cook over low heat for 10 minutes, pour over chicken and sprinkle with remaining Parmesan. Bake, covered with aluminum foil, at 325⁰F for approximately 45 minutes. Remove aluminum foil and finish baking for approximately 15 minutes or until nicely browned on top. Remove from oven, arrange on a platter, and serve. Garnish with finely chopped fresh parsley. SERVES 6.

*Off the coast of British Columbia, between Vancouver and Vancouver Island, there is delightful island, Galiano, with an equally delightful French restaurant called "La Berengerie." On numerous occasions we have been treated to Huguettes's wonderful <u>Lamb Ragout</u>. It was with these in mind that we have developed this recipe, which works equally well with leftover cooked leg of lamb. We felt, in fact, that the flavor was enhanced by the charred surface caused by spit roasting. There are a number of ways this recipe could be varied, as it is basic. We encourage you to be creative with it. We also found that this dish paired beautifully with a 1994 Callaghan Vineyard "Buena Suerte" (Good Luck) Cuvee. Fresh peaches with crème fraiche finished it off pleasantly. We hope you experience the joy we found at Huguette's!*

# Lamb Ragout With Vegetables

2-3 Pounds Boneless Lamb, cut into 1-2" chunks

2 Tablespoons Soy Sauce

½ Cup Port Wine

4 Teaspoons Mustard Seeds

1½ Teaspoons Fresh Thyme leaves, chopped

½ Teaspoon Fresh Tarragon, chopped & Black Peppercorns, ground

2-3 Bay Leaves

1½ Cups Chicken Broth

1 Cup Dry Red Wine (Cabernet Sauvignon)

6-8 Medium Size New Potatoes, scrubbed & left whole

6-8 Medium Size Carrots, peeled & cut into 3" chunks

4-6 Parsnips (or turnips, if you prefer), scrubbed & cut into 3" chunks

1 Cup Heavy Cream

1 Tablespoon Dijon Mustard

¼ Cup Butter

Sprigs Of Rosemary, Thyme Or Sage For Garnish

Place lamb chunks in a large heavy fry pan, add soy sauce. Cover tightly, bring to a boil over medium heat; let simmer in its own juices for 30 minutes. Uncover and boil over high heat until juices have evaporated, stirring frequently. When lamb starts to sizzle, stir often until richly browned. Add the port wine and stir well; add mustard seeds, thyme, tarragon, peppercorns, bay leaves, chicken broth, and wine. Lay potatoes, carrots, and parsnips or turnips on meat. Bring to a boil, reduce heat, cover tightly, simmer until meat and vegetables are tender when pierced, approximately 1½ hours. With a slotted spoon, lift vegetables and lamb from broth and mound individually on a large platter. Cover with foil and keep hot in a 150°F oven for 30 minutes. Add cream and mustard to pan juices. Boil over high heat until reduced to 1¾ cups. Reduce heat to medium and add butter in 1 chunk, stirring constantly until blended into sauce. Pour sauce into a serving dish. Garnish with fresh herbs. Serve platter, garnished with fresh herbs, and dish of sauce in center. SERVES 4-6.

# Glazed Chicken Breasts With Rosemary

1  Chicken Breast, halved with skin on
1  Garlic Clove, finely chopped

Preheat oven to 350°F.  Sprinkle chicken pieces with salt and pepper.  Rub with garlic.  Place in 9 x 13-inch pan, skin side up.  Bake 45 minutes.  Meanwhile, prepare the sauce.

## SAUCE

1  Cup Water
1  Cup Dry White Wine
1  Tablespoon Lemon Juice
¼  Cup Honey
1  Teaspoon Hot Dry Mustard
1  Teaspoon Fresh Rosemary, finely chopped
½  Cup Pitted Prunes
½  Cup Dried Apricots
1  Large Apple, cored & sliced in rings

In saucepan, combine water, wine, lemon juice, honey, mustard and rosemary.  Bring to a boil, reduce heat and simmer for 15 minutes.  Add the fruit and simmer for another 15 minutes, or until the liquid is reduced by ½ and the fruit is tender.

ASSEMBLY:  Remove chicken from the oven, pour off fat, and remove skin (if desired).  Spoon sauce over chicken.  Turn oven to 400°F.  Return chicken to the oven and bake 15 minutes, basting once or twice.  Serve the chicken with some of the sauce and fruit spooned on top, garnish with chopped parsley.  SERVES 6.

**ABOUT RED WINES:**  *Red wines are, usually, best with red meats. Barolo, Hermitage, Chateauneuf du Pape, Bandol (and so many other deep, intense reds) with herb-crusted lamb make for memorable dining experiences. Your best bet is to match the weight and intensity of the wine to the dish. A lighter Cabernet, Syrah, or Cotes du Rhone might be best with roast pork (even grilled chicken). A richer, deeper version of any of these wines (possibly a result of vintage differences) would merit pairing with full-blooded red meats. As with white wines, sauces complicate matters. With big, tannic (astringent) reds, look for meat/mushroom reduction sauces and cream sauces. Lighter reds work well with light herb-based sauces on pork or even chicken. Any dish that has a noticeable amount of spice heat (chiles) is best approached with extreme caution with regard to red wines. Repeat after me - tannic (astringent) red wine and chiles are not a felicitous match.*

Kent Callaghan, Wine Maker for Callaghan Vineyards

# Stuffed Beef Tenderloin

## (With A Balsamic Vinegar Sauce)

*Seems difficult but it really isn't.  It makes a very nice  party dish.*

### SAUCE

3  Pounds Meaty Veal Bones (or beef if veal is difficult to obtain)

1  Tablespoon Vegetable Oil

2  Celery Stalks, chopped

1  Carrot, chopped

1  Onion, chopped

1  Garlic Head, halved

2  Bacon Slices, chopped

2  Cups Dry Red Wine

2  Cups Balsamic Vinegar

6  Cups Chicken Stock

Salt & Freshly Ground Pepper

### BEEF

1  Red Bell Pepper

1  2-Pound, Center-Cut Beef Tenderloin

3  Tablespoons Olive Paste (look for this in Italian Specialty Foods section of the supermarket)

6  Anchovy Fillets

FOR SAUCE: Preheat oven to 400°F.  Place bones in baking pan.  Roast until well-browned, about 1 hour.  Heat oil in heavy large stockpot over medium high heat.  Add celery, carrot, onion, garlic, and bacon; sauté until light brown, about 15 minutes.  Add roasted bones and wine.  Bring to boil, scraping up any brown bits.  Boil until reduced to glaze, about 15 minutes.  Add vinegar and boil until reduced to ½ cup, about 15 minutes.  Add stock and simmer until liquid is reduced to 2 cups, about 1½ hours.  Strain sauce and degrease.  Season to taste with salt and pepper.  (Can be prepared 1 day ahead and refrigerated.)

FOR BEEF: Char bell pepper over gas flame, or in broiler, until blackened on all sides.  Wrap in paper bag and let stand for 10 minutes.  Peel and seed.  Rinse if necessary, pat dry, and cut julienne.  Cut beef lengthwise down center, cutting ⅔ of the way through.  Open beef flat, cut side up.  Using meat mallet, pound to thickness of 1¼ inch all over.  Spread with olive paste.  Arrange alternate rows of red pepper strips and anchovy fillets on top of olive paste.  Fold long sides of beef to meet at center.  Roll edges to form cylinder and tie every 2 to 3 inches with string.  (Can be prepared 6 hours ahead, wrap tightly and refrigerate.  Bring to room temperature before continuing).  Preheat oven to 500°F.  Roast beef until thermometer registers 130°F, about 40 minutes.  Let rest 10 minutes.  Meanwhile, rewarm sauce, stirring frequently.  Slice Tenderloin.  Place on plate, surround with sauce.  Garnish with blanched asparagus tips.  SERVES 6.

# Karen's Roasted Vegetable Lasagna

*The roasted vegetables really make this lasagna.*
*Even meat lovers like this one! To make it easier on yourself, do it in stages.*

10  Garlic Cloves, thinly sliced
½  Cup Olive Oil
1  Eggplant, washed, trimmed & sliced crosswise ¼" thick
2  Medium Size Zucchini, washed, trimmed, & sliced lengthwise ¼" thick
1  Yellow Onion, washed, trimmed & sliced ¼" thick
4  Roasted Red Bell Peppers, drained & sliced ¼" thick
4  Medium Size Tomatoes, washed, trimmed & sliced ¼" thick
2  Portabello Mushrooms, washed, stemmed & sliced ¼" thick

1  Package Lasagna Noodles, cooked, rinsed & tossed lightly with oil
1  3-Pound Container Ricotta Cheese
1  Cup Italian Parsley, chopped
½  Cup Thyme, chopped Or 2 Tablespoons Dry Thyme
1  Cup Chives, chopped
4  Eggs
2  Cups Romano Cheese, grated
1  Cup Mozzarella Cheese, grated
1  Cup Dry Vermouth
1  Cup Parmesan Cheese, shredded

Preheat oven to 450°F. Place olive oil and garlic in bottom of large roasting pan. Place in oven for 5 minutes. Remove pan from oven and lay eggplant slices in single layer over bottom of pan. Bake for another 20 minutes. Remove pan from oven and place zucchini slices over eggplant slices and roast for another 10 minutes. Remove from oven and layer on onion slices, return to oven and bake for another 20 minutes. Remove from oven and place red bell peppers, tomato, and mushroom slices on top, drizzle with ¼ cup more olive oil. Salt and pepper to taste (Approximately 2 teaspoons salt and 1 tablespoon pepper). Return to oven and bake for 20 minutes. Remove from oven and cool. In large bowl of food processor, place parsley, thyme, and chives. Process till very fine. Put ricotta cheese and eggs in processor with herbs and process till well combined. Set aside. When roasted vegetables have cooled enough to handle, chop all (including red bell peppers) very coarsely.

TO ASSEMBLE: Place enough lasagna noodles to completely cover bottom of 13 x 9-inch pan. Spread ½ of the Ricotta-Egg-Herb mixture over the noodles. Sprinkle with ½ of the Romano Cheese. Cover with another layer of noodles. Spread chopped vegetables evenly over the noodles. Cover evenly with Mozzarella Cheese. Cover again with noodles and spread the remaining Ricotta-Egg-Herb mixture evenly over the top. Carefully pour the dry vermouth around the edges. Cover tightly with aluminum foil and bake in a 350°F oven approximately 60 minutes. Remove foil and bake until browned on top, approximately 20-30 minutes. Remove from oven and allow to sit for 30 minutes. Cut into 3 x 3-inch squares. Serve topped with Tomato Basil Butter (see recipe below). SERVES 12-15.

## TOMATO BASIL BUTTER
*A general purpose sauce which works well with lots of different dishes!*

20  Ripe Roma Tomatoes, washed & stemmed
10  Large Basil Sprigs, washed & patted dry
1  Cup Butter

Process tomatoes and basil in food processor, pulsing, until coarsely chopped. Place in a saucepan and cook over medium heat approximately 30 minutes. Add butter and continue to cook until butter is melted. Add salt and pepper to taste. (Approximately 2 teaspoons salt and 1 tablespoon pepper.) Serve warm with pasta.

# Lamb Curry

4 Cups Onions (diced to ¼")  
1¾ Pounds Ripe Tomatoes  
3 Pounds Lean, Boneless Lamb Shoulder or Leg, trimmed  
7 Tablespoons Vegetable Oil  
3 Tablespoons Fresh Ginger, grated  
2 Tablespoons Fresh Garlic, minced  
4 Tablespoons Ground Coriander Seeds  

1 Teaspoon Cayenne Pepper  
2 Teaspoons Turmeric  
4 Teaspoons *Garam Masala* (see recipe below)  
Salt  
4 Serrano or Jalapeño Chiles  
1 Cup Coriander Leaves (Cilantro), loosely packed  
½ Cup Half & Half  

In the work bowl of a food processor equipped with a metal blade place the tomatoes (quartered); puree and set aside. Cut lamb into 1-inch cubes and pat dry with paper toweling.

Heat 2 tablespoons oil in a 4-quart soup kettle. Working in batches, sear lamb over medium-high heat until well browned; set aside. Heat the remaining 5 tablespoons oil in the kettle. Add the onions and sauté over low heat, stirring occasionally, until softened and lightly colored, about 20 minutes. Add the ginger and garlic and sauté until fragrant, 1 to 2 minutes longer. Add the ground coriander, cayenne pepper, turmeric, *garam masala*, tomato puree, lamb, 2½ teaspoons salt, and 2 cups water. Bring to a boil, cover and simmer slowly for 1 hour. Set cover ajar and simmer until the lamb is tender and the liquid thickens and reduces to a saucelike consistency, 30 to 45 minutes longer. (Can cool, cover, and set aside for 4 to 5 hours or refrigerate up to 3 days.)

SERVING: Reheat curry if it has been set aside or refrigerated. Stem, seed, and cut chiles into ⅛-inch julienne strips. Mince the coriander (cilantro). Stir in the half & half, coriander (cilantro), and chiles into the curry. Simmer until hot, then serve immediately. SERVES 6.

## GARAM MASALA
### *(A spice blend used in Northern India)*

1 Tablespoon Whole Cumin Seeds  
1 Tablespoon Whole Coriander Seeds  
1 Tablespoon Whole Cardamom Seeds  
½ Cinnamon Stick  
1½ Tablespoons Black Peppercorns  
½ Teaspoon Whole Cloves  

Put the spices in a nonstick skillet and toast until fragrant and lightly colored, about 3 minutes. Cool and grind in a coffee grinder or with a mortar and pestle. Transfer to a jar with an airtight lid. (Can store up to 3 months.)
MAKES ¼ CUP.

Wine Recommendation:
Gigondas (Trignon)

# Rolled Leg Of Lamb With Spinach & Bell Peppers

| | |
|---|---|
| 2 Large Red Bell Peppers | 2 Teaspoons Salt |
| 1 Large Garlic Clove | 1½ Teaspoons Freshly Ground Pepper |
| 2 Tablespoons Unsalted Butter | 1 3½-Pound Leg Of Lamb, loin end, boned, butterflied & trimmed |
| 1 Pound Young Spinach, stemmed, rinsed & patted dry | 1 Large Garlic Clove, thinly sliced |

**SAUCE**

6 Tablespoons Unsalted Butter

1 Large Garlic Clove, thinly sliced

⅓ Cup Dry Marsala Wine

¼ Cup Beef Stock

¼ Teaspoon Dried Oregano, crumbled

Salt & Freshly Ground Pepper

FOR LAMB: Char bell peppers over gas flame or in broiler until blackened on all sides. Transfer to paper bag and let stand 10 minutes to steam. Peel and seed; rinse with cold water and pat dry. Cut into ½-inch strips. In a food processor with a steel blade, drop garlic clove through feed tube and mince.

Melt butter in heavy skillet over low heat. Add minced garlic from work bowl and cook until tender but not brown, stirring occasionally, about 3 minutes; set aside in small bowl. Increase heat to high. Add spinach, ½ teaspoon salt, and ½ teaspoon pepper and stir until spinach wilts, about 1 minute. Remove from heat and cool.

Place lamb between 2 large sheets of plastic. Using meat pounder, flatten lamb to thickness of 1 inch, scoring surface if necessary. Make small slits in lamb. Press garlic slices into slits. Season with 1 teaspoon salt and ½ teaspoon pepper. Arrange bell peppers over; spread spinach over, leaving 1-inch border around edge. Starting at one short end, roll up jellyroll style, enclosing peppers, and spinach completely. Tie with string at 1½-inch intervals to hold shape. Season Lamb with remaining salt and pepper. Position rack in center of oven and preheat oven to 350⁰F. Line shallow roasting pan with foil. Place lamb in prepared pan, seam side down. Bake 30 minutes. Increase temperature to 450⁰F and continue baking until baking thermometer, inserted in center of lamb, reaches 145⁰F for medium-rare, about 30 minutes. Transfer lamb to heated platter, tent with foil to keep warm.

SAUCE: Pour pan juices into a measuring cup. Melt 1 tablespoon butter in heavy small saucepan over low heat. Add garlic slices and cook until tender, stirring occasionally, about 3 minutes. Add reserved pan juices, Marsala, stock, and oregano. Bring to boil. Reduce heat to medium-low. Whisk in remaining 5 tablespoons butter, 1 tablespoon at a time, incorporating each before adding next. Season with salt and pepper.

TO SERVE: Carve lamb into ¼-inch thick slices. Arrange on platter. Spoon sauce over. SERVES 6.

# Smoked Chicken Lasagna

*This is a terrific variation of traditional lasagna. Lighter too!*

1¼ Cups Dried Porcini Mushrooms

¼ Pound Mixed Fresh Mushrooms, sliced ¼" thick

2 Large Garlic Cloves, chopped

¾ Pound Fresh Spinach, stems removed

⅓ Cup Plus 2 Tablespoons Extra-Virgin Olive Oil

4 Cups Smoked Chicken, chopped

1 Fresh Rosemary Sprig (or ½ teaspoon dried)

2 Tablespoons Fresh Oregano, chopped (or ½ teaspoon dried)

1 Pound Fresh Mozzarella, cut into ¼" x ¼" dice, Plus ½ Cup Shredded Mozzarella

2 Cups Ricotta Cheese

1⅓ Cups Freshly Grated Romano Cheese

½ Cup Freshly Chopped Basil

5 6" x 9" Sheets Of Pasta

Tomato-Basil Butter Sauce (see recipe on page 37)

2 Tablespoons Chives, cut into 1" lengths for garnish

In a small bowl, soak the dried porcini mushrooms in hot water to generously cover until softened, about 20 minutes. Drain and rinse carefully; pat dry and coarsely chop. Set aside.

In a large nonreactive skillet, heat ⅓ cup olive oil over moderately high heat until hot, about 2 minutes. Add the fresh mushrooms and the garlic and cook, stirring, until the mushrooms are softened, about 3 minutes. Add the reserved porcini and cook until heated through, about 2 minutes. Add the spinach; reduce the heat to moderate and cook, stirring, until almost half of the liquid has evaporated, about 10 minutes. Add the oregano, 1 teaspoon of the salt, and the ½-teaspoon pepper. Remove from the heat and stir in the chopped chicken. Season with additional salt and pepper, if necessary. Set aside. In a large bowl combine the diced mozzarella, ricotta, Romano, and basil.

In a large saucepan, combine the remaining 1 tablespoon salt with 4 quarts of water and bring to a boil over high heat. Add the pasta sheets, one at a time, and boil until tender, about 1½ minutes (or use lasagna noodles prepared according to the package directions). Using two slotted spoons or spatulas, carefully remove each sheet and transfer to a work surface. Using your fingers, coat each side with a little of the remaining olive oil to prevent sticking. Repeat with the 4 remaining sheets of pasta.

Preheat oven to 350⁰F. Lightly oil the bottom of a 13 x 9 x 2-inch glass baking dish. Line the bottom of the dish with one layer of the pasta. Spread evenly with half of the cheese mixture and then cover with another single layer of the pasta. Spread all of the spinach-mushroom-chicken mixture on the pasta and cover with another single layer of the pasta. Spread with the remaining cheese mixture and top with a final layer of pasta. Sprinkle the shredded mozzarella on top. Bake the lasagna for about 30 minutes, until heated through. Do not let it come to a boil or the cheese will become rubbery.

Preheat the broiler. Broil the lasagna 4 inches from the heat until the top is browned, about 1 minute. Cool for about 10 minutes before cutting into 6 portions. Spoon a heaping ¼ cup of the Tomato-Basil Butter Sauce onto 6 warmed dinner plates. Place the lasagna in the center and garnish with the chives. Serve immediately, with the remaining sauce passed separately. SERVES 6.

# Southwestern Sandwich

### (With Karen's Black Beans)

1   Loaf Karen's Golden Corn Bread (see recipe on page 43)
3   Cups Monterey Jack Cheese, grated
6-8   Canned Whole Green Chiles, split lengthwise in strips

Preheat oven to 450⁰F.  Slice cornbread into ½-inch thick slices.  Place cornbread on ovenproof plate.  Sprinkle with jack cheese and place strips of one whole chile over the top.  Place in oven and bake until cheese is melted and beginning to brown.  Remove from oven and serve with Karen's Black Beans (see recipe on page 20), and Tomato Salsa (see recipe on page 214).

*Southwest Sandwich, Karen's Black Bean's and Fresh Tomato Salsa*

# Cranberry — Orange Muffins

| | |
|---|---|
| 1 Cup Dried Cranberries | ½ Teaspoon Salt |
| ¾ Cup Sugar | ½ Cup Vegetable Oil |
| 2 Teaspoons Grated Orange Zest | ½ Cup Orange Juice |
| 2 Cups All-Purpose Flour | 2 Large Eggs |
| 2 Teaspoons Baking Powder | ½ Cup Chopped Pecans |

Preheat oven to 375°F.  Grease muffin pan.  In bowl combine cranberries, ¼ cup sugar, and the orange zest; set aside.  In a large bowl, combine flour, remaining ½ cup sugar, the baking powder, and salt.  In 2 cup measuring cup, combine oil, orange juice, and eggs.  Pour all at once into dry ingredients, and stir only until moistened.  Blend in cranberry mixture and nuts.  Spoon batter into muffin pan, dividing evenly.  Bake 25 minutes.  Let muffins cool in pan 5 minutes before removing.  MAKES 6 MUFFINS.

# Multi Grain Bread

1 Cup Milk, scalded

¼ Cup Molasses

2 Teaspoons Salt

1 Tablespoon Shortening

⅓ Cup Cracked Wheat

⅓ Cup Rolled Oats

⅓ Cup Cornmeal

2 Packages Active Dry Yeast

½ Cup Warm Water

⅓ Cup Whole Wheat Flour

2¾-3 Cups Bread Flour

Combine milk, molasses, salt, shortening, cracked wheat, rolled oats, and cornmeal in a large mixer bowl.  Cool to lukewarm.  Dissolve yeast in warm water.  Add yeast, whole-wheat flour, and 1 cup of bread flour to the cracked wheat mixture.  With dough hook on mixer, beat 2 minutes on medium speed, scraping bowl frequently.  Mix in enough flour to make a stiff dough, not sticky to the touch, until the dough balls up around dough hook and cleans sides of bowl.  Place in a greased bowl and rotate greased side up.  Cover and let rise in warm place until doubled, about 1 hour.  Punch dough down.  Shape into 2 loaves and place in two lightly greased loaf pans.  Let rise until doubled.  Heat oven to 375°F.  Bake until loaf sounds hollow when tapped, approximately 30 to 35 minutes.  Remove from pan and cool on a wire rack.  MAKES 2 LOAVES.

# Karen's Golden Corn Bread

*A very old recipe – we had so many requests for this recipe we started packaging a mix.*

| | |
|---|---|
| 1 Cup Bread Flour | 4 Teaspoons Baking Powder |
| 1 Cup Yellow Cornmeal | 2 Eggs |
| ½ Teaspoon Salt | ⅓ Cup Butter, melted |
| ⅓ Cup Sugar | 1 Cup Milk |

Preheat oven to 425°F. Grease loaf pan. Combine dry ingredients. Beat liquid ingredients together. Add to dry ingredients and mix until just blended. Bake 30 to 35 minutes or until golden brown. Let cool 5 to 10 minutes before removing from loaf pan. MAKES 1 LOAF.

# Sourdough French Bread

| | |
|---|---|
| 4-5 Cups Bread Flour | 1 Cup Very Warm Water |
| 2 Tablespoons Wheat Germ | 1 Cup Sour Cream, at room temperature |
| 1 Teaspoon Sugar | 2 Tablespoons Vinegar |
| 2 Teaspoons Salt | 1 Egg White |
| ½ Teaspoon Ginger | 1 Tablespoon Water |
| 2 Package Fast-Acting Dry Yeast | 2 Teaspoons Poppy Seeds |

Lightly spoon flour into measuring cup; level off. In large bowl, combine 1½ cups flour, wheat germ, sugar, salt, ginger, and yeast; blend well. Add 1 cup very warm water (120F° to 130F°), sour cream, and vinegar to flour mixture. Blend at low speed until moistened; beat 3 minutes at medium speed. By hand, stir in 2 to 2½ cups flour until dough pulls cleanly away from sides of bowl.

On a floured surface, knead in remaining ½ to 1 cup flour until dough is smooth and elastic, about 5 minutes. Place dough in greased bowl; cover loosely with plastic wrap and cloth towel. Let rise in warm place (80F° to 85F°) until light and doubled in size, 25 to 30 minutes.

Grease large cookie sheet. Punch dough down several times to remove air bubbles. Allow to rest on counter covered with inverted bowl for 15 minutes. Divide dough in half; roll each half to a 14 x 8-inch rectangle. Starting with 14-inch side, roll up; pinch edges firmly to seal. Place seam side down on greased cookie sheet; taper ends to a point. With sharp knife, make five ¼-inch deep diagonal slashes on top if each loaf. Cover; let rise in warm place until doubled in size, about 15 minutes.

Heat oven to 375°F. Uncover dough. Bake 25 minutes. In small bowl, beat egg white and 1 tablespoon water. Brush top of loaves with egg white mixture. Sprinkle with poppy seed. Bake an additional 5 or 10 minutes or until golden brown and loaves sound hollow when lightly tapped. Remove from cookie sheet immediately; cool on wire racks. MAKES 2 17-SLICE LOAVES.

# Pistachio Wheat Bread

*A real favorite at Karen's – we served it with our homemade preserves!*

2 Cups Milk

⅓ Cup Sugar

1 Tablespoon Salt

4 Tablespoons Butter

2 Eggs, beaten

2 Tablespoons Dry Yeast

½ Cup Warm Water

3 Cups White Bread Flour

3 Cups Whole Wheat Flour

1 Cup Shelled Pistachios, chopped

*Directions:* Scald milk; add sugar, salt, butter, and eggs, stirring constantly. Mix yeast and warm water and stir into mixture. Add flours and pistachios and blend with a dough hook until dough becomes smooth and resilient, normally when dough cleans side of bowl and balls around dough hook. Place in an oiled bowl, cover and let rise until doubled. Punch down and shape into loaves, placing in 2 well-greased loaf pans. Allow to rise until doubled. Bake in a 350°F oven approximately 30 to 35 minutes. Remove from oven. Remove loaves from pans, place on a wire rack, and allow to cool completely. MAKES 2 LOAVES.

# Focaccia Bread With Sun Dried Tomatoes & Herbs

2 Loaves Frozen White Bread Dough

¼ Cup Sun Dried Tomatoes, finely chopped

1 Teaspoon Dried Oregano

2 Teaspoons Granulated Garlic

½ Teaspoon Chile Flakes

Thaw bread dough. Place all ingredients in a mixer bowl with a dough hook; mix on low speed until well combined. Place on a well-greased cookie sheet and pat and roll out to an even thickness of approximately 1 inch. Let rise until doubled. Make slashes in 3 or 4 places and sprinkle lightly with kosher salt. Place in a preheated 350°F oven and bake until evenly browned. Remove from oven and let cool slightly. Cut into squares and serve with garlic oil or pesto. SERVES 8-10.

*Some of the earliest settlers and explorers in the area were Jesuits who traveled through the region establishing missions and mapping territories. Later the Franciscans came to the area and continued the work of the Jesuits.*

# Thimble Cookies

*A recipe from my high school home economics class.*
*A traditional Christmas cookie at the Callaghan house.*

3 Cups Butter
2 Cups Sugar
4 Egg Yolks
6 Cups All-Purpose Flour
Jam
Powdered Sugar

Cream the butter, add sugar gradually, add egg yolks, and continue beating until light and fluffy; add flour and continue mixing until well combined. Form the dough into balls the size of walnuts. Place on a greased cookie sheet. Make an indentation in each ball and fill with jam. Bake at 350°F for 10 minutes. Sift powdered sugar over cookies and allow to cool. MAKES 6-8 DOZEN.

*These three cookies make a wonderful trio for the holidays.*

*Thimble Cookies, Oatmeal-Coconut-Macadamia Nut Cookies and Shortbread Stars*

# Oatmeal – Coconut – Macadamia Nut Cookies

*A crispy cookie – a good accompaniment to flan, mousse, or just by itself.*

| | |
|---|---|
| ½ Cup Sugar | ½ Teaspoon Baking Soda |
| ½ Cup Light Brown Sugar, firmly packed | ¼ Teaspoon Salt |
| ½ Cup Butter, softened | 1 Cup Uncooked Quick-Cooking Oats |
| 1 Large Egg | ½ Cup Flaked Coconut |
| 1 Teaspoon Vanilla Extract | 1 Cup Macadamia Nuts, coarsely chopped |
| 1¼ Cups All-Purpose Flour | |

Beat first 5 ingredients at medium speed with an electric mixer until fluffy. Combine flour and next 5 ingredients. Add half of mixture at a time to butter mixture, beating at low speed until blended.

Drop dough by heaping teaspoonfuls 2 inches apart onto lightly greased baking sheets. Bake at 350°F for 7 to 10 minutes or until edges are golden. Cool on baking sheets 1 minute. Remove to wire racks to cool. MAKES 3 DOZEN.

# Shortbread Stars

*A pretty and tasty Christmas cookie. It reminds me of the shortbread cookies we had in Ireland.*

1 Pound Unsalted Butter, softened

1 Cup Icing Sugar (confectioner's)

1 Tablespoon Brandy

Juice Of One Orange

1 Teaspoon Vanilla

1 Teaspoon Almond Extract

5-6 Cups Flour

½ Cup Ground Almonds

Whip butter for 10 minutes until light and fluffy. Gradually add ½ cup icing sugar. Combine brandy, orange juice, vanilla, and almond extract. Add liquid and part of flour alternately to butter-sugar mixture, ½ cup of flour at a time, until all liquid has been added. Add ground almonds. Add remaining flour, ¼ cup at a time until dough forms a ball, and sides of bowl come clean. Roll out dough on a lightly floured work surface to ⅛-inch thickness. Cut out stars with a star cutter and place on baking sheet lined with parchment. Bake in a 350°F oven until lightly browned, about 10 to 15 minutes. When done, remove from oven, allow to cool 5 minutes, and remove from baking sheet. MAKES 5-6 DOZEN.

# Kahlua Orange Cake

| | | | |
|---|---|---|---|
| 1 | Dark Chocolate Cake Mix | 4 | Eggs |
| 1 | Small Package Instant Chocolate Pudding Mix | ¼ | Cup Vodka |
| ½ | Cup Vegetable Oil | 2 | Tablespoons Kahlua |
| 2 | Tablespoons Sugar | ½ | Cup Orange Juice |

Preheat oven to 350ºF. In a large bowl, mix all ingredients. Beat 3 to 4 minutes on medium-high speed of mixer. Pour into a well-greased and lightly floured bundt pan. Bake 50 to 55 minutes. Remove from oven and allow cake to cool approximately 10 minutes before inverting onto a plate and removing from pan. Cool completely before glazing.

## GLAZE

| | | | |
|---|---|---|---|
| 1 | Cup Bittersweet Chocolate Chips, melted | 1 | Tablespoon Vodka |
| 2 | Tablespoons Heavy Cream | 1 | Tablespoon Triple Sec |
| 1 | Tablespoon Kahlua | | |

Beat all ingredients together well. Drizzle over cake when cool. SERVES 12.

# Baked Ricotta Pudding With Strawberry Sauce

| | | | |
|---|---|---|---|
| 2 | 15-Ounce Containers Ricotta Cheese | 3 | Tablespoons Flour |
| ½ | Cup Sugar | ½ | Teaspoon Grated Lemon Peel |
| 1 | Egg Yolk | 2 | Egg Whites, at room temperature |
| 1 | Teaspoon Vanilla Extract | | Pinch of Salt |
| ¼ | Teaspoon Almond Extract | | Sliced Fresh Strawberries |
| ¼ | Teaspoon Cinnamon | | Strawberry Sauce (see recipe on page 208) |

Place ricotta cheese in sieve over bowl. Cover and refrigerate overnight.

Preheat oven to 350ºF. Coat shallow 1¾-quart baking dish with vegetable spray or grease lightly. Puree drained ricotta with ½ cup sugar and next 4 ingredients in processor or blender until light, about 5 minutes; mixture will be grainy. Transfer to a large bowl. Fold in flour and peel. Beat egg whites with salt to form soft peaks. Gradually add 1 tablespoon sugar and beat until stiff but not dry. Fold whites into ricotta mixture. Spoon ricotta mixture into prepared baking dish. Set dish in larger baking pan. Pour enough boiling water into larger pan to come half way up sides of dish. Place in oven. Bake until pudding is puffed and golden, about 45 minutes. Remove pudding from water bath. Cool on rack to room temperature. Garnish with sliced berries. Serve with Strawberry Sauce. MAKES 8 SERVINGS.

# Apple Almond Tart

*This is especially good with a late harvest riesling!*

*Apple Almond Tart*

Make into 6 small tartlets (3-4 inch), or one 9" tart.

6  Unbaked Tart Shells, chilled

**FILLING**
½  Cup Sliced Toasted Almonds
1  Cup Sugar
4  Tablespoons Butter
3  Eggs
3  Baking Apple (Granny Smith)

**GLAZE**
¼  Cup Strained Apricot Jam
2  Tablespoons Triple Sec

In food processor, process the almonds and sugar until blended. Add butter and eggs and process until smooth and creamy. Peel and core apples, slice lengthwise into thin pieces, and arrange decoratively in each tart pan. Spoon filling into prepared crust with apples. Bake at 375⁰F for 15 to 20 minutes, or until golden brown. Prepare glaze by mixing ingredients in a small bowl while tart is baking. When tart(s) is almost done, remove from oven and brush tops with glaze. Return to oven and bake until custard is set and lightly browned. Cool completely before serving. SERVES 6.

Wine Recommendation:
German Riesling Auslese

# Bittersweet Chocolate & Cranberry Terrine

## CRANBERRIES

1 Cup Sugar

1 Cup Water

1½ Cups Cranberries

## FILLING

| | |
|---|---|
| 1 Cup Whipping Cream | 1 Cup (2 Sticks) Unsalted Butter, at room temperature |
| 4 Egg Yolks | 1 Cup Unsweetened Cocoa Powder |
| ¾ Cup Sugar | ¾ Cup Whipping Cream, chilled |
| 12 Ounces Bittersweet Chocolate | 1 Cup Toasted Almonds, chopped |
| 1 Teaspoon Vanilla Extract | Whipped Cream |
| 1 Teaspoon Orange Zest | 8 ⅛" x 2" Orange Peel Strips |
| | Cranberry Coulis (see recipe below) |

FOR CRANBERRIES: Place wire rack atop cookie sheet. Stir sugar and water in a heavy medium saucepan over medium heat until sugar dissolves. Boil without stirring until syrup registers 234⁰F on a candy thermometer. Stir in cranberries until cranberries are coated with syrup and begin to pop, about 4 minutes. Using slotted spoon, transfer cranberries to prepared rack. Can prepare 1 day ahead. (Cover and refrigerate).

FILLING: Bring I cup cream to a simmer in a heavy medium saucepan. Whisk yolks and sugar in a small bowl to blend. Gradually whisk hot cream into yolk mixture. Return mixture to saucepan and stir over medium heat until mixture thickens and leaves a path on the back of a spoon when finger is drawn across the back, about 6 minutes; DO NOT BOIL. Remove from heat and add chocolate. Stir until chocolate melts and mixture is smooth. Add vanilla and orange zest. Cool custard to room temperature.

Line 8-cup rectangular terrine, or bread pan, with foil. Using electric mixer, beat unsalted butter and cocoa powder in a large bowl until light and fluffy. Gradually beat in custard. Whip ¾ cup of chilled whipping cream, in a large bowl, to soft peaks. Fold into chocolate mixture. Spoon filling into prepared pan. Cover with plastic and refrigerate overnight. (Can prepare 4 days ahead.)

Unmold terrine onto platter; remove foil. Smooth top and sides with spatula if necessary. Spoon whipped cream into pastry bag fitted with a medium star tip. Pipe 16 rosettes down center of terrine. Top rosettes alternately with reserved cranberries and orange peel strips. Cut terrine into thin slices and serve with Cranberry Coulis. SERVES 16.

## CRANBERRY COULIS

| | |
|---|---|
| 4 Cups Cranberries | 2 Tablespoons Orange Zest |
| 1½ Cups Orange Juice | 2 Tablespoons Grand Marnier Or Triple Sec |
| 1 Cup Sugar | |

Combine cranberries, orange juice, sugar, and orange zest in heavy large saucepan. Simmer over medium heat until cranberries lose their shape and mixture thickens slightly, stirring occasionally, about 12 minutes. Transfer mixture to processor and blend until smooth. Stir in liqueur. (Can be prepared 4 days ahead). MAKES 4 CUPS.

# Mexican Chocolate Spice Cake

*(With Kahlua Crème Anglaise)*

Mexican Chocolate Spice Cake

*This is simple and delicious. It is also good with a few dots of raspberry puree swirled through the Crème Anglaise.*

1   Milk Chocolate Cake Mix
1   Tablespoon Ground Cinnamon
1   Teaspoon Nutmeg
3   Large Eggs
1   Tablespoon Instant Espresso Powder
¾   Cup Plain Yogurt
1   Cup Water

Place all ingredients in a mixing bowl and beat with whisk for approximately 2 minutes. Pour into a well greased 10-inch cake pan. Place in preheated 350°F oven and bake for approximately 30 minutes or, until top springs back when touched slightly. Remove from oven and let cool 7 to 8 minutes. Remove from pan and cool completely. Slice and serve with Kahlua Crème Anglaise. SERVES 12.

## KAHLUA CREME ANGLAISE

6  Egg Yolks          1  Tablespoon Vanilla
⅛  Cup Granulated Sugar   1  Tablespoon Kahlua
2  Cups Milk, scalded & cooled slightly   1  Teaspoon Instant Espresso Powder

Using an electric mixer, beat the egg yolks lightly and add the sugar, beating until the mixture forms a ribbon when the beaters are lifted. Slowly stir in the scalded milk as you continue to beat. Transfer the mixture to a heavy pan and cook over moderately low heat, stirring constantly, until thickened to the consistency of heavy cream. Remove from the heat and stir in the vanilla. Add the Kahlua. Transfer to a bowl, cover with a round of wax paper placed directly on the surface, and refrigerate to chill. Serve pooled around a slice of Mexican Spice Cake. Sprinkle with Espresso Powder.

Wine Recommendation:
Banyuls or Tawny Port  (Especially Australian Vin Santo)

# Pineapple Upside Down Cake

*A recipe for those who love the homey taste of desserts – this is special!*

½   Cube (4 tablespoons) Butter
¼   Cup Brown Sugar
1   #303 Can Pineapple Rings
Maraschino Cherries
1   Yellow Cake Mix

In a 10-inch round cake pan melt butter with brown sugar.  Place pineapple rings in bottom of pan to cover, then place a cherry in the center of each pineapple ring.  Prepare cake mix according to directions.  Pour batter carefully into pan over pineapple rings and cherries.  Bake in preheated 375⁰F oven for approximately 45 minutes making sure it is well done in the center (a toothpick inserted in the center should come out clean).  SERVES 12.

*Pineapple Upside Down Cake*

# Georgia Chess Pie

½ Cup Butter  
1½ Cups Sugar  
3 Eggs  
1 Teaspoon Cornmeal  
1 Teaspoon Vinegar  

1 Tablespoon Vanilla Extract  
1 Teaspoon Cornstarch  
1 Cup Flaked Coconut  
1 9" Pie Shell, unbaked  

Cream butter and sugar until light. Add eggs, one at a time, beating thoroughly after each addition. Add next 4 ingredients and beat well. Stir in coconut and pour into pie shell. Bake in a 325°F oven for 1 hour or until firm. Serve slightly warm. This is a very rich pie so serve it in small wedges. SERVES 6-8.

# Kahlua — Chocolate — Espresso Mousse

*My favorite mousse recipe – no eggs.*

12 Ounces Bittersweet Chocolate, melted  
2 Tablespoons Espresso Beans, finely ground  
⅓ Cup Kahlua  
3¾ Cups Whipping Cream  

Melt chocolate in top of double boiler. Remove from heat and add espresso, Kahlua, and ¾ cup of cream. Mix well. Beat the remaining 3 cups of cream until stiff peaks form. Gently fold in chocolate mixture by hand until well combined. Refrigerate till ready to serve. SERVES 6-8.

# Greek Rice Pudding

½ Cup Rice  
2 Quarts Milk  
½ Cup Sugar  
Grated Rind Of 1 Orange  
Cinnamon  

Boil the rice for 5 minutes in 2 cups of water. Drain. Bring the milk to a boil. Remove from heat and keep hot. Pour 1 cup of hot milk into a saucepan. Bring to a boil and add the rice. Cook on low heat, stirring constantly and adding milk every time it has been absorbed, until all of the milk has been used. The whole process from the time you begin adding the hot milk will take approximately 45 to 50 minutes. During the last 15 minutes of cooking, stir in sugar and orange rind. Serve cold sprinkled with cinnamon. SERVES 6-8.

# Karen's Pecan Pie

*The best I have ever found – not so sweet!*

1 Cube (8 tablespoons) Butter, melted

1 Cup Sugar

⅛ Cup Dark Karo Syrup

3 Eggs

2 Cups Pecans, whole

1 Unbaked 9" Pie Shell

Combine butter, sugar, Karo, and eggs in a bowl and mix well.  Add pecans and stir until well combined.  Pour into the pie shell and bake in a 350°F oven approximately 25 to 30 minutes or, until the filling is set.  Remove from oven and allow to cool until ready to serve.  SERVES 6–8.

# Cappuccino Cheesecake

1 Cup Chocolate Wafer Cookie Crumbs

3 Tablespoons Sugar

3 Teaspoons Butter, melted

4 Packages (8 ounces each) Philadelphia Cream Cheese

1 Cup Sugar

2 Tablespoons Flour

2 Teaspoons Vanilla Extract

4 Eggs

1 Tablespoon Instant Espresso

3 Tablespoons Kahlua

Mix crumbs, 3 tablespoons sugar, and butter; press onto bottom and 2 inches up the sides of a 9-inch springform pan. Bake at 325°F for 10 minutes.

Mix cream cheese, 1 cup sugar, flour, and vanilla with electric mixer on medium speed until well blended.  Add eggs, one at a time, mixing on low speed after each addition, just until blended.  Stir instant espresso into Kahlua until dissolved.  Blend into batter.  Pour into crust.  Bake at 325°F for 55 minutes to 1 hour until center is almost set.  Run knife or metal spatula around rim of pan to loosen cake; cool before removing rim of pan.  Refrigerate 4 hours or overnight.  SERVES 12.

# Bread Pudding With A Whiskey Sauce

*Our favorite – it is lighter than most versions and the unusual dried fruit adds color and unique flavor.*

Bread Pudding With A Whiskey Sauce

4   Tablespoons Butter, softened
½   Pound Sliced Egg Bread, such as Brioche
1   Cup Dried Apricots, chopped
4   Large Eggs
4   Egg Whites
⅓   Cup Sugar
½   Teaspoon Salt
3   Cups Half & Half
2   Teaspoons Vanilla Extract
1   Cup Dried Cranberries

Use 4 tablespoons butter to coat one side of the slices of bread.  Set aside.  In a large bowl, beat the eggs, egg whites, sugar, and salt.  In a saucepan over moderate heat, heat the half & half until scalded (a skin will begin to form on top).  Slowly whisk the hot cream into the egg mixture, taking care that the eggs don't "scramble."  Stir in the vanilla.

Preheat the oven to 350⁰F.  In an 8-cup soufflé dish, arrange the bread, apricots, and cranberries in alternate layers, making sure that you end with a layer of bread.  Pour the egg mixture over and allow to stand for 30 minutes.  Place the soufflé dish in oven and bake for 45 minutes or until the center of the custard is just set.  Remove and allow to stand for 15 minutes before serving.  Serve warm or at room temperature with Whiskey Sauce.  SERVES 8.

### WHISKEY SAUCE
3   Tablespoons Butter
½   Cup Brown Sugar
50   Milliliters Whiskey
1½   Cups Heavy Cream

Melt butter and add sugar.  Boil until syrupy, add whiskey, and boil until all sugar is combined and mixture is again thick and syrupy.  Add cream and bring back to a boil.  Boil until sauce is thick and caramel colored.  Place in a covered container and refrigerate until ready to serve.  Reheat to warm before serving.

# Chocolate Cappuccino Cake With Coffee Cream Ganache

*A not so sweet chocolate cake. We love it!*

Chocolate Cappuccino Cake With Coffee Cream Ganache

1  Butter Chocolate Cake Mix
2  Tablespoons Instant Coffee Granules

Prepare cake mix according to package directions, adding coffee granules dissolved in the water.  Pour into a 10-inch cake pan sprayed with pan release spray.  Bake at 350°F approximately 50 minutes (test for doneness – cake will spring back when lightly touched).   When done, remove from oven and cool 7 minutes on a wire rack.  Invert cake onto plate and allow to cool completely.  Frost with Coffee Cream Ganache (see recipe below).  SERVES 12.

## COFFEE CREAM GANACHE

8  Tablespoons Butter
½  Cup Brown Sugar
1  Tablespoon Instant Coffee Granules, dissolved in whipping cream

1  Cup Whipping Cream
2  Cups Confectioner's Sugar
2  Teaspoons Vanilla

Melt butter in medium sized saucepan.  Add brown sugar and heat, stirring until sugar is melted and bubbly.  Add coffee and cream and stir till boiling.  Remove from heat and add confectioner's sugar and vanilla, mixing well.  Allow to cool.  Beat well with mixer fitted with a whisk.  Spread over top and sides of cake.  Garnish with whole coffee beans.

*desserts*

# *Spring*

The migrating birds – the Sonoita/ Patagonia area, renowned for its bird life, attracts birders from around the world. Tourists looking for relief from the frenetic pace of Tucson and Phoenix head to Sonoita in droves. This impacts the restaurant business dramatically. Many times you must have reservations to be seated at Karen's Wine Country Café. I will never forget the first patron we had to turn away for lack of room and her remark, "who would believe that a small, remote restaurant could possibly be that busy!"

Indian paintbrush, baby cottontail rabbits, shy pronghorn antelope, baby Red Tailed Hawks along with mom and dad screeching in the skies above – all herald the emergence of Spring in Sonoita. This is my favorite time of year. It is a time of renewing. I love to garden and have a difficult time disciplining myself not to start planting flowers while the danger of frost is still here. We can have frost as late as mid-May.

# Cheese & Spinach Pastries

*These flavors are reminiscent of Spanakopita without quite so much work.*

## PASTRY

1⅓ Cups All-Purpose Flour     ½ Teaspoon Salt

½ Cup Butter     3-4 Tablespoons Cold Water

In the bowl of a food processor, mix flour and salt, cut in butter with steel blade until mixture resembles coarse crumbs.  Sprinkle with cold water, 1 tablespoon at a time, while pulsing blender, until all flour is moistened and pastry almost cleans the sides of the bowl.  Additional water may be added if necessary.

## FILLING

1  Egg, separated

1  Cup Fresh Spinach, chopped

1  Tablespoon Onion, finely chopped

1  Cup Ricotta Cheese

2  Tablespoons Grated Parmesan Cheese

¼  Teaspoon Pepper

1  Garlic Clove, finely chopped

Combine egg yolk, remaining ingredients, and mix well.

ASSEMBLY:  Heat oven to 425⁰F.  Gather pastry into ball.  Shape into flattened round on lightly floured, cloth covered, board.  Roll into rectangle, 14 x 12 inches; brush with egg white.  Cut into 2-inch squares.  Spoon 1 level teaspoon of filling onto the center of each square.  Bring 2 diagonally opposite corners of pastry up and over filling, overlapping slightly.  Press down to seal.  Do the same with the other 2 opposite corners, pressing to seal.  Brush top of pastry with egg white.  Bake on an ungreased cookie sheet until the crust is golden brown, 12 to 15 minutes.  Immediately remove from cookie sheet; serve hot.  MAKES 42 APPETIZERS.

# Jalapeño Cheddar Canapés

1  Cup Extra Sharp Cheddar, grated

1  Large Egg, beaten lightly

2½  Teaspoons Pickled Jalapeño Pepper, minced

16  1½"-Rounds, cut from sliced whole wheat bread, toasted lightly

In a small bowl stir together the Cheddar, egg, and jalapeño pepper until the mixture is well combined.  Spread 1 teaspoon of mixture on each toast round, mounding it, and broil the canapés in a jelly-roll pan under a preheated broiler about 4 inches from the heat for 2 to 3 minutes, or until they are puffed and golden. MAKES 16 CANAPÉS.

# Phyllo Wrapped Brie With Caramelized Onions

1 Tablespoon Butter

4 Medium Onions, in thinly sliced wedges

2 Teaspoons Sugar

¼ Cup Hazelnuts, toasted & chopped

In saucepan melt butter, add onions and cook over medium low heat about 15 minutes, or, until onions are tender and golden, stirring occasionally. Sprinkle sugar over onions. Cook covered for 10 to 15 minutes or, until brown. Stir in hazelnuts. Cool.

8 Sheets Phyllo Dough (purchased frozen & thawed)

¼ Cup Butter, melted

2 Brie Rounds (4½ ounces)

¼ Cup Apricot Spread (jam)

Place 2 stacks of 4 layers of Phyllo, buttering each layer. Cut layers into a 12-inch circle. Slice Brie horizontally in half. Place 1st half on circle; rind at bottom, spread 1 tablespoon apricot jam and ½ onion mixture. Place 2nd half of Brie on top of 1st half and repeat. Top 2nd half (rind at bottom to finish) with ½ of onion mixture. Wrap Phyllo up and over Brie and filling, pleating Phyllo and twisting slightly. Repeat with 2nd Phyllo circle and other ingredients. Brush both slightly with butter. Bake at 400°F for about 20 minutes. Let stand for 5 to 10 minutes. Serve with sliced baguette and sliced apples and/or pears. SERVES 6-8.

# Bacon & Roasted Red Pepper Swirls

*These make a pretty presentation and taste really good!*

1 8-Ounce Can Refrigerated Crescent Rolls

1 3-Ounce Package Cream Cheese

4 Bacon Slices, cooked crisp & crumbled

2 Tablespoons Onion, minced

1 Teaspoon Milk

2 Tablespoons Roasted Red Pepper, chopped & well drained

Grated Parmesan Cheese

Unroll crescent roll dough, and separate into 4 rectangles; press perforations to seal. Stir together cream cheese, bacon, onion, roasted peppers, and milk until well blended; spread mixture evenly on rectangles. Roll up, jellyroll fashion, starting at long side; press edges to seal. Cut each roll into 8 slices; and place on ungreased baking sheets. Sprinkle swirls evenly with Parmesan cheese. Bake at 375°F for 12 to 15 minutes or until lightly browned. Serve warm. MAKES 2-2½ DOZEN.

# Wild Mushroom — Walnut Turnovers

*This is a really fun item to make and people love it!*
*Great for a large party because they can be made ahead and frozen.*

¼ Cup Shallots, finely minced
1 Stick Unsalted Butter
¼ Pound Wild Mushrooms (porcini, morels or shiitakes) cleaned well, finely chopped
1 Teaspoon Dried Thyme
¼ Cup Chicken Broth
½ Cup Toasted Walnuts, finely chopped
¼ Cup Sour Cream
2 Teaspoons Dijon Mustard
24 Slices Homemade Style White Bread, thinly sliced, crusts removed

In a large skillet over moderate heat, cook the shallots in 1 tablespoon of the butter about 3 minutes or until softened. Add mushrooms and continue cooking until all the liquid is evaporated. Add thyme and stock and simmer until mixture is almost dry. Remove from heat; stir in the walnuts, sour cream, mustard, and salt and pepper to taste. Melt remaining butter in a small saucepan.

Keep bread wrapped in plastic wrap so that it does not dry out. Roll out a piece of bread with a rolling pin until paper-thin. Mound 1 rounded teaspoon of the filling in the center of each bread slice, brush the edges with melted butter and fold the edges over to enclose the filling and form a triangle, pressing the edges together tightly. Be sure the edges are tightly sealed. Repeat with remaining bread and filling. Brush each turnover with melted butter. The turnovers may be made up to this point and frozen. Arrange turnovers in one layer on a baking sheet and bake for 10 minutes (12 to 15 if frozen) or until golden. MAKES 24.

# Stuffed Cherry Tomatoes

*Simple, very simple. Great for a last minute item.*

1 Package French Boursin (herbed cream cheese)
2 Containers (50-60) Cherry Tomatoes

Bring Boursin to room temperature. Wash and trim top ¼ off cherry tomatoes. Remove seeds from tomatoes and allow to drain upside down on piece of paper toweling. Using a teaspoon, fill each cherry tomato with Boursin (can be made ahead and kept covered in refrigerator). When ready to serve, place tomatoes on a baking sheet and place under broiler for 5 to 6 minutes. Serve immediately. SERVES 10-15.

# Wild Mushroom Raviolis In Broth

*These work as a soup or entrée. Very tasty and light!*

1 Cup Button Mushrooms, cleaned, stemmed & chopped
1 Cup Shiitake Mushrooms, cleaned, stemmed & chopped
½ Cup Sherry
1 Cup Button Mushrooms
2 Teaspoons Fresh Thyme
2 Tablespoons Butter
Salt & Pepper, to taste

Sauté mushrooms and thyme in butter till most of the liquid has evaporated. Add sherry and continue sautéing until liquid has again evaporated. Add salt and pepper and remove from heat. Place in a covered bowl and chill.

### TO ASSEMBLE

1 Cup Shredded Parmesan Cheese     1 Package Wonton Skins
Mushroom Mixture     8 Cups Chicken Broth

On a lightly floured cutting board place 8 individual wonton skins separately and flat. Place approximately 2 to 3 tablespoons of mixture on each skin and place 1 to 2 tablespoons of Parmesan on top of mixture. Using a pastry brush and cold water, brush edges of wonton skin and place another skin on top and press edges together well (re-wet if necessary). Place finished ravioli on a foil lined baking sheet. Continue until all mushrooms and cheese are used up (can be frozen at this point).

TO SERVE: Heat chicken broth to boiling. Add raviolis and cook till they float. Ladle 3 raviolis into bowl and add broth to fill. Garnish with Parmesan Chip Crisp (see recipe on page 212). SERVES 4.

# Cream Of Sorrel Soup

*One of our favorite herbs – a very lemony taste and a great hit as a soup. Try growing some!*

2 Tablespoons Butter     4 Cups Fresh Sorrel Leaves, rinsed & patted dry
5 Small Leeks, white part only     1 Cup Heavy Cream
6 Cups Chicken Broth     Salt & Pepper
2 Medium Baking Potatoes, peeled & diced

Heat butter and gently sauté leeks for 10 minutes, then add chicken stock and potatoes and simmer until potatoes are tender, about 20 minutes. Add sorrel leaves and simmer 5 minutes longer. Puree soup, leaving flecks of green; add cream and heat just to a boil. Serve immediately garnished with a fresh sprig of parsley. SERVES 4-6.

# Tortellini Soup

*Another quick and tasty soup. Pesto is available ready made
if you don't have the time or fresh basil to make it yourself.*

1 Tablespoon Olive Oil  
1 Medium Onion, chopped  
½ Cup Diced Carrots  
2 Garlic Cloves, minced  
4 Cups Chicken Broth  
4 Ounces Cheese Tortellini  

1 Cup Spinach Leaves, chopped  
½ Cup Frozen Green Peas  
2 Tablespoons Pesto (see recipe on page 114)  
2 Tablespoons Freshly Grated Parmesan Cheese  
Salt & Freshly Ground Pepper  

In large saucepan heat oil over medium heat.  Add onion, carrot, and garlic; cook, stirring frequently, until onion is translucent.  Add broth and bring to a boil.  Reduce heat and stir in tortellini.  Simmer until tortellini is cooked, 5 to 8 minutes.  Stir in spinach, peas, cheese, pesto, and salt and pepper to taste.  Serve garnished with chopped chives. SERVES 4.

# Creamy Thyme – Garlic Soup

*A comfort food.  Many people have told us it is a wonderful for what ails you!*

1 Garlic Head, cleaned & peeled, then chopped  
3 Large Onions, coarsely chopped  
4 Tablespoons Olive Oil  
6 Cups Chicken Broth  

Herbs In Cheesecloth, wrapped & tied with 6" strings; 8-10 Parsley Springs; 4-5 Thyme Sprigs; 1 Bay Leaf

4 Cups 1" Chunks Of French Bread  
½ Cup Heavy Cream  
2 Tablespoons Fresh Thyme Leaves, chopped  
Fresh Chives  

In a 4-quart pan, combine 3 tablespoons garlic and 2 tablespoons of the oil.  Cook over medium heat, stirring, just until garlic is golden, about 5 minutes.  Lift out garlic and set aside.  Add remaining garlic, oil, and onion.  Stir often over medium heat till mixture is a light golden, about 30 minutes.  Add broth, herb bundle, bread, and thyme.  Simmer, covered, 20 to 30 minutes.  Lift out and discard herb bundle.  In a food processor, whirl soup, a portion at a time, until smoothly pureed.  Return to pan and add cream.  Stir over medium heat until hot.  Add salt and pepper to taste.  Ladle into 6 to 8 bowls.  Add equal amounts of the fried garlic and chives to each bowl.  SERVES 6-8.

# Sweet Red Pepper & Corn Chowder

| 6 Slices Bacon | 2 Tablespoons Margarine Or Butter |
| 1 Large White Onion, finely chopped | 2 Large Red Peppers, seeded & diced |
| 2 Cups Water | 4 Cups New Red Potatoes, diced |
| 2 Cups Chicken Broth | 2 Cups Milk |
| 2 Pounds Cream Style Corn | Salt & Pepper, to taste |
| 2 Cups Half & Half | |

*Sweet Red Pepper & Corn Chowder*

In a 5-quart pan, cook bacon until crisp. Remove bacon, crumble, and set aside. Discard all but 2 tablespoons of drippings. Add onion and red bell peppers to drippings and sauté until soft. Add water, chicken broth, potatoes, and corn. Bring to a boil, reduce heat, cover, and simmer for about 20 minutes. Add milk, half & half, and season to taste with salt and pepper. Heat and stir in margarine or butter. Top with bacon and serve. SERVES 8.

Wine Recommendation:
Austrian Gruner Veltliner (Weingartner)

# Five Onion Soup

## (Onions, Shallots, Leeks, Garlic & Chives)

*This was extremely successful at a wine dinner we served.*
*It pairs very well with some of the Sauvignon Blancs available.*

3 Tablespoons Olive Oil
4 Cups Yellow Onions, finely diced
¼ Cup Shallots, cleaned & sliced
1 Tablespoon Garlic, chopped
1 Cup Dry White Wine
1 Bay Leaf
6 Cups Chicken Broth
2 Teaspoons Thyme, minced (or 1 teaspoon dried thyme)
2 Teaspoons Oregano, minced (or 1 teaspoon dried oregano)
½ Cup Celery, minced
1 Cup Sliced Leeks, white & green tender parts
2 Tablespoons Dry Sherry
2 Tablespoons Chives, minced
Garnish With Gremolata (see recipe below)

### GREMOLATA GARNISH
1 Tablespoon Garlic, minced
2 Tablespoons Parsley, minced
2 Tablespoons Lemon Zest

GREMOLATA GARNISH:  Combine ingredients in a small bowl.

In a medium saucepan, heat the olive oil.  Add the onions, shallots, and garlic and sauté until they just begin to color.  Puree half of this mixture and return to the pan.  Add wine, bay leaf, and chicken stock and simmer for 10 minutes.

Season with salt and pepper (may be prepared to this point and refrigerated).
Just before serving, add the thyme, oregano, celery, leeks, and sherry to the hot soup base.  Bring to a simmer and simmer for 2 minutes.  DO NOT OVERCOOK;  The vegetables should be crunchy.  Remove the bay leaf; stir in the chives, and garnish with a sprinkle of gremolata.  SERVES 6-8.

# Basic Chicken Broth

| | |
|---|---|
| 1 Chicken (2½-3 pounds), rinsed & cut in half | 3 Celery Ribs, trimmed & chopped |
| 2½ Quarts Cold Water | 2 Carrots, pared & thinly sliced |
| 2 Medium Onions, chopped | 10 Sprigs Fresh Parsley |

Place chicken and water in 6-quart stockpot. Over medium heat, heat to simmering. Skim off foam and add vegetables and parsley. Reduce heat to maintain simmer. Simmer, partially covered, until chicken is tender, about 1 hour. Using slotted spoon, remove chicken to plate and let cool. When cool to handle, remove meat from chicken. Return bones to pot and simmer, partially covered, for 1 hour longer. Meanwhile, discard chicken skin and tear meat into bite sized shreds. Freeze in portions for recipes calling for cooked chicken.

Strain broth through fine sieve to extract as much liquid as possible; discard solids. If using immediately, spoon off fat from broth. To store broth and chicken, let cool separately to room temperature, then refrigerate, covered, up to 3 days. Remove fat from cold broth before using. MAKES 1-1½ QUARTS.

# Carrot Vichyssoise

3 Tablespoons Butter
1½ Pounds Carrots, peeled & sliced
2 Leeks (white part only), sliced
1¾ Pounds Potatoes, peeled & cut into ½" dice
1 Teaspoon Fresh Thyme, minced, Or ½ Teaspoon Dried, crumbled
7 Cups Chicken Broth
½ Cup Dry Vermouth
2 Cups Heavy Cream
Salt & Freshly Ground White Pepper
Fresh Lemon Juice
Fresh Thyme, minced

Melt butter in heavy saucepan over medium-low heat. Add carrots and leeks and cook until leeks are tender, stirring occasionally, about 10 minutes. Mix in potatoes and 1 teaspoon thyme. Add stock and vermouth. Simmer until potatoes are tender, about 25 minutes.

Puree soup in batches in food processor or hand held immersion blender. Return to saucepan. Add cream. Season to taste with salt, pepper, and lemon juice. (Can be prepared 2 days ahead. Cover and refrigerate.) Stir over medium heat until warmed through. Garnish with minced fresh thyme and serve. MAKES 12 SERVINGS.

*appetizers, small dishes, soups*

# French Garlic Soup

24  Plump Cloves Of Garlic, peeled, cut in half lengthwise

1  Bouquet Garni, consisting of 1 bay leaf, 1 dried fennel stem, 1 sprig rosemary &

1  2"-piece dried orange peel, bound together with cotton string

3  Cups Chicken Broth

1  Cup Dry White Wine

¼  Teaspoon Fresh Ground Black

Pepper & Salt, to taste

12  Slices Stale French Bread, oven toasted

2  Teaspoons Light Olive Oil

Simmer the garlic with the broth, wine, and the bouquet garni until the garlic is completely soft, approximately 15 to 20 minutes.  Discard the bouquet garni.  Press the cooked garlic through a sieve and put the puree back into the soup.  Reheat the soup to a boil, cover the pot, and remove it from the stove to steep.  Arrange the toasted bread into 4 bowls and sprinkle the toasts with black pepper.  Salt the soup to taste, reheat it to the boiling point, and pour it over the toasted bread. Drizzle the toasts in each bowl with ½ teaspoon of the olive oil.  Serve at once while very hot.  SERVES 4.

# Chunky Minestrone Soup

1  Medium Carrot, thinly sliced

2  Teaspoons Instant Beef Bullion Granules

½  Teaspoon Dried Oregano, crushed

½  Teaspoon Dried Basil, crushed

1  Garlic Clove, minced

1  Small Zucchini, halved lengthwise & sliced

⅛  Teaspoon Pepper

½  Cup Tiny Shell Macaroni

1  Can Cannellini Or Kidney Beans (15 ounces)

In a large saucepan combine all ingredients *except zucchini, macaroni, and beans.*  Bring to boiling, stirring occasionally.  Reduce heat; simmer, covered, 15 to 20 minutes or until tender.  Stir in zucchini, macaroni, and beans.  Cook, uncovered for 5 minutes. Serve garnished with chopped parsley if desired.  SERVES 4.

# Béchamel Sauce

⅓ Cup Butter

5 Tablespoons Flour

3 Cups Hot Water

Salt & Pepper

¼ Teaspoon Nutmeg

Melt the butter in a heavy saucepan and stir in flour until smooth. Add gradually the hot milk, stirring constantly, and season with salt, pepper, and nutmeg. Simmer on medium low heat until mixture thickens, about 15 to 20 minutes, stirring constantly. *Use as a sauce for any cooked vegetable.*

# Roasted New Potatoes With Garlic & Mint

8 Small New Potatoes, scrubbed

3 Tablespoons Olive Oil

8 Fresh Garlic Cloves (1 per potato)

Fresh Mint Leaves (2-3 per potato), chopped

Greek Seasoning (available in the supermarket or substitute salt & freshly ground pepper)

Steam potatoes in the top of a steamer until almost done. Remove from steamer and chill. Slice potatoes in ⅛-inch slices, and arrange over bottom of roasting pan. Mix olive oil and garlic, and pour over potato slices. Sprinkle with chopped mint leaves and Greek seasoning. Bake at 350°F approximately 1 hour. Remove and serve. SERVES 4.

# Garlicky Mashed Potatoes

*A great potato recipe – it is easy to eat only these!*

8 Large Russet Potatoes, peeled & cubed (can substitute half thin skinned Red Potatoes)

¼ Cup Butter

¾ Cup Sour Cream

1 Tablespoon Dill Weed, finely chopped (substitute rosemary or thyme, if desired)

1 Tablespoon Chives, finely chopped

8 Cloves Of Garlic

Boil potatoes and garlic in water until soft. Drain and mash. Add butter, sour cream, dill weed, and chives. Mix well. Salt and pepper to taste. SERVES 8-10.

*vegetables, salads and grains*

# Savory Pasta Custards

*These make such a nice change of pace with any entrée as well. The ingredients can be put together ahead of time and assembled just before baking.*

| | | | |
|---|---|---|---|
| ½ | Pound Capellini Or Angel Hair Pasta | 1 | Teaspoon Hot Pepper Sauce |
| | 3 Eggs | ½ | Cup Heavy Cream |
| 1½ | Cups Low Fat Ricotta Cheese | 1 | Cup Chicken Broth |
| 1½ | Tablespoons Parsley, minced | 1 | Tablespoon Butter |
| 1 | Teaspoon Salt | 2 | Tablespoons Freshly Grated Parmesan Cheese |
| ¼ | Teaspoon Freshly Ground Black Pepper | | |

Preheat oven to 350°F. Generously butter a 2-quart, shallow, ovenproof casserole or, alternatively, 6, 1-cup individual ramekins. Break the pasta in half and drop into a large pot of boiling water. Separate the pasta strands with a fork if necessary. Cook for 1½ minutes, or until the pasta is half cooked. Drain and rinse under cold water. Shake off excess moisture and place in the prepared dish or divide and place in the individual ramekins. In a large bowl, beat together the eggs and ricotta cheese. Whisk in the parsley, salt, black pepper, hot pepper sauce, cream, and chicken broth. Pour over the pasta and dot with butter. Bake for 45 minutes, if using the casserole dish or, for 25 minutes if using the individual ramekins; or until the custard is set and the top is lightly browned. Allow to cool for a few minutes before running a knife around the edge(s) and un-molding. Serve with Roasted Red Pepper-Tomato Sauce (see recipe on page 207). SERVES 6.

# Brandied Creamy Potatoes

| | |
|---|---|
| 1½ | Pounds Thin-Skinned White Potatoes, scrubbed |
| 2 | Tablespoons Butter |
| ½ | Cup Brandy |
| ½ | Cup Chicken Broth |
| 1 | Cup Heavy Cream |
| 4 | Green Onions, ends trimmed |
| | Freshly Ground Black Pepper |
| | Freshly Grated Nutmeg |

Cut potatoes into ¼-inch sticks. In a 10 to 12-inch skillet, over medium-high heat, melt butter and add potatoes. Using a wide spatula, occasionally turn potatoes just till they begin to turn pale gold, about 10 minutes. Add brandy and broth; cover and simmer till potatoes are very tender when pierced, about 15 minutes. Add cream. Gently turn potatoes over with spatula. Cook over high heat till boiling vigorously, about 5 minutes. Spoon equal portions of potatoes onto 4 salad plates and place green onions along side. Sprinkle generously with pepper and nutmeg. SERVES 4.

# Roasted Peppers Napoli

*Roasted Peppers Napoli with Vienna Bread*

| ½ Cup Olive Oil | 1 Cup Chopped Greek Kalamata Olives, loosely packed |
|---|---|
| 2 Garlic Cloves, finely minced | ½ Cup Capers, drained |
| 6 Roasted Red Bell Pepper Halves | 1 Cup Romano Cheese, grated |

Heat 2 tablespoons of olive oil in a small sauté pan until hot. Add chopped garlic and cook, stirring constantly, until golden. Remove from heat and set aside. In a 9-inch square pan, begin layering vegetables. Place half of roasted peppers on bottom of pan. Sprinkle with ½ the olives, ½ the garlic, ½ the capers, and ½ the Romano. Using the same ingredients, do a second layer the same as the first layer. Finish by sprinkling olive oil over the entire top. Place in a 375⁰F oven for approximately 30 minutes or, until very hot and slightly bubbly. Remove from oven and serve with lots of French Bread. SERVES 4-6.

*vegetables, salads and grains*

# Spinach & Bulgur Salad

½ Cup Bulgur

½ Cup Boiling Water

1 Cup Plain Yogurt

¼ Cup Olive Oil

2 Tablespoons Red Wine Vinegar

2 Garlic Cloves, minced

1 Teaspoon Ground Cumin

Salt & Fresh Ground Pepper

8 Cups Fresh Spinach Leaves, torn into bite size pieces

½ Large Red Onion, sliced

½ Cup Sliced Black Olives

¼ Cup Freshly Grated Parmesan,

Combine the bulgur and boiling water in a small bowl.  Let stand until bulgur has absorbed the water, about 10 minutes.  Cool bulgur completely.  For dressing, stir yogurt and next 4 ingredients in another small bowl.  Season to taste with salt and pepper.

Place spinach, onion, olives, Parmesan, and bulgur in a large bowl.  Add enough dressing to season to taste. Toss well.  MAKES 4 SERVINGS.

# Corn Pudding

*We love this dish – it is another side dish that it is easy to eat all by itself!*

3 Eggs

2 Cups Milk

1 Tablespoon Butter Or Margarine, melted

1 Tablespoon Flour

1 Tablespoon Sugar

2 Cups Whole-Kernel Corn

Preheat oven to 400ºF. Grease a 1½-quart casserole.  In mixing bowl beat eggs and milk until smooth.  Add butter (or margarine), flour, sugar and salt. Beat until blended. Stir in corn. Pour into greased casserole and bake in preheated oven for 45 minutes, or until set.  SERVES 4-6.

# Grilled Salmon Fillet Salad

*A nice, fresh way to serve grilled salmon – the flavors are delicious!*

16  Ounces Mixed Greens
4  Salmon Fillets, marinated in Karen's® Lemon-Herb Vinaigrette & grilled until firm
8  Young Asparagus Spears, steamed & chilled
Fresh Red Bell Pepper Rings
Shredded Parmesan Cheese
Cucumber-Dill Dressing (see recipe below)

Arrange greens on each of 4 plates.  Place salmon fillet in center of each plate.  Arrange remaining ingredients on each plate paying attention to your presentation.  Dress with Cucumber-Dill Dressing.  SERVES 4.

## CUCUMBER-DILL DRESSING

½  Medium Cucumber, peeled, seeded & chopped into very fine dice
1  Cup Sour Cream
2  Tablespoons Miracle Whip
1  Tablespoon Rice Vinegar
Salt & Fresh Ground Pepper

Mix well and chill until ready to serve.

# Chicken & Pasta Salad

*(With A Jalapeño -Tomato Vinaigrette)*

2  Cloves Garlic                         ¼  Cup Olive Oil
1  Tablespoon Fresh Ginger, minced       Salt & Fresh Ground Pepper
2  Teaspoons Ground Cumin                 8  Chicken Thighs
3  Tablespoons Red Wine Vinegar          1  Pound Angel Hair Pasta

Mince the garlic and ginger.  In a bowl combine the garlic, ginger, cumin, vinegar, oil, ½ teaspoon salt, and 1 teaspoon pepper.  Add the chicken, stir to coat, and let stand at room temperature, stirring twice, for at least 2 hours. Heat the grill.  Grill the chicken, turning occasionally and brushing with the marinade, until crisp and dark brown on both sides, about 15 to 18 minutes total.  Or, broil for 20 minutes.

Meanwhile, cook the pasta in a large pot of boiling water until just tender, 4 to 6 minutes.  Drain and toss immediately with the Jalapeño-Tomato Vinaigrette (see recipe on page 209).  Season pasta to taste and put on plates.  Top each serving with 2 grilled chicken thighs and garnish with mint or cilantro sprigs.  SERVES 4.

Grilled Salmon Fillet Salad

# Endive & Tomato Salad With Balsamic Vinegar

4   Cups Belgian Endive, sliced
4   Large Roma Tomatoes, sliced
2   Tablespoons Water
4   Teaspoons Balsamic Vinegar
4   Tablespoons Olive Oil
2   Teaspoons Dijon Mustard
1   Clove Garlic, finely chopped

Arrange endive on platter.  Place sliced tomatoes on top.  Cover with plastic wrap and refrigerate up to 1 hour.  Combine water, vinegar, oil, mustard, and garlic in a small bowl and whisk together until blended.  Before serving whisk vinaigrette and spoon over prepared salad.  Serve immediately.  SERVES 4.

<u>Wine Recommendation:</u>
Simple, off-dry Riesling (Hogue)

# Salami & Cheese Salad

*(With A Balsamic-Mustard Seed Dressing)*

4   Scallions
2   Red Bell Peppers
1   Pound Salami
¾   Pound Gruyere Cheese
2½  Cups Frozen Corn Kernels
Salt & Fresh Ground Pepper
1   Head Romaine Lettuce

Trim and cut the scallions, including green tops, into thin slices.  Seed the peppers and cut them into ¼-inch dice.  Cut both the salami and cheese into ½-inch cubes.  Cook frozen corn in small amount of water. Drain and cool.  In a bowl, combine the scallions, peppers, salami, cheese, and corn and toss with Balsamic-Mustard Seed Dressing (see recipe on page 208).  Season to taste with salt and pepper.  To serve, put romaine lettuce leaves on plates and top with a mound of salad.  Garnish with basil sprigs or chopped chives (optional).  SERVES 4.

*vegetables, salads and grains*

# Rice & Sour Cream

*This is an old family favorite – we serve it often with other Southwestern dishes.*

| | |
|---|---|
| 1 Cup Long Grained White Rice, uncooked | ½ Pound Monterey Jack Cheese |
| 1 Small Can Whole Green Chiles | 2 Cups Sour Cream |
| 2 Tablespoons Butter | Salt & Pepper, to taste |

Cook rice in 2 cups salted water till done and water is absorbed. Cut chiles into 3 strips lengthwise. Cut cheese in small oblongs. Wrap a chile strip around each cheese piece. Butter casserole dish and put a layer of rice, then ⅔ of the wrapped chiles and cover with sour cream. Repeat above until all ingredients are used up, reserving some of the sour cream for the top. Sprinkle with grated cheese and dot with butter. Bake at 350⁰F until browned on top. SERVES 4-6.

# Pan Grilled Salmon Salad With Vegetables & Eggs

*(With An Oregano Dressing)*

6 New Potatoes

3 Eggs

1 Pound Green Beans

2 Tomatoes

1½ Pounds Salmon Fillets

Salt & Fresh Ground Pepper

2 Tablespoons Olive Oil

⅓ Cup Mediterranean Black Olives

Put potatoes in a pot of cold, salted water to cover. Cover pot and bring to a boil. Uncover and continue cooking until tender, about 15 minutes. Drain. Put eggs in a saucepan, cover with water, and bring to a simmer. Cover; remove from heat, let sit at least 15 minutes, drain. Peel the eggs. Cook the beans in a pot of boiling, salted water until tender, about 6 minutes. Drain, refresh under cold, running water, and drain well. Peel and seed the tomatoes and cut into small dice. Recipe can be completed to this point several hours ahead.

Pat the salmon dry and season with salt and pepper. In a heavy, nonstick frying pan, heat the oil until very hot. Add the fish and cook over high heat, turning once, until well-seared but still moist inside, about 3 minutes total. Remove and cool to room temperature.

Bring dressing back to room temperature. Slice the potatoes. Quarter the eggs. Cut fish into thin slices and arrange on plates along with the beans, potatoes, eggs, and diced tomatoes. Drizzle each salad with Oregano Dressing (see recipe on page 210) and scatter olives over all. Pass remaining dressing. SERVES 4.

# Thyme Marinated Pork Roast

*Pork is always a personal favorite and was extremely popular at the Café.*

| | |
|---|---|
| 3 Garlic Cloves, peeled | 1 6-Pound Boneless Pork Loin |
| ¼ Cup Fresh Parsley, finely chopped | Freshly Ground Black Pepper |
| 1 Tablespoon Dried Thyme | 1 Small Onion, finely chopped |
| 1 Tablespoon Olive Oil | 2 Garlic Cloves, peeled & finely minced |
| Salt | 1 Cup Tomato Sauce, homemade if possible |
| 1 Cup Dry White Wine | 1 Tablespoon Unsalted Butter |

In a food processor, process 3 cloves of garlic, parsley, thyme, olive oil, 1 teaspoon salt, and 1 tablespoon of wine until they form a smooth paste. With a sharp knife, make small slits in the roast approximately ¾ of an inch apart. Force generous quantities of the paste into the slits. Rub the remaining paste all over the roast. Put the roast in a large roasting pan and pour on the remaining wine. Cover and marinate for several hours or, overnight, turning the meat several times.

Preheat the oven to 450°F. Drain the roast and discard the marinade. Sprinkle the top of the roast with salt and pepper and roast for 10 to 15 minutes. Lower the oven temperature to 325°F and cook for approximately 2 hours or, until meat thermometer, inserted into the center of the roast, reads 160°F. Transfer the roast to a platter and keep warm. Cut the strings.

Pour off all but 2 tablespoons of juice from the roasting pan. Add the onion and the remaining garlic and sauté gently for 2 to 3 minutes. De-glaze the sauté pan with the remaining wine over high heat. Add the tomato sauce and cook until it is reduced by ½. Remove from heat and swirl in butter. Adjust seasoning to taste with pepper and salt. DO NOT OVER SALT! Carve the roast into thin slices and serve with spoonfuls of the sauce. SERVES 8-10.

# Grilled Lamb Chops

*(Served With A Port-Mustard Cream Sauce)*

*This sauce is exceptional – be sure to trim your chops well.*

| | |
|---|---|
| ½ Cup Port | Salt & Fresh Ground Pepper |
| ¾ Cup Heavy Cream | 12 Lamb Loin Chops, 1½" thick |
| 2 Tablespoons Hot Mustard | 2 Tablespoons Olive Oil |
| 1 Tablespoon Dijon Mustard | |

SAUCE: Heat port in small pan over high heat 1 to 2 minutes to burn off alcohol. In a second pan, over medium high heat, reduce cream by ½. Add port and mustards to cream and whisk until well blended. Season to taste with salt and pepper.

LAMB PREPARATION: Heat grill or broiler. Brush lamb chops with oil and lightly sprinkle with salt and pepper. Grill 4 minutes on each side.

Heat sauce to a simmer and spoon over each serving of lamb chops. Garnish with a sprig of fresh rosemary. SERVES 6.

# Spicy Herb Crusted Leg Of Lamb

1   Leg Of Lamb, butterflied (4 to 5 Pounds)
1   Tablespoon Chile Powder
1   Tablespoon Fresh Oregano, chopped
2   Teaspoons Salt
1   Teaspoon Ground Cumin
½   Teaspoon Ground Clove
2   Garlic Cloves, finely chopped
2   Tablespoons Red Wine Vinegar
3   Tablespoons Olive Oil

Combine chile powder and the next seven ingredients in a blender; blend to a paste. Rub paste into lamb. Wrap tightly in plastic wrap and marinate overnight in the refrigerator. Remove from refrigerator and allow to come to room temperature before cooking. To roast, place meat, fat side up, on a rack in a shallow roasting pan. Roast at 500°F until the internal temperature reaches 135°F for rare, about 25 minutes. Remove from oven. Cover lightly with aluminum foil; let rest for 15 minutes. Carve in thin slices across the grain. SERVES 6-8.

# Pecan Crusted Halibut

*(With A Creamy Shallot Sauce)*

*This is an exceptional fish dish and guests loved it!*

4-6   Fresh Halibut Fillets, 6-8 ounces each
2   Eggs, beaten with 2 tablespoons of milk
1   Cup All-Purpose Flour
2   Cups Pecans, finely chopped
2   Tablespoons Butter

Preheat oven to 375°F. Rinse the fillets and pat them dry. Melt the butter in a skillet large enough to hold all fillet pieces. Working quickly, dip each fillet in flour, then in egg mixture, then, pressing lightly, in pecans to make them adhere well. Sauté each piece in butter, turning once, until light golden. Remove to a baking sheet and place in oven until fish flakes easily with a fork (approximately 10 minutes per inch of thickness of the fillets). Remove and place on warmed plates. Spoon Shallot Sauce (see recipe below) over fillets and serve immediately. SERVES 4-6.

## CREAMY SHALLOT SAUCE

3   Tablespoons Shallots, chopped
1   Tablespoon Butter
1   Cup Of White Wine
½   Cup Of Heavy Cream
Salt & Pepper, to taste

In a large saucepan sauté the shallots in butter till lightly browned. Add the white wine and reduce by ½. Add the heavy cream and simmer till thickened. Salt and pepper to taste.

# Icelandic Cod With Savory Stuffing

*(Served With Hollandaise Sauce)*

## SAVORY STUFFING

2  Teaspoons Butter
¼  Cup Celery, chopped
¼  Cup Carrots, shredded
2  Tablespoons Onion, finely chopped
1  Teaspoon Lemon Peel, grated
¼  Teaspoon Salt
1  Teaspoon Dried Thyme
Dash Of Pepper
3  Tablespoons Water
2  Cups Soft Bread Crumbs

Melt butter over medium heat, add vegetables, and cook and stir until tender.  Remove from heat and stir in remaining ingredients, tossing lightly.

## ASSEMBLY

1  Pound Icelandic Cod Fillets
1  Tablespoon Butter

Heat oven to 375⁰F.  Spray baking dish with pan release spray.  Spoon stuffing evenly over each fillet.  Carefully roll fillet to enclose stuffing and secure with toothpick.  Place seam side down in pan.  Brush with butter and bake for 20 minutes; Serve with Hollandaise Sauce (see recipe below).  SERVES 4.

## HOLLANDAISE SAUCE

1  Cup Unsalted Butter
3  Egg Yolks
Pinch Of Salt & White Pepper
1  Tablespoon Fresh Lemon Juice

Melt butter over low heat and keep warm.  Place egg yolks, salt, pepper, and lemon juice in blender.  Mix at high speed until blended thoroughly.  While blending at high speed, add hot butter in a thin stream; do not add the milky residue at the bottom of the pan.  DO NOT OVERPROCESS!  Taste and adjust seasonings.

Wine Recommendation:
White Burgundy (Verget)
U.S. Sauvignon Blanc (Spottswoode)

# Poached Snapper With A Capered Salsa

*The capered salsa works well with almost any fish – chicken as well.*

Poached Snapper With A Capered Salsa
served with Pasta Custard

1   Medium Tomato, chopped

2   Tablespoons Green Onions, sliced

1   Tablespoon Capers, drained

1   Tablespoon Vinegar Or Lemon Juice

1   Tablespoon Olive Oil

2   Cups Dry White Wine

2   Tablespoons Mrs. Dash® Seasoning (Lemon Blend)

2   4-Ounce Red Snapper Fillets; fresh or defrosted if previously frozen

In small bowl combine tomato, onions, capers, vinegar or lemon juice, and oil. Toss well to mix. Cover and refrigerate at least 4 hours to blend flavors. POACHING LIQUID: In medium saucepan bring wine, mixed with Mrs. Dash®, to boil. Reduce heat and simmer, covered, 5 minutes. Reduce heat to barely simmering. Add fish fillets and, keeping liquid to below the boil, cook until fish is opaque and flakes with a fork. Remove fish from liquid with a spatula, draining well. Place on plate, spoon salsa over, and garnish with lemon or lime slices. SERVES 2.

# Cornish Hens With A Basil Walnut Sauce

*I like to serve this to guests – it has really nice flavors and makes a very attractive presentation.*

1   Bunch Fresh Basil, approximately 1 ounce
½   Cup Grated Parmesan Cheese
1   Garlic Clove
Salt & Pepper, to taste
¼   Cup Shelled Walnuts
Vegetable Shortening Spray (i.e. Pam)

Lemon Pepper (i.e. Mrs. Dash)
4   Cornish Hens, 24 Ounces, if possible
½   Cup Chicken Broth
½   Cup Heavy Cream
Basil Leaves, for garnish
Walnut Pieces, for garnish

To prepare the sauce base, combine the first 5 ingredients in a food processor and puree to make a smooth paste. Refrigerate till ready to make sauce.

Remove giblets from hens and discard. Rinse thoroughly, and pat dry. Arrange in baking dish just large enough to hold them and tie legs together with kitchen twine. Fold wings under. Spray with vegetable shortening and sprinkle with lemon pepper. Place a sliver of garlic and 2 basil leaves in the cavity of each hen. Tent to cover with aluminum foil. Roast in a preheated 350°F oven approximately 1¼ hours, remove the foil tent and bake for 15 minutes, or until the juices run clear when a leg or thigh is pierced with a fork. Remove from oven and place hens on a serving platter. Cover and keep warm while preparing the sauce.

## BASIL—WALNUT SAUCE

Drain the grease from the roasting pan (above) and add the chicken stock to the pan. Over medium-high heat, reduce the stock by ½. Add the cream and reduce by ½ again, stirring constantly. Swirl in the Basil-Walnut Sauce, and adjust the seasonings. Pour the sauce over the hens, garnish with basil leaves, and walnut pieces. SERVES 4.

Cornish Hens With A
Basil Walnut Sauce

# Pasta With Prosciutto, Peas & Roasted Garlic Cream Sauce

*For those who love pasta – this one is excellent and very simple!*

4   Ounces Prosciutto
¼   Cup Butter
2   Shallots, very finely chopped
½   Cup Frozen Peas, thawed
⅔   Cup Heavy Cream
6   Cloves Roasted Garlic, mashed (see recipe on page 212)
12   Ounces Fettuccine
½   Cup Grated Parmesan
Salt & Ground Black Pepper
Fresh Parsley Sprig, to garnish

Cut the fat from the Prosciutto and chop both lean and fat parts separately into small squares.

Melt the butter in a medium frying pan and add the shallots and the squares of fat.  Cook until golden.  Add the lean Prosciutto, and cook for 2 minutes more.  Season with black pepper.  Stir in the cream, peas, and garlic, mix well, and warm over low heat while the pasta is cooking.

Cook the pasta in plenty of boiling water until *al dente*.  Drain into a warm serving dish and toss with the sauce.  Stir in the cheese and serve immediately, garnished with a sprig of parsley.  SERVES 4.

# Linguine With Arugula & Goat Cheese

1   Cup Fresh Arugula
½   Cup Plain Yogurt
½   Cup Ricotta Cheese
3   Tablespoons Goat Cheese
1   Teaspoon Salt
Freshly Ground Black Pepper, to taste
8   Ounces Linguine

Place linguine in boiling water and cook according to package directions.  Trim, wash, and thoroughly dry arugula.  In food processor blend yogurt, ricotta, and goat cheese until creamy.  Add arugula to cheese mixture and blend till arugula is thoroughly blended.  Season with salt and pepper.  When linguine is cooked, drain, top immediately with sauce, and serve.  SERVES 2.

# Pasta Rollups With A Red Pepper Coulis

*This is great as an entrée or, in smaller portions, as an appetizer.*

8-10  Lasagna Noodles
8  Ounces Fresh Spinach Leaves, well washed
4  Ounces Mushrooms, sliced
4  Ounces Mozzarella Cheese, shredded
2  Ounces Chives, chopped

### RED PEPPER COULIS

1  Cup Roasted Sweet Red Peppers
6  Cloves Garlic

### BÉCHAMEL SAUCE

½  Cup All-Purpose Flour    Salt & Ground Black Pepper
3  Tablespoons Butter    Freshly Grated Nutmeg
2½  Cups Milk    Freshly Grated Parmesan Cheese, to serve
1  Bay Leaf

Cook the lasagna noodles according to the instructions on the package.  Drain and let cool.

Cook the spinach in the tiniest amount of water for 2 minutes, then add the sliced mushrooms and cook for 2 minutes more.  Drain very well, pressing out all the excess liquid, and chop the spinach coarsely.

Place the roasted peppers and the garlic cloves in a food processor equipped with a metal blade and pulse to a puree.  Place in a bowl, cover, and refrigerate till ready to serve.

Put all the béchamel ingredients into a saucepan and bring slowly to a boil, stirring until the sauce is thick and smooth.  Simmer for 2 minutes with the bay leaf, then season well and stir in the nutmeg to taste.

Lay out the pasta sheets and spread with the béchamel sauce, spinach, mushrooms, chives, and mozzarella.  Roll up each one and place in a large, shallow casserole with the seam face down in the dish.

Remove and discard the bay leaf and then pour the sauce over the pasta.  Sprinkle on the cheese and place under a hot broiler to brown.

TO SERVE: Heat the Red Pepper Coulis to just before a boil.  Place a pasta rollup on each of four serving plates, ladle coulis over each pasta roll, sprinkle with parmesan, and serve immediately.  SERVES 4.

# Tomato Basil Bread

*Out of the ordinary – it is reminiscent of pizza and makes really good grilled cheese sandwiches!*

| | | | |
|---|---|---|---|
| 1 | Package Active Dry Yeast | 3 | Teaspoons Dried Basil |
| ½ | Cup Warm V-8 Juice | ½ | Teaspoon Salt |
| ½ | Cup Warmed Cottage Cheese | ¼ | Teaspoon Baking Soda |
| 2 | Tablespoons Sugar | 1 | Egg |
| 1 | Tablespoon Dried Minced Onions | 2½ | Cups All-Purpose Flour |
| 1 | Tablespoon Butter | | |

Dissolve the yeast in warm V-8 juice. Add cottage cheese to yeast mixture. Combine sugar, onion, butter, basil, salt, soda, and egg. Add to yeast mixture. Sift in flour and mix in a mixer bowl fitted with a dough hook until forms soft ball and cleans sides of bowl. Cover with a light cloth or dishtowel and let dough rise to double in size. Punch down dough. Turn out dough into a greased 1½-quart loaf pan. Cover and let rise for 30 minutes. Bake in a 350ºF preheated oven for 45 minutes. Remove from pan onto a wire rack and cool; brush with butter. MAKES 1 LOAF.

# Oatmeal – Raisin Scones

| | | | |
|---|---|---|---|
| 1 | Cup All-Purpose Flour | 1 | Cup Quick-Cooking Rolled Oats |
| 3 | Tablespoons Brown Sugar | ½ | Cup Raisins, chopped |
| 1½ | Teaspoons Baking Powder | 2 | Egg Whites |
| ½ | Teaspoon Ground Cinnamon | 2 | Tablespoons 2% Milk |
| ⅓ | Cup Butter | | |

Mix flour, sugar, baking powder, and cinnamon. Cut in butter. Add oats and raisins, then egg whites and 2 tablespoons milk; mix well (dough will be sticky). On a floured surface roll or pat the dough into a 7-inch circle. Cut into 12 wedges; dip knife in flour as needed. Place on an ungreased baking sheet; brush lightly with milk. Bake in a preheated 400ºF oven 10 to 12 minutes. MAKES 12.

# Crusty Cornbread

| | | | |
|---|---|---|---|
| 1 | Cup Cornmeal | ½ | Teaspoon Salt |
| ½ | Cup All-Purpose Flour | 1 | Egg, beaten |
| 1 | Tablespoon Sugar | 1 | Cup Buttermilk |
| ½ | Teaspoon Baking Soda | ¼ | Cup Butter |

Combine the first 5 ingredients; mix well. Add egg and buttermilk; stir until smooth. Place butter in an 8-inch skillet; heat at 425ºF for 5 minutes. Remove from oven and pour hot butter into batter; mix well. Quickly pour batter into skillet. Bake at 425ºF for 25 minutes or until golden brown. 6 SERVINGS.

# Wheat Germ Cornmeal Muffins

1 Cup All-Purpose Flour

½ Cup Toasted Wheat Germ

½ Cup Cornmeal

2 Tablespoons Sugar

1 Tablespoon Baking Powder

½ Teaspoon Salt

1 Egg, beaten

1 Cup Milk

¼ Cup Butter, melted

Mix the flour, wheat germ, cornmeal, sugar, baking powder, and salt. Make a well in center. In small bowl mix egg, milk, and butter. Add all at once to flour mixture, stirring just till moistened. Spoon batter into greased muffin cups and bake at 400°F for 20 minutes or till lightly browned. MAKES 12.

# Raisin Pumpernickel Bread

| | |
|---|---|
| 2 Packages Active Dry Yeast | ½ Teaspoon Salt |
| 1¼ Cups Warm Water | 1 Cup All-Purpose Flour |
| 1 Cup Rye Flour | ½ Cup Raisins |
| 1 Cup Whole-Wheat Flour | 1 Tablespoon Vegetable Oil |
| ¼ Cup Dark Molasses | 2 Tablespoons Cornmeal |
| 2 Tablespoons Unsweetened Cocoa | 1 Large Egg White |
| 1 Tablespoon Instant Coffee Powder | 1 Tablespoon Warm Water |

In a large bowl, combine yeast and warm water; let stand until softened, about 5 minutes. Add rye and whole-wheat flours, molasses, cocoa, coffee powder, and salt. With an electric mixer, equipped with a dough hook, beat dough until flour is moistened. Mix in the 1 cup of all-purpose flour and continue mixing at medium speed until the dough is stretchy and pulls cleanly from mixer bowl, about 3 minutes (if needed, add more all-purpose flour, 1 tablespoon at a time). Push raisins into dough. Place dough in a greased bowl; turn to grease top of dough. Cover bowl loosely and let dough rise, in a warm place, until doubled, about 1 hour. Sprinkle cornmeal in the center of a 12 x 15-inch baking sheet; set aside. Punch down dough. On a lightly floured board, knead dough to shape into a ball. Place dough on cornmeal and press to form a 6-inch round. Cover loaf lightly with plastic wrap; let rise in a warm place until puffy, about 30 minutes.

Preheat oven to 350°F. Beat together egg white and water; lightly brush loaf with egg mixture. Bake in oven until loaf is rich, dark brown, about 30 minutes. Transfer to a wire rack. MAKES 1 LOAF.

# Oatmeal Cornmeal Bread

2 Cups Oatmeal
⅔ Cups Cornmeal
2 Cups Boiling Water
1 Cup Cold Milk
¼ Cup Molasses
2 Tablespoons Yeast
⅓ Cup Vegetable Oil
2 Teaspoons Salt
1 Cup Whole Wheat Flour
4 Cups Bread Flour

Mix oatmeal and cornmeal together and pour boiling water over. Allow to stand about 20 minutes. Add milk, molasses, and stir. When cool enough, warm, but not hot, sprinkle on the yeast. Mix with dough hook adding the oil, salt, whole-wheat flour, and bread flour. Mix until the dough forms a soft ball. Cover mixer bowl with plastic wrap and let rise until doubled. Form into loaves and place in well-greased loaf pans and allow to double. Place in a 350°F oven and bake 30 to 35 minutes until browned and hollow sounding when tapped. Turn out on a wire rack and allow to cool completely. MAKES 2 LOAVES.

# Cracked Wheat Bread

*Great taste, texture, appearance – healthy, too.*

1 Cup Milk, scalded
¼ Cup Molasses
2 Teaspoons Salt
1 Tablespoon Shortening
1 Cup Cracked Wheat
2 Packages Active Dry Yeast
½ Cup Warm Water (105°F-115°F)
1 Cup Stone-Ground Whole Wheat Flour
2¾-3 Cups Bread Flour

Combine milk, molasses, salt, shortening, and 1 cup cracked wheat in a large mixer bowl. Cool to lukewarm. Dissolve yeast in warm water. Add yeast, whole-wheat flour and 1 cup of the bread flour to the cracked wheat mixture. Beat 2 minutes on medium speed in mixer fitted with a dough hook. Scrape bowl frequently. Mix in enough flour to make stiff dough that is not sticky. Place dough in a greased bowl and flip dough greased side up. Cover loosely and let rise in a warm place until double, about 1 hour. Punch dough down. Shape into loaves and place in greased loaf pans. Let rise until double in a warm place free of drafts. Heat oven to 375°F. Bake until loaf sounds hollow when tapped 30 to 35 minutes. Remove from pan and cool on a wire rack. MAKES 2 LOAVES.

# Apple Bread

1½ Cups All-Purpose Flour

1 Teaspoon Baking Powder

¼ Teaspoon Baking Soda

1¼ Cups Apple, shredded & peeled

⅔ Cup Packed Brown Sugar

1½ Teaspoons Instant Coffee Crystals

1 Egg, beaten

3 Tablespoons Vegetable Oil

¼ Cup Walnuts, chopped

In a small bowl, mix the flour, baking powder, and baking soda.  In a large bowl combine apple, sugar, and coffee crystals; let stand 5 minutes, stirring once.  Add egg and oil; mix well.  Stir in flour mixture just till combined.  Fold in nuts.  Spray an 8 x 4 x 2-inch loaf pan with nonstick coating; pour in batter.  Bake in a preheated 350⁰F oven about 50 minutes.  Cool in the pan for 10 minutes.  Remove from pan and cool completely on a wire rack.  Wrap and store overnight before slicing.  MAKES 1 LOAF.

# Refrigerator Potato Rolls

*An easy recipe to make and the dough keeps very well in the refrigerator.*

| | |
|---|---|
| 1 Envelope Active Dry Yeast | 1 Teaspoon Salt |
| ½ Cup Lukewarm Water | ⅔ Cup Butter |
| 1 Teaspoon Sugar | 2 Eggs, slightly beaten |
| 1 Cup Hot Mashed Potatoes | 1 Cup Lukewarm Milk |
| ½ Cup Sugar | About 6½ Cups Presifted Flour |
| ½ Cup Water | Butter, melted |

Soften yeast in water with 1 teaspoon sugar.  In mixing bowl combine potatoes, ½ cup sugar, ½ water, salt, butter, and eggs.  Beat well.  Stir in enough flour to make soft dough.  Cover; let rise for about 3 hours or until doubled in bulk.  Punch down dough; brush top generously with melted butter; refrigerate until ready to use.  About 2 hours before baking.  Grease muffin cups.  *Form dough into tiny balls.  Place in cups.  Cover; let rise for 2 hours.  Preheat oven to 450⁰F.  Bake in preheated oven for 20 minutes.  MAKES 36.

*NOTE:  The dough can be formed into fist sized balls and baked individually on a sheet pan.

# Irish Brown Soda Bread

¾ Cup All-Purpose Flour
½ Teaspoon Salt
1 Teaspoon Baking Soda
2⅓ Cups Whole Wheat Flour
2 Tablespoons Sugar

3 Tablespoons Wheat Germ
⅓ Cup Miller's Bran
2 Tablespoons Butter, cold
1-1½ Cups Buttermilk

Preheat oven to 425⁰F. Place flour, salt, baking soda, whole wheat flour, sugar, wheat germ, and bran in bowl of food processor. Using quick pulsing, add butter in pieces, till mixture resembles fine crumbs. Add enough buttermilk, pulsing quickly, to make a soft dough. On a floured board, knead the dough lightly and form into a circle about 1½ inches thick. Place on a greased baking sheet, make a deep cross in the top with a floured knife, and bake in the preheated oven for 45 minutes, or until browned and hollow sounding when tapped on the bottom. Turn the baking sheet around halfway through the baking. MAKES ONE LOAF.

# Vienna Bread

*My favorite bread to make – the loaves turn out really pretty. This makes fantastic french toast.*

1 Package Dry Yeast
1 Cup Warm Water
5½-6 Cups Bread Flour
3 Tablespoons Sugar
1 Cup Milk

2 Teaspoons Salt
2 Tablespoons Butter
1 Egg White, slightly beaten
Sesame Seeds

In large bowl, dissolve yeast in warm water. Stir in 2 cups flour and 1 tablespoon sugar. Cover and let rise in warm place 1 hour. In small saucepan scald milk. Remove from heat. Stir in 2 tablespoons sugar, salt and butter. Cool to lukewarm. Add to yeast mixture. Stir in enough flour to form a stiff dough. On floured surface, knead in remaining flour till dough is smooth and elastic, 8 to 10 minutes.

Place in greased bowl. Turn to grease all sides. Cover loosely with plastic wrap and cloth towel. Let rise in warm place until light and doubled in size, 1 to 1¼ hours.

Punch dough down. Cover and let rise again until doubled in size, 50 to 60 minutes. Punch down dough. Divide in half. Shape each loaf into a 14-inch oblong loaf. Place loafs on generously greased large baking sheet. With scissors, cut five 1-inch slits in top of each loaf. Cover and let rise in warm place until doubled, 30 to 40 minutes.

Brush tops and sides of loaves with egg white. Sprinkle with sesame seeds. Bake at 350⁰F 40 to 50 minutes or until loaves sound hollow when lightly tapped. Remove at once from baking sheets and cool on wire racks.
MAKES 2 LOAVES.

*The high desert grasslands of the Sonoita area become filled with flowering native plants and cacti in the spring.*

# Kahlua Brownies

*We served this brownie frequently at the Café – it was also a favorite for red wine tasting at Callaghan Vineyards!*

8 Ounces Unsweetened Chocolate
1¼ Cups Butter
2½ Cups Granulated Sugar
2½ Teaspoons Vanilla
2½ Teaspoons Kahlua
5 Eggs
1⅞ Cups Flour
1¼ Cups Chopped Walnuts

*Kahlua Brownie with Chocolate-Orange-Cinnamon Ice Cream*

Melt butter and chocolate.  Remove from heat and stir in sugar until well combined.  Add eggs, one at a time, beating well after each addition.  Add vanilla and Kahlua.  Stir in flour and nuts and mix well.  Pour into a greased 9 x 13-inch pan.  Bake at 350⁰ for 30 minutes or until set. Cool slightly and frost with dark chocolate frosting to which Kahlua has been added. Serve with Chocolate-Orange-Cinnamon Ice Cream (see recipe on page 150).  SERVES 15 LARGE PIECES, OR 30 SMALL PIECES.

# Bittersweet Chocolate Mousse

24 Ounces Chocolate Chips (Ghirardelli®)
1 Egg Yolk
⅓ Cup Amaretto
1 Quart Whipping Cream

Melt chocolate chips in top of double boiler.  Add egg yolk and Amaretto and stir until smooth.  Remove from heat. Whip 3½ cups cream until heavy peaks form.  Add slightly cooled chocolate mixture and mix until well combined. Cover; place in refrigerator, and chill until ready to serve.  Garnish with fresh fruit and cookies.  SERVES 4-6.

# White Chocolate Cheesecake With Cranberry Swirl

| | |
|---|---|
| 1½ Cups Cranberries | ½ Teaspoon Ground Cinnamon |
| ¾ Cup Orange Juice | 6 Ounces White Chocolate |
| ¼ Cup Sugar | 3 8-Ounce Packages Cream Cheese, room temperature |
| 3 Tablespoons Dried Currants | ¾ Cup Sugar |
| 2 Tablespoons Grand Mariner | 4 Large Eggs |
| 1 Tablespoon Orange Zest | Dark & White Chocolate Curls Or Shavings (optional) |

CRANBERRIES: Combine first 7 ingredients in small saucepan. Simmer over medium heat until cranberries lose their shape and mixture thickens slightly, stirring occasionally, about 8 minutes. Transfer to food processor and blend until smooth. (Can be prepared 1 to 2 days ahead.) Cover and refrigerate.

FILLING: Preheat oven to 350⁰F. Stir 6 ounces of white chocolate in top of double boiler over barely simmering water until melted and smooth. Cool slightly. Using electric mixer beat cream cheese in a large bowl until smooth. Mix in sugar. Beat in eggs 1 at a time, beating well after each addition. Gradually mix in white chocolate.

FINAL PREPARATION: Pour ½ of filling into a 9-inch diameter springform pan. Drop half of cranberry mixture atop filling by 2 tablespoons, spacing evenly. Use small sharp knife to swirl cranberry mixture into filling. Carefully pour remaining mixture over. Drop remaining cranberry mixture atop filling by 2 tablespoons, spacing evenly. Use small sharp knife to swirl cranberry mixture into filling. Bake cheesecake until edges are puffed and golden, about 40 minutes. (Center will not be set). Cool on rack. Chill overnight. (Can be prepared 3 days ahead.)

Run small sharp knife around sides to loosen cheesecake. Release pan sides. Press white chocolate swirls onto edges of cheesecake if desired. Top with dark and white chocolate swirls. SERVES 8.

# Chocolate Chess Pie

| | |
|---|---|
| 2 Eggs | ¾ Cup Milk |
| 1½ Cups Sugar | 1 Teaspoon Vanilla |
| 3 Tablespoons Cocoa | 1 Stick Butter |
| 2 Tablespoons Flour | 1 9" Pie Shell, unbaked |

Beat eggs until foamy. Add sugar, cocoa, and flour, mix well. Add milk, vanilla, and butter, combine thoroughly. Pour into pie shell. Bake at 375⁰F oven for 35 to 40 minutes, or until set. SERVES 6-8.

# Piña Colada Cheesecake

*Delicious and a new twist on an old favorite!*

## CRUST

3  Cups Vanilla Wafer Crumbs, finely ground
1  Cup Unsweetened Coconut, shredded
2  Cups Granulated Sugar
½  Cup Unsalted Butter, melted

In a large bowl, toss together the cookie crumbs, ¾ cup of the coconut, and ¼ cup of the granulated sugar. Using a fork, stir in the melted butter. Transfer the crumb mixture to a 9 x 13-inch springform pan and press evenly all over the bottom and up the sides of the pan. Refrigerate for 15 minutes. Preheat the oven to 350°F. Toast ¼ cup coconut till lightly browned. Remove from oven and cool. Prepare filling.

## FILLING

4  8-Ounce Packages Cream Cheese, softened
1  Cup Granulated Sugar
1  Teaspoon Vanilla
4  Eggs
⅔  Cup Frozen Piña Colada Tropical Fruit Mixer, concentrate, defrosted

Mix cream cheese, sugar, and vanilla at medium speed with electric mixer until well blended. Add eggs and mix until blended. Blend in Piña Colada mixer. Pour into pie shell and bake for 40 minutes or until center is almost set. Garnish with fresh fruit and toasted coconut. SERVES 12.

# Orange Crème Brulee

2  Cups Heavy Cream          ½  Teaspoon Orange Peel, grated
4  Egg Yolks                 3  Tablespoons Orange Juice
¼  Cup Sugar                 ⅓  Cup Brown Sugar, sifted

Preheat oven to 325°F. In medium saucepan scald cream. Meanwhile, in medium bowl whisk egg yolks and sugar until thick and light. Slowly pour in hot cream, whisking constantly. Return mixture to saucepan and cook over medium-low heat stirring constantly, until mixture coats the back of a spoon, about 10 minutes. Remove from heat. Add orange peel and orange juice. Pour into 6 individual ramekins. Place ramekins in a baking pan; fill pan with hot water halfway up sides of ramekins. Bake 20 minutes or until centers are set. Cool on wire rack. Place in freezer 15 minutes or cover loosely with plastic wrap and refrigerate overnight.

To serve, preheat broiler. Sprinkle custard evenly with brown sugar. Broil until sugar is melted and a thin crust forms, about 3 minutes. SERVES 6.

# Buttermilk Pie

3 Cups Granulated Sugar

6 Tablespoons All-Purpose Flour

1½ Cups Buttermilk

5 Eggs, beaten

¾ Cup Butter, melted

2 Teaspoons vanilla

1 Teaspoon Nutmeg

2 Pie Crusts, unbaked

Combine sugar, flour, and ¾ cups of buttermilk, add the eggs and mix well. Add the remaining buttermilk and vanilla, blend well. Pour mixture into the pie crusts. Bake in a 425⁰F oven for 10 minutes. Reduce heat to 350⁰F and bake until knife inserted into center of pie comes out clean, about 30 minutes. EACH PIE SERVES 6–8.

*We discovered this dessert on Galiano Island – I experimented with many recipes before we decided this was the closest to the one we had at the Galiano Lodge.*

Buttermilk Pie

# Russian Cream & Strawberries Romanoff

*A very pretty, special dessert...we served it around Valentine's Day when the first strawberries of the season were available – we did the Russian Cream in small heart molds and people loved it.*

*Russian Cream & Strawberries Romanoff*

## RUSSIAN CREAM

2½  Cups Half & Half
1  Cup Sugar
2  Envelopes (¼ ounces each) Unflavored Gelatin
1  Pint Sour Cream
1  Teaspoon Vanilla
¼  Teaspoon Almond Extract

Combine half & half, sugar, and gelatin in a 2-quart saucepan; let stand 5 minutes.  Stir over low heat until gelatin is thoroughly dissolved; cool to lukewarm.  Whisk in sour cream, vanilla, and almond extract; whisk until mixture is smooth.  Pour into individual dishes, sprayed with pan release, or a 6 cup mold.  Refrigerate, covered, until set, at least 4 hours.  To unmold, dip mold in warm water until edges begin to liquefy.  Invert onto serving platter.  Top and surround with Strawberries Romanoff.  SERVES 8-10.

## STRAWBERRIES ROMANOFF

Clean and slice 2 pints fresh strawberries.  Add 1 cup sugar, ¼ cup Triple Sec, and ¼ cup vodka.  Mix well and let marinate for at least 2 hours.

Wine Recommendation:
U.S. Orange Muscat Dessert Wine (Quady Essencia)

# Chocolate —Orange —Frangelico® Soufflé With Grand Marnier Sauce

⅓ Cup, Plus 3 Tablespoons, Granulated Sugar

¼ Cup All-Purpose Flour

1 Cup Milk

½ Cup Ghirardelli® Chocolate Chips

2 Tablespoons Unsalted Butter

4 Egg Yolks, at room temperature

1 Tablespoon Vanilla

1½ Tablespoons Frangelico® Liqueur

Zest From 1 Orange

5 Egg Whites, at room temperature

Pinch Of Salt

1 Teaspoon Cream Of Tartar

Sifted Confectioner's Sugar

Butter 6 1-cup soufflé dishes and sprinkle with granulated sugar, knocking out the excess sugar.

In a bowl combine the ⅓ cup sugar, the flour, and ¼ cup of the milk and whisk the mixture until smooth. In a heavy saucepan bring the remaining ¾ cup of milk to a simmer and add it, whisking, in a stream to the flour mixture. Return the mixture to the pan, add the chocolate chips, bring it to a simmer, whisking, and cook it over moderately low heat, whisking for 2 minutes. Remove the pan from the heat, beat in 1 tablespoon of the butter, and allow the mixture to cool for 2 to 3 minutes. Beat in the egg yolks, one at a time, beating well after each addition, the vanilla, and Frangelico. Strain the soufflé base into a bowl, mix in the orange zest, and dot the top with small bits of the remaining 1 tablespoon of butter. Cover with plastic wrap and keep cool for up to 3 hours.

Preheat the oven to 400°F. In a mixer bowl beat the egg whites with the salt until foamy. Add the cream of tartar and beat the egg whites until they hold soft peaks. Add the remaining 3 tablespoons of sugar, a little at a time, and beat the whites until they hold stiff peaks. Stir ¼ of the egg whites into the soufflé mixture and fold in the remaining whites gently but thoroughly. Spoon the mixture into the prepared dishes. Set the soufflé dishes in a baking dish and add enough hot water to reach one third up the sides of the soufflé dishes.

Bake the soufflés in the middle of the oven for 20 minutes, or until they are puffed. Dust the tops of the soufflés with confectioner's sugar. Serve immediately and, at the table, open a small hole in the top of the soufflé and pour 2 to 3 ounces of warm Grand Marnier Sauce into the soufflé. SERVES 6.

# Lemon Cake Pudding With Strawberries & Whipped Cream

|                    |                          |
|--------------------|--------------------------|
| 1 Cup Sugar        | 1 Cup Milk               |
| ¼ Cup Flour        | ¼ Cup Fresh Lemon Juice  |
| ¼ Teaspoon Salt    | 1 Teaspoon Grated Lemon Peel |
| 2 Eggs, separated  | 1 Cup Sliced Strawberries |

### SWEETENED WHIPPED CREAM

| | |
|---|---|
| ½ Cup Heavy Cream | 1 Tablespoon Sugar |

Preheat oven to 350⁰F. In medium bowl sift sugar, flour, and salt; set aside. In mixer bowl beat 2 egg yolks at medium speed until lemon-colored. Stir in milk, lemon juice, and peel. Beat in dry ingredients until well combined. In another mixer bowl beat 2 egg whites until stiff but not dry; fold into lemon mixture. Pour pudding into a 1½-quart ovenproof casserole. Set in a baking pan; fill with 1 inch hot water. Bake 50 minutes. Serve warm or cold with sliced strawberries and Sweetened Whipped Cream. MAKES 4-6 SERVINGS.

Sweetened Whipped Cream: In mixer bowl beat cream until slightly thickened. Add sugar and continue beating until stiff peaks form. SERVES 4-6.

# Crème Renversee

*This is the <u>best</u> custard dish ever – very light and tender.*

|                |                           |
|----------------|---------------------------|
| ¼ Cup Sugar    | 1 Teaspoon Vanilla Extract |
| 4 Eggs         | ¼ Teaspoon Salt           |
| ¼ Cup Sugar    | Lemon Peel Twists         |
| 2 Cups Milk    |                           |

Grease 6 custard cups. Put ¼ cup of sugar in a small pan; heat over medium heat until melted and a light caramel color, stirring constantly. Pour immediately into the greased cups.

Using a whisk or fork beat the eggs and ¼ cup of sugar in a large mixing bowl until well blended. Add in the milk, vanilla, and salt; blend well. Divide the mixture between the custard cups. Put the cups into a 13 x 9-inch baking pan. Fill the pan with hot water to come halfway up the sides of the cups. Bake in a 325⁰F oven for 50 to 55 minutes, until a knife inserted in the center of the custard comes out clean. Remove the cups from the pan and allow to cool. Cover and refrigerate until cool, about 1½ hours.

To serve, unmold each custard onto a chilled dessert plate, allowing the caramel topping to drip from the cup onto the custard. Garnish with lemon peel twists. SERVES 6.

# Earthquake Cake With Raspberry Puree & Truffle Sauce

*Earthquake Cake With Raspberry Puree & Truffle Sauce*

*This was always on our dessert menu – try it with a glass of port for a marvelous finish.*

24  Ounces Semi-Sweet Chocolate Bits, preferably Ghirardelli®
1  Cup (2 sticks) Butter
8  Large Eggs, at room temperature
3  Cups Sifted Confectioner's Sugar
½  Cup Instant Potato Flakes, pulverized in a food processor

Preheat oven to 350⁰F.  Grease a 9-inch springform pan well with pan release.  Melt the chocolate and butter in the top of a double boiler.  Cool.

In a large bowl beat the eggs until pale and thick and heavy ribbons form when the beaters are lifted.  Fold in the cooled chocolate mixture and the confectioner's sugar.  Fold in the potato flakes.  Pour the batter into the prepared pan and bake for approximately 45 minutes.  The cake will seem slightly soft in the middle, cracked and fallen.  Covered and held at room temperature, it will keep for 1 week.  Serve small slices with raspberry puree and Truffle sauce.  SERVES 12.

## TRUFFLE SAUCE

4  Cups Chocolate Chips      1  Tablespoon Raspberry Liqueur Or Vanilla
2  Cups Whipping Cream

Place all ingredients in a bowl.  Cover with plastic wrap and allow to sit in a 200⁰F oven till chocolate chips are melted.  Stir to combine well.  Place in covered storage container and store in refrigerator.  MAKES 3 CUPS.

## RASPBERRY PUREE

1  12-Ounce Package Frozen Unsweetened Raspberries, thawed      3  Tablespoons Sugar
½  Cup Water      1  Tablespoon Fresh Lemon Juice

Puree raspberries with remaining ingredients in processor.  Strain through sieve into bowl to eliminate seeds, pressing to extract as much pulp as possible.  Cover and refrigerate until chilled (*Can be prepared 2 days ahead*).
MAKES ABOUT 1¼ CUPS.

# Chocolate Raspberry Mousse Cake

### CAKE

⅔ Cup All-Purpose Flour

½ Teaspoon Baking Powder

¼ Teaspoon Salt

6 Tablespoons (¾ Stick) Butter

½ Cup Sugar

1 Egg

¼ Cup Milk

1 Teaspoon Vanilla

*This may sound complicated but really isn't – it serves beautifully and is very impressive!*

*Chocolate Raspberry Mousse Cake*

## RASPBERRY MOUSSE

| | |
|---|---|
| 1 6-Ounce Package White Chocolate Baking Bars (3 Foil-Wrapped Bars), broken up | 2 Tablespoons Water |
| 1¾ Cups Heavy Cream | 1 Teaspoon Cornstarch |
| ⅓ Cup Sugar | 2 Cups Frozen Raspberries |
| | 1 Teaspoon Vanilla |

## CHOCOLATE LAYER

1 8-Ounce Package Semi-Sweet Chocolate Bars, broken up

¾ Cup Heavy Cream

2 Tablespoons Water

1 Cup Heavy Cream, for garnish

1 Tablespoon Sugar, for garnish

Fresh Raspberries, for garnish

Fresh Mint Leaves, for garnish

CAKE: Preheat oven to 350°F. Grease 9-inch springform pan. In small bowl, combine Flour, baking powder, and salt; set aside. In small mixer bowl, beat butter and ½ cup sugar till creamy. Beat in egg. Blend in milk and 1 teaspoon vanilla. Gradually beat in flour mixture. Spread in prepared pan and bake 22 to 25 minutes until lightly browned. Cool completely.

RASPBERRY MOUSSE: In small saucepan over low heat melt white chocolate with ½ cup heavy cream, stirring until smooth. Transfer to large bowl; set aside. In medium saucepan, combine ⅓ cup sugar, 2 tablespoons water, and cornstarch. Add frozen raspberries. Cook, stirring constantly, until mixture comes to boil. Boil 1 minute, stirring constantly. Remove from heat; stir into white chocolate mixture. Cool completely. In small mixer bowl, beat 1¼ cups heavy cream with 1 teaspoon vanilla until stiff peaks form. Fold into raspberry mixture; set aside.

CHOCOLATE LAYER: In small saucepan over low heat, melt semi-sweet chocolate with ¾ cup heavy cream and 3 tablespoons water, stirring constantly until smooth; set aside.

PREPARATION: Loosen and remove sides of springform pan. Wrap inside of pan tightly with plastic wrap.* Reattach side of pan. Spread ¾ cup chocolate mixture over cake layer. Freeze 5 minutes. Spread Raspberry Mousse over chocolate layer. Freeze 10 minutes. Gently spread remaining chocolate mixture over mousse. Refrigerate 3 to 4 hours until set. Loosen and remove side of pan.

In small mixer bowl, beat 1 cup heavy cream with 1 tablespoon sugar until stiff peaks form. Spread side of cake with whipped cream. If desired, spoon remaining whipped cream into pastry bag fitted with rosette tip; decorate cake. Garnish with fresh raspberries and mint leaves. MAKES 10-12 SERVINGS.

*Plastic wrap prevents aluminum pan from discoloring raspberry mixture.

# Lemon Cake Roll

*Our granddaughter Caitlin's favorite cake – she asks for it for her birthday.*

1   Duncan Hines® White Cake Mix
1   Cup Water
6   Egg Whites
⅓   Cup Oil

Preheat oven to 350°F.  Grease and line with parchment a jelly roll pan (12 x 17-inch) and then spray parchment with Pam.  Place all ingredients in a mixer bowl and mix on low speed until combined.  Beat on high-speed 2 minutes. Pour batter into prepared pan and bake in preheated oven 10 to 15 minutes until done but not browned.  While baking spread a tea towel on a large baking rack and sprinkle the tea towel with sifted confectioner's sugar.  When the cake is done invert the tea towel/baking rack on top of the cake and then quickly invert the cake onto the tea towel. Quickly roll the cake up in the tea towel, like a jellyroll.  Let cool.  When cooled, unroll and trim away crusty edges. Spread with approximately ¾ cup Lemon Curd (see recipe on page 211) and re-roll.  Wrap in plastic wrap and chill completely.  When chilled, spread with Lemony Cream Cheese Frosting (see recipe below).  To serve, slice cross ways into 1-inch slices and serve.  SERVES 6-8.

## LEMONY CREAM CHEESE FROSTING

1   8-Ounce Package Cream Cheese, softened
2   Cups Sifted Confectioner's Sugar
3   Tablespoons Lemon Juice

Beat all ingredients together well adding a little half & half if necessary to reach desired consistency.  Chill till ready to use.

# Strawberries With Lemon Cream

1   8-Ounce Package Cream Cheese, softened
⅓   Cup Confectioner's Sugar
1   Teaspoon Lemon Peel, grated
1   Tablespoon Lemon Juice
2   Pints Fresh Strawberries, about 42

In bowl, with electric mixer, beat cream cheese, sugar, lemon peel, and juice until smooth.  Cover; refrigerate.  Remove hulls from strawberries; place on paper-towel-lined tray, hulled end down.  With a sharp knife cut an X through the top of each berry (don't cut all the way through).  Pull sections apart slightly.  Spoon filling into pastry bag fitted with a ½-inch star tip.  Pipe a heaping teaspoon in center of each berry.  (Berries may be filled 2 hours before serving.)  To serve place in petit-four cups.  SERVES 10-12.

# Summer

Summer in Sonoita is quite warm; days
are normally 85⁰ to 95⁰ and can often
reach 100⁰ plus. During July and August
the summer monsoons and the spectacular
lightning displays are breathtaking. People
often sat in our dining room, looking out
over the adjacent ranch, and were trans-
fixed by the tremendous storms rolling in
over the Whetstone Mountains and across
the Empire-Cienega Preserve. We said it
was the best show in town. The temperatures can drop to the low 60s in a matter
of minutes during these storms. In mid to
late August the straw colored grassland
turns to a beautiful green landscape.

People from as far away as Tucson,
Phoenix, Mesa and Scottsdale will drive to
Sonoita for lunch or dinner to escape the
scorching temperatures in those areas.

# Burnet & Salmon Tea Sandwiches

⅔ Cup Sour Cream
1 Tablespoon Prepared Horseradish
3 Tablespoons Burnet* Leaves, firmly packed
8 Slices Firm White Bread
About ¾ Pound Salmon, cooked
32 Sprigs Burnet Or ½ Of A Cucumber, seeded & peeled

In a food processor whirl sour cream, horseradish and burnet or cucumber until burnet is minced and sour cream is pale green; chill to firm. Trim crusts from bread; slice each piece into 4 triangles. Spread each with sour cream mix, using all. With fingers, gently pull salmon apart into 32 equal-size pieces; remove and discard skin and bones. Place 1 piece of salmon on each triangle; top each with 1 sprig of burnet. SERVES APPROXIMATELY 12-16.

*Burnet is an herb which tastes like cucumber. Look for seeds to grow your own or plants at your local nursery.

# Mozzarella & Sun – Dried Tomato Crostini

*One of my favorite quick-to-prepare appetizers – guests love it!*

1 Jar Marinated Sun-Dried Tomatoes (8 ounces)
1 Medium Shallot
½ Cup Heavy Cream
10 Slices Crusty Italian Bread (½" thick)
6 Basil Leaves, stemmed
10 Slices Mozzarella Cheese

Drain tomatoes and reserve the oil. Thinly slice the shallot. Heat 4 tablespoons of the reserved oil in a medium skillet. Add the shallot and cook over low heat until softened, about 5 minutes. Stir in the cream, bring to a boil, reduce heat to low and simmer until cream is absorbed and mixture is thickened, about 5 minutes. Transfer mixture into the workbowl of a food processor fitted with the metal blade and pulse until tomatoes are chopped but not pureed. (Can be covered and refrigerated overnight.)

COOKING: Place oven rack to middle position and heat oven to 400°F. Put bread on a baking sheet and bake until golden brown, about 5 minutes. Reduce oven temperature to 375°F. Put one slice of mozzarella on each slice of bread and top with tomato mixture. Bake until cheese is melted and tomato mixture is bubbly, about 10 minutes
SERVES 10.

*appetizers, small dishes, soups*

# Cocktail Meatballs With Karen's®
## Honey – Jalapeño Sauce

*This has been a favorite of mine for many years – another really quick appetizer.*

### MEATBALLS
2 Pounds Lean Ground Beef

1 Egg

¼ Cup Bread Crumbs

2 Teaspoons Worcestershire Sauce

1 Teaspoon Salt

¼ Teaspoon Pepper, fresh ground preferably

2 Tablespoons Fresh Parsley, chopped

1 8-Ounce Jars Karen's® Honey-Jalapeño Sauce

¼ Cup Dry Vermouth, approximately

Combine all ingredients, *with the exception of the Honey-Jalapeño Sauce*. Roll into tiny balls (about the size of a walnut). These can be placed on a sheet pan and frozen until ready to use.

When ready to cook, place 2 tablespoons of oil in a large skillet and heat on high heat. Brown meatballs quickly on all sides. Alternatively bake in a 350°F oven.

In a saucepan, bring Karen's® Honey-Jalapeño Sauce to a boil over medium-high heat (if too thick, add dry vermouth to thin). Place meatballs in saucepan and simmer approximately 46 to 60 minutes. Serve in a chafing dish with toothpicks.
SERVES APPROXIMATELY 16.

Another sauce that makes a good *Sweet and Sour Meatball* is as follows:

1 12-Ounce Bottle Chile Sauce

Juice Of ½ Lemon

¾ Cup Grape Jelly

Combine ingredients in saucepan and follow same method as above.

Wine Recommendation:
Alsatian Gewurtztraminer (Weinbach)

# Corn & Sour Cream Cakes With Smoked Salmon & Dill

*We served this many times as an evening appetizer – a very pretty presentation.*

1½ Cups Corn Kernels, fresh (from 3 ears) or frozen
1⅓ Cups Milk

1 Tablespoon Yellow Cornmeal
1 Tablespoon Sugar
¼ Teaspoon Salt
½ Teaspoon Baking Soda
2 Eggs
3 Tablespoons Cake Flour
1 Cup Sour Cream
¼ Cup Oil

## SMOKED SALMON-DILL TOPPING
2 Ounces Smoked Salmon, chopped
3 Ounces Fresh Dill Weed, chopped
¼ Cup Sour Cream

Cut corn kernels from the cobs. Cook kernels with the milk over medium heat until milk is evaporated and the corn is tender. Put mixture in a food processor or blender and puree until smooth. Cool.

SMOKED SALMON TOPPING: In a bowl fold the salmon and dill into the sour cream. Refrigerate. Recipe can be made to this point one day ahead.

COOKING AND SERVING: In a food processor, combine the corn puree, cornmeal, sugar, salt, baking soda, eggs, cake flour, and sour cream and blend until thoroughly mixed. Let rest for 15 minutes.

Heat a nonstick frying pan over medium heat and brush lightly with oil. Working in batches, drop batter by tablespoons onto pan and cook, turning once, until browned, about 1 minute per side.

Put a dollop of topping on each cake and garnish with a fresh dill sprig. MAKES 30 APPETIZERS.

# Boursin —Sage Custard Tartlet

*Always a hit and really fun to serve.*

1  Loaf White Bread, each slice rolled thin
6-12  Fresh Sage Leaves

Cut out round from each slice of bread and place in a muffin tin, lightly pressing down into cavities.  Bake at 350°F until lightly browned.

When cool, pour Boursin Custard (see recipe below) filling equally into each cavity.  Place a fresh sage leaf on top of each custard and bake in preheated 350°F oven until set, approximately 10 to 15 minutes.  When done, a knife inserted in the center of the custard will come out clean.  SERVES 6.

### BOURSIN  CUSTARD

1  Package (4 to 5 ounces)  Herb-Flavored Boursin Cheese
1  Package (3 ounces)  Cream Cheese
1  Large Egg

In a food processor or with a mixer, beat Boursin, cream cheese, and egg until smooth.

# Monterey Jack —Jalapeño Quesadillas

| | |
|---|---|
| 8  7"-Flour Tortillas | ½  Cup Bottled Pimento, drained & minced |
| ½  Stick Unsalted Butter | 4  Bottled Pickled Jalapeño Peppers, minced |
| ¾  Pound Monterey Jack, grated | 2  Teaspoons Fresh Cilantro, minced |
| 8  Scallions, minced | 1  Teaspoon Ground Cumin |

Preheat oven to 400°F.  Spread the tortillas on one side with the butter and put them buttered side up on ungreased baking sheets.  Toast them in the middle of the oven for 5 minutes, or until barely golden.

In a bowl toss together the remaining ingredients and sprinkle on the tortillas.  Bake in the middle of the oven for 5 to 8 minutes, or until the cheese is bubbly.  Serve the quesadillas cut into wedges.  MAKES ABOUT 48.

*appetizers, small dishes, soups*

# Herbed Cream Cheese With Sweet Peppers

*(Broiled On Toasted Rounds)*

6 Slices Day Old Wheat Bread

1 8-Ounce Package Cream Cheese, softened

¼ Cup Mixed Dried Herbs Such As Dill, Parsley & Thyme (or your choice)

1 Sweet Red Pepper, finely diced

1 Sweet Green Pepper, finely diced

PREPARE CRUSTS: Cut bread slices into 2-inch rounds using sharp cookie cutter. Toast until browned.

PREPARE CREAM CHEESE: In food processor fitted with steel blade, combine cream cheese and dried herbs. Store in refrigerator until ready to use.

FINAL PREPARATION: Spread cream cheese on toast rounds, sprinkle with red and green peppers. Broil until cheese begins to bubble, approximately 3 to 5 minutes. SERVES 6.

# Tomato Burgundy Soup

*There is nothing like the taste of freshly made tomato soup – especially when you grow your own tomatoes!*

2¼ Pounds Ripe Tomatoes (preferably Roma tomatoes)

1 Cup Celery, coarsely chopped

1 Large Onion, coarsely chopped

3 Tablespoons Basil, chopped fresh or 1 teaspoon dried

¼ Cup Butter (½ stick)

¼ Cup All-Purpose Flour

2 Cups Chicken Broth

½ Cup Red Burgundy Wine

½ Cup Heavy Cream

Salt & Pepper, to taste

Chopped Fresh Parsley, for garnish

Bring large pot of water to boiling. Drop in tomatoes. When skins begin to split, immediately remove tomatoes with a slotted spoon and plunge into cold water. Drain. Peel tomatoes, core, and halve. Seed, if you wish. Cut into small pieces and set aside.

Sauté celery, onion, and basil in a large saucepan over medium-low heat until vegetables are tender, stirring occasionally. Sprinkle flour over all; cook and stir 1 minute. Add chopped tomatoes, chicken broth, and wine. Cook over medium heat, stirring constantly, until mixture thickens and boils. Lower heat, cover and simmer 8 minutes. Uncover and simmer 2 minutes more. Cool slightly. Pour soup into electric blender or food processor; whirl until pureed.

Return to saucepan. Stir in cream. Heat to serving temperature; DO NOT BOIL. Season with salt and pepper; serve garnished with chopped parsley. SERVES 6–8.

# Tomato & Sweet Red Pepper Soup

| | |
|---|---|
| 5 Tablespoons Unsalted Butter | 2 Teaspoons Sweet Paprika |
| 1 Teaspoon Olive Oil | ⅛ Teaspoon Sugar |
| 1 Large Onion, peeled, quartered & thinly sliced | 6 Cups Chicken Broth |
| 4 Tomatoes, peeled, seeded & chopped (3 cups) | 1½ Tablespoons All-Purpose Flour |
| 2 Red Bell Peppers, cored, seeded & diced (2½ cups) | ¾ Cup Heavy Cream |
| 1 Tablespoon Fresh Thyme Leaves Or 1½ Teaspoons Dried | Salt & Pepper, to taste |

**GARNISH**

1 Cup Ripe Tomatoes, finely diced

1 Cup Green Bell Peppers, cored, seeded & finely diced

3 Tablespoons Fresh Chives, chopped

Melt 3 tablespoons butter and the olive oil over moderate heat in a large soup pot. Add onion and cook until translucent, but not browned, about 5 minutes. Stir in tomato, red pepper, thyme, paprika, and sugar. Cook over moderately low heat until all tomato juices have evaporated, about 25 minutes. Stir in chicken broth, salt, and pepper to taste. Bring to boiling. Lower heat and simmer, partially covered, for 25 minutes, or until vegetables are tender. Using an immersion blender, puree the soup in the pot until smooth.

In a small saucepan melt the remaining butter, add the flour and cook, stirring constantly, for 1 minute; DO NOT LET BROWN. Slowly whisk into soup. Bring soup to a boil, lower heat, and simmer, partially covered, for 10 minutes.

Whisk in cream and just heat through; DO NOT LET BOIL. Season to taste with salt and pepper. Serve in hot individual bowls., garnish with diced tomato, bell pepper, and chives. MAKES 8 SERVINGS.

# Cold Cucumber — Yogurt Soup

1 Large Cucumber, peeled & seeded

2½ Cups Plain Yogurt

¼ Cup Green Onions, thinly sliced (including tops)

¼ Cup Celery, thinly sliced

1 Tablespoon Fresh Dill Weed, minced, Or, 1 Teaspoon Dry Dill Flakes

1 Garlic Clove, minced

2 Tablespoons Olive Oil

Shred enough of cucumber to make ¼ cup; set aside. Coarsely chop remaining cucumber and place in food processor, add yogurt, and whirl until smooth. Transfer mixture to a bowl and mix in shredded cucumber, green onions, celery, dill, garlic, and oil. Season to taste with salt. Cover and refrigerate until cold, at least 1 hour, or up to a day. Stir well before serving. Garnish each serving with a sprig of fresh dill weed. SERVES 4.

*appetizers, small dishes, soups*

# Tomato, Green Chile & Lime Soup

1   Small Onion, finely chopped
1   Garlic Clove, pressed
1   Tablespoon Olive Oil
½   Teaspoon Ground Cumin
½   Teaspoon Chile Powder
½   Cup Chicken Broth
1   14½-Ounce Can Whole Tomatoes, coarsely chopped (with liquid)
1   Tablespoon Canned Chopped Chiles, hot or mild
1   Lime
1   Tablespoon Cilantro, coarsely chopped
2   Tablespoons Sour Cream

*Served with crispy tortilla chips this is virtually the same as tortilla soup.*

*Tomato, Green Chile & Lime Soup*

Combine onion, garlic, and oil in 1 to 2 quart pan and sauté over medium-high heat until onion is translucent, tossing frequently, about 5 minutes.  Add cumin and chile powder and stir until completely blended.  Add chicken broth, tomatoes with liquid, and chiles.  Bring to a boil.  Cut 2 thin slices from center of lime and set aside.  Squeeze juice from lime halves into soup and stir in chopped cilantro.  Ladle soup into 2 bowls and top each with a lime slice and a dollop of sour cream.  SERVES 2.

# Vegetable Soup With Pesto

*This soup was always a hit when we served it – these flavors are really delightful!*

| | |
|---|---|
| 3 Cups Water | Pepper |
| ¾ Cup Dry Navy Beans | 1½ Cups Sliced Green Beans |
| 4 Tablespoons Olive Oil | 1½ Cups Zucchini, diced |
| 1 Cup Onions, diced | ½ Cup Broken Pasta |
| 1 Pound Tomatoes, finely chopped | 2 Pinches Saffron |
| 3 Quarts Water | 3 Cloves Garlic |
| 1½ Cups Carrots, diced | ½ Cup Fresh Basil |
| 1½ Cups Potatoes, diced finely | 1 Tablespoon Tomato Paste |
| 1 Cup Leeks, chopped | ¼ Cup Parmesan |
| 1 Tablespoon Salt | 3 Tablespoons Olive Oil |

Bring water to boil in I-quart saucepan, add beans, and boil 2 minutes. Remove from heat and let soak I hour. Return to low heat and simmer, uncovered, for 1 to 1½ hours, adding water, if necessary or, until beans are tender. Drain beans and reserve liquid. Heat oil in heavy soup pot. Stir in onions and cook until limp. Add tomatoes and cook 3 to 4 minutes. Pour in 3 quarts of water and bring to a boil, stirring occasionally. Add carrots, potatoes, leeks, salt, and pepper. Reduce heat and simmer, uncovered, for 15 minutes. Stir in beans, reserved liquid, green beans, zucchini, pasta, and saffron. Simmer 15 minutes.

PESTO: Mince garlic and basil to a fine paste. Work in tomato paste and Parmesan. Beat in olive oil, 1 tablespoon at a time.

Ladle soup into bowls; add a dollop of pesto, and garnish with parsley sprigs or, chopped parsley.

# Gazpacho

*My favorite cold soup – this is a recipe that was served at a Tucson restaurant for many years.*

| | |
|---|---|
| 3 Pounds Tomatoes, peeled, seeded & chopped | 3 Tablespoons Balsamic Vinegar |
| 2 Cucumbers, peeled, seeded & chopped | 1 Garlic Clove, minced |
| ½ Cup Green Bell Pepper, minced | Juice Of 1 Lemon |
| ½ Cup Onion, minced | ¼ Teaspoon Tabasco Sauce |
| 2 Cups Tomato Juice | ½ Teaspoon Paprika |
| ⅓ Cup Olive Oil | Salt & Pepper, to taste |

In a large bowl, combine tomatoes, cucumbers, bell pepper, onion, and tomato juice. In a small bowl mix oil, vinegar, garlic, lemon juice, Tabasco sauce, and paprika. Add to tomato mixture. Salt and pepper to taste. Cover and chill for 4 hours or more. Serve in chilled bowls with a dollop of sour cream. SERVES 6.

# Chilled Chicken In Pineapple Broth

*This is a really unusual soup with very pleasant flavors – with a little bread it makes a complete meal*

4½ Cups Chicken Broth

⅓ Cup Brown Sugar, firmly packed

1 Tablespoon Fresh Ginger, minced

1 Fresh Jalapeño Pepper, seeded & minced

1 Small Pineapple

⅓ Cup Cilantro Sprigs

1¼ Cups Lemon Or Lime Juice

6 Cold Grilled Chicken Breast Halves, skinless & boneless

Cilantro Sprigs

6 Nasturtium Blossoms (optional)

1 Lemon, cut into wedges

In a 3 to 4-quart pan, over high heat, bring sugar, ginger, and chile to a boil; set aside. Meanwhile, trim ends off pineapple; also cut off 3 crosswise slices. Peel remaining pineapple and coarsely chop enough fruit to make 3 cups. Whirl chopped fruit with the ⅓ cup cilantro in a food processor or blender until smoothly pureed, about 10 minutes. Stir puree and lemon juice into chicken broth; cover and chill until cold, about 2 hours or up to 1 day. Cover pineapple slices and chill too.

Place 1 piece of chicken in each of 6 wide, shallow soup bowls. Cut pineapple slices into quarters and add to bowls as garnish, along with cilantro sprigs and Nasturtiums. Stir broth mixture and ladle around breasts. Offer lemon wedges to season soup to taste. SERVES 6.

# Chilled Curried Zucchini Soup

1 Pound Zucchini

1 Cup Onion, minced

1 Teaspoon Curry Powder

1 Teaspoon Cumin Powder

2 Cups Chicken Broth

3 Cups Buttermilk

Sauté zucchini and onion in butter. Add curry and cumin. Stir in chicken broth. Using food processor or blender, add buttermilk to mixture and whirl until smooth. Serve chilled with yogurt or sour cream on top. SERVES 6-8.

# Cream Of Zucchini Soup With Rosemary & Thyme

*A wonderful recipe from Huguette – a great way to use an abundant zucchini crop.*

2  Tablespoons Olive Oil

4  Cloves Garlic, finely minced

1  Large Onion, diced

6  Medium Size Zucchini, coarsely chopped

2  Tablespoons Fresh Thyme Leaves Or 1 Tablespoon Dried

2  Tablespoons Fresh Rosemary Leaves Or 1 Tablespoon Dried

4  Cups Chicken Broth

1  Quart Milk

1  Quart Half & Half

In a heavy stockpot, sauté garlic in olive oil over medium heat until golden. Add onions and sauté, stirring frequently, until onion is limp. Add zucchini and sauté lightly. Add thyme and rosemary, and toss for 1 minute with other vegetables. Add chicken broth, cover, and barely simmer approximately 2 hours. Remove from heat and, using an immersion blender (or a food processor, in small batches) puree the vegetables. Return to a low heat; add the milk, and half & half. Heat to just before boiling – DO NOT BOIL OR IT WILL CURDLE. Taste and adjust seasonings. Serve, garnished with grated Swiss or Parmesan cheese, and chopped chives or sprigs of fresh thyme. SERVES 6.

# Wild Mushroom Soup

3½  Cups Chicken Broth (2 13¾-ounces canned)

3  Cups Water

1½  Pounds Assorted Fresh Mushrooms, such as shiitake, porcini, oyster mushroom, cleaned, trimmed to remove stems & dried.

2  Tablespoons Unsalted Butter

8  Green Onions, trimmed & thinly sliced, both green & white parts (1 cup)

Salt & Freshly Ground White Pepper, to taste

Combine chicken broth and water in saucepan. Bring to a simmer. Slice mushroom caps and stems into thick shreds. Heat butter in large saucepan until foamy. Add mushrooms; toss to coat. Cover and cook gently over low heat, stirring occasionally. Add ¾ cup green onion, reserving remainder for garnish. Cover and cook 5 minutes until mushrooms are tender. Add broth mixture and simmer rapidly, partially covered, for 15 minutes. Strain soup into colander over a bowl. Return liquid to saucepan; boil uncovered until reduced to about 4½ cups, about 8 to 10 minutes. Return solids to saucepan. Gently heat through. Serve in soup bowls. Garnish with remaining green onions. SERVES 6-8.

In the late summer after the intense rainy season, grasshoppers arrive sporting colorful and intricate designs. While they like to munch on a wide variety of vegetables and herbs, they especially love mint!

# Melange Of Summer Garden Vegetables

*Even if you don't like squash this is a very tasty dish.*

1    Medium Green Zucchini
1    Yellow Summer Squash
1    Leek, white part only, well cleaned
1    Carrot, well scrubbed
1    Red Bell Pepper, well cleaned

Remove top, stem, and bottom knob from squash. Cut in half and julienne in fine strips. Julienne the carrot and leek in same manner. Cut pepper into fine strips. Mix all vegetables in a bowl and refrigerate until ready to cook. In a medium skillet, heat 2 tablespoons of roasted garlic oil and add vegetables. Toss till crisp tender. Season with kosher salt and fresh ground pepper to taste.

ALTERNATIVELY: Mix all vegetables with olive oil, place in roasting pan, uncovered, and place in a 350ºF preheated oven until slightly browned, tossing well every 10 minutes during roasting. Remove and serve immediately. SERVES 4-6.

# Horiatiki (Greek Country Salad)

*Of all the foods we had in Greece this was my favorite. Contrary to many American versions it does <u>not</u> contain any lettuce.*

4    Roma Tomatoes, trimmed & chopped to a ¾" dice
½    Cucumber, washed, ends trimmed & chopped to a ¾" dice
2    Thin Slices Red Onion, peeled & trimmed
8-10    Greek Olives, drained
½    Cup Crumbled Feta Cheese
Dry Oregano Flakes

Scatter cucumber cubes on 2 plates. Scatter tomato cubes over the cucumbers. Toss the cucumbers and tomatoes gently to mix. Break onion slices into rings and scatter across tomatoes and cucumbers. Scatter the crumbled feta cheese and oregano leaves over the onions and then place the Greek olives randomly on top of the feta cheese. Drizzle Greek Vinaigrette (see recipe on page 124) over all and serve immediately. SERVES 2.

# Tami's Chinese Chicken Salad

*My daughter-in-law, Tami, shared this recipe with me – it is a delicious whole meal salad!*

1 Pound Fresh Mesclun Greens Mix Or 1 Head Romaine Lettuce
1 Pound Boneless & Skinless Chicken Breasts
1 Bottle Karen's® Soy-Ginger Glazing-Marinade Sauce
1 2-Ounce Package Sai Fun (noodles-bean threads)
½ Package Won Ton Skins (20-25 skins), cut lengthwise into ¼" strips
2 Tablespoons Toasted Sesame Seeds
3 Green Onions, chopped (including tops)

Marinate chicken breasts in Karen's® Soy-Ginger Marinade for at least 4 hours. Remove from marinade, grill until done, and cut into ½ to ¾-inch cubes. Separate the Sai Fun Noodles and deep fry. Slice the Won Ton Skins into ½-inch strips and deep fry. Combine all ingredients and top with dressing or *dress with* Karen's® Soy-Ginger Vinaigrette. SERVES 4.

### DRESSING
½ Cup Salad Oil
4 Tablespoons Wine Vinegar
2 Tablespoons Sugar
1 Teaspoon Salt
½ Teaspoon Pepper

Combine and mix well. Allow to sit for 1 hour and remix.

# Steamed Broccoli With Sesame – Cumin Butter

1 Pound Fresh Broccoli; cut into 1½" florets, the stems peeled & cut diagonally into ¼" slices
4 Teaspoons Sesame Seeds
3 Tablespoons Unsalted Butter
1½ Teaspoons Cumin, or to taste
Fresh Lemon Juice, to taste

Steam the broccoli in a steamer over simmering water, covered, for 6 minutes, or until it is crisp tender. In a heavy skillet toast the sesame seeds over moderately high heat, stirring constantly, until they are golden; add the butter, cumin, salt to taste, and heat the mixture, stirring, until the butter is melted. Transfer the broccoli to a bowl and add the herb-butter mixture. Toss the broccoli to coat it and sprinkle it with lemon juice. SERVES 4.

# Farfalle Salad

½ Pound Farfalle Pasta, cooked according to package directions, rinsed & drained

2 Roma Tomatoes, finely diced

6 Large Fresh Basil Leaves, finely julienned

1 Green Onion, cleaned & thinly sliced

½ Cup Shredded Parmesan Cheese

¼ Cup Toasted Pine Nuts

1 Bottle Karen's® Lemon-Herb Vinaigrette (or see recipe below)

Arrange half of farfalle on each of two plates. Sprinkle half of the tomatoes on each plate. Sprinkle basil and green onions on each plate. Top with cheese and pine nuts. Dress with Lemon-Herb Vinaigrette. SERVES 2.

## LEMON HERB VINAIGRETTE

1 Cup Canola Oil

¼ Cup Fresh Lemon Juice

¼ Cup Rice Vinegar

1 Tablespoon Chives Or Green Onions, finely chopped

2 Teaspoons Fresh Thyme Leaves Or 1 Teaspoon Dry Thyme Leaves

Salt & Fresh Ground Pepper, to taste

Whisk all ingredients together and refrigerate until ready to use.

*Farfalle Salad*

*Our granddaughter Caitlin's favorite. She always asked for "Folly Salad."*

# Sauté Of Zucchini, Garlic & Herbs

3 Medium Size Zucchini, washed with ends removed
3 Cloves Garlic, finely minced
1 Tablespoon Fresh Rosemary Leaves
1 Tablespoon Fresh Thyme Leaves
¼ Teaspoon Freshly Ground Black Pepper
1 Tablespoon Olive Oil
2 Tablespoons Dry White Wine

Chop zucchini into ¾-inch cubes, approximately. In a medium sized sauté pan, heat olive oil over medium-high heat, add garlic, and cook until garlic is golden, stirring constantly. Add zucchini, rosemary, and thyme; toss until zucchini is coated and barely cooked. Add white wine, cover, and simmer until zucchini is crisp tender, approximately 3 to 5 minutes. Remove from heat and, using a slotted spoon, place in a serving dish. Serve immediately, garnishing with freshly grated Parmesan cheese. SERVES 6.

# Vegetable Ribbons With Shallot Butter

*Very pretty presentation and very tasty as well.*

2 Carrots, peeled
2 Small Zucchini, scrubbed
2 Small Yellow Summer Squash, washed well
2 Tablespoons Butter
4 Medium Shallots, peeled & thinly sliced

With a vegetable peeler or mandolin (preferable) cut the carrots, zucchini, and the yellow squash, lengthwise, into thin "ribbons," reserving the cores for another use. In a glass dish microwave the vegetables, covered, at high power for 2 minutes or, until they are crisp-tender. In a small glass dish, or glass cup, combine the butter and the sliced shallots and microwave on high power for 30 seconds, covered, until the shallots are limp and the butter is melted. Pour the shallot butter over the vegetables, adjust the seasonings, and toss them well. SERVES 4.

# Green Beans With Bacon & Hazelnuts

*This is my favorite green bean recipe – if I can't find hazelnuts, I separate them from a can of mixed nuts!*

1½ Pounds Fresh Green Beans, cleaned & trimmed
½ Cup Chopped Hazelnuts Or Almonds
½ Cup Bacon, minced

Steam green beans till bright green. Chill and set aside. In a 375°F oven, roast chopped hazelnuts on a baking sheet till lightly toasted. Fry minced bacon till crisp and place on paper towels to drain. When ready to serve; reheat beans and toss with bacon and hazelnuts. Salt and pepper to taste. SERVES 4-6.

# Vinegared Cucumbers With Burnet

1 Medium Size Cucumber

1 Teaspoon Salt

¼ Cup White Wine Vinegar

2 Tablespoons Minced Burnet Leaves, firmly packed

2 Teaspoons Sugar

½ Teaspoon Dry Dill Weed

½ Teaspoon Pepper

Burnet Sprigs

Peel cucumbers and thinly slice.  In a bowl, mix cucumber slices with salt.  Cover and chill 30 minutes or up to 24 hours.  Drain accumulated liquid from cucumbers.  Stir in vinegar, burnet, dill weed, and pepper.  Mound cucumbers on a serving plate; garnish with burnet sprigs.  SERVES 2-4.

# Karen's Potatoes Au Gratin

| | |
|---|---|
| 7-8 Russet Potatoes | 1 Pint Heavy Cream |
| 8 Ounces Sharp Cheddar Cheese, grated | ¼ Cup Bread Crumbs |
| 1 Teaspoon Salt | 1 Tablespoon Butter |

Boil potatoes with skins on.  Cool, peel, and shred using a medium shredder.  Butter 2-quart casserole.  Alternate layers of potatoes and cheese in casserole, then sprinkle with salt.  Pour cream over layers.  Combine crumbs and butter and sprinkle over top.  Bake uncovered until heated through, 45 to 55 minutes.  This dish can be refrigerated until ready to bake.  If refrigerated increase baking time 10 minutes.  SERVES 6.

# Michoteta

*(Feta & Vegetable Salad )*

| | |
|---|---|
| 7 Ounces Crumbled Feta Cheese | 2 Tablespoons Fresh Lemon Juice |
| 1 Cucumber, peeled, seeded & chopped | Fresh Ground Pepper |
| ½ Large Red Onion, chopped | Fresh Parsley, chopped |
| 3 Tablespoons Olive Oil | |

Combine the first 5 ingredients together in a large bowl.  Season with pepper and toss well.  Place on individual salad plates; garnish with parsley and serve.  SERVES 4.

*vegetables, salads and grains*

# Karen's Grilled Chicken Breast Salad

### (With Karen's® Soy-Ginger Glazing/Marinade Sauce)

Karen's Grilled Chicken Breast Salad

*We had customers at the Café who never ordered anything but this salad!*

16 Ounces Mixed Greens

4 Roma Tomatoes, washed & quartered lengthwise

12 Diagonal Slices Of Cucumber

4 Boneless, Skinless Chicken Breasts, grilled & sliced diagonally

8 Ounces Angel Hair Pasta, cooked according to package directions, drained & tossed lightly in olive oil

2 Green Onions, cleaned & sliced on the diagonal

½ Cup Shredded Parmesan Cheese

4 Tablespoons Red Bell Peppers, minced

4 Tablespoons Cashews

Karen's® Soy-Ginger Glazing/Marinade Sauce (or see recipe on page 210)

Arrange greens on 4 plates. Place ¼ of pasta on top of greens and in the center of each plate. Place 1 chicken breast on top of the pasta. Sprinkle Parmesan over chicken breasts, then green onions, bell pepper, and cashews. Garnish with tomatoes and cucumbers. Dress with Soy-Ginger Vinaigrette. SERVES 4.

# 24-Hour Greek Pasta Salad

6 Ounces Cut Ziti (tube shaped pasta)
½ Cup Plain Yogurt
½ Cup Greek Salad Dressing (see recipe below)
½ Teaspoon Dried Oregano, crushed
1 Small Cucumber, halved lengthwise & thinly sliced
½ Cup Pitted Greek Olives
1 Cup Crumbled Feta Cheese
12 Cherry Tomatoes Quartered Or 1 Large Tomato, chopped
1 Cup Alfalfa Sprouts
Onion & Garlic Croutons

In large saucepan cook pasta, uncovered, in boiling water about 14 minutes or till tender but still slightly firm, stirring occasionally. Immediately drain in a large colander. Rinse with cold water; drain well. Transfer to large bowl and set aside.

For dressing, in a small bowl combine yogurt, dressing, and oregano. Stir in ⅓ cup of the dressing into the drained pasta. Place in bottom of 2-quart straight-sided clear bowl. Layer the cucumber, olives, cheese, and tomatoes on top. Spread remaining dressing over top. Top with sprouts. Cover tightly; chill up to 24 hours. To serve top with croutons. MAKES 4-6 SIDE DISH SERVINGS.

## GREEK SALAD DRESSING

¾ Cup Olive Oil
¼ Cup Red Wine Vinegar
⅛ Teaspoon Dry Mustard
½ Teaspoon Salt
¼ Teaspoon Freshly Ground Pepper

Put ingredients in a small jar and shake thoroughly. Chill before serving.

# Sautéed Cherry Tomatoes

1 Pint Cherry Tomatoes, cleaned & halved
¼ Cup Olive Oil
¼ Cup Mixed Mediterranean Herbs Such As Basil, Chives & Oregano, finely chopped

Heat oil in sauté pan until hot. Add tomatoes and herbs and toss till heated. SERVES 2.

# Shrimp & Chicken Salad With Lemon & Basil Mayonnaise

## LEMON AND BASIL MAYONNAISE

| | |
|---|---|
| 2 Lemons | ⅓ Cup Vegetable Oil |
| 2 Cups Fresh Basil Leaves, loosely packed | 4 Boneless Chicken Breasts |
| 1 Egg | 2 Teaspoons Salt |
| 1 Egg Yolk | ¾ Pound Shelled & Deveined Shrimp (about 20) |
| Salt & Freshly Ground Pepper | Radiccio & Boston Lettuce Leaves |
| 1 Cup Olive Oil | Fresh Basil Sprigs, for garnish |

LEMON AND BASIL MAYONNAISE: Squeeze 5 tablespoons juice from lemons. In a food processor, combine the basil, whole egg, egg yolk, lemon juice, 1½ teaspoons salt, and ½ teaspoon pepper and process until smooth. With the machine running, slowly add both oils. Season to taste with salt and pepper. DO NOT OVERPROCESS!

Put chicken breasts in a frying pan just large enough to hold them in a single layer and cover with cold water. Add 2 teaspoons salt and bring to a simmer over medium heat, about 5 minutes. Turn the chicken, add the shrimp, and simmer until just cooked through, about 4 minutes. Remove the shrimp with a slotted spoon and cool. Cool the chicken in the poaching water, about 30 minutes. Drain, reserving the chicken broth for another use. Slice the chicken.

To serve, put radiccio and Boston lettuce leaves on plates, alternating colors. Arrange the chicken and shrimp on lettuce, top with some of the mayonnaise, and garnish with basil sprigs. Pass remaining mayonnaise. SERVES 4.

# Thai Cucumber Salad

½ Cup Rice Vinegar

2 Tablespoons Light Brown Sugar, firmly packed

1 Teaspoon Salt

1 Large Cucumber, peeled & cut crosswise into ¼" slices

½ Cup Shallots, thinly sliced

2 Tablespoons Seeded Fresh Red *Prig Chee Fah (Chiles)*, thinly sliced

1 Tablespoon Fresh Coriander, chopped

In a bowl stir together the vinegar, sugar, and the salt until the sugar and the salt are dissolved. Add the cucumbers, shallots, and the chiles and combine the mixture well. Let the salad stand, chilled or at room temperature, for up to 1 hour and just before serving sprinkle it with the coriander. MAKES ABOUT 2 CUPS.

# Polenta Tamales With Roasted Tomato — Garlic Sauce

*A very nontraditional tamale but fun to serve and delicious as well!*

| | |
|---|---|
| 1 Package Dry Corn Husks | 1¼ Cups Monterey Jack Cheese, grated |
| 1¼ Cups Of Polenta | 1⅞ Cups Chicken Breast, grilled & diced |
| 3¾ Cups Of Chicken Broth | ⅓ Cup Green Chiles, chopped |
| 5 Tablespoons Of Butter | 1¼ Cups Colby Jack Cheese, grated |
| ⅓ Cup Green Onion, thinly sliced | 1¼ Cups Roasted Tomato-Garlic Sauce |

Place husks in hot water, covering completely. Allow to absorb water while preparing other ingredients.

Sauté green onions in butter till soft. Add chicken stock and bring to a boil. Add polenta, slowly, stirring constantly, till polenta is thickened. Add the shredded monterey jack cheese, stirring to combine. Cover and set aside. Chop chicken into ¼-inch dice.

TO ASSEMBLE: Drain husks. Tear smaller pieces into strips to be used for tying tamale ends. Spread 2 to 3 husks flat. Spread approximately ½ cup of polenta over the husks. Sprinkle approximately 2 tablespoons of diced chicken over polenta and sprinkle 2 tablespoons chopped chiles over chicken. Sprinkle 1 tablespoon shredded colby jack over all. Wrap husks to enclose filling completely and tie ends with small husk strips. Continue until all ingredients are used up. At this point, the tamales can be frozen on a flat pan and, when frozen can be stored in freezer bags until ready to serve.

TO SERVE: Steam tamales in a ziploc bag in the microwave approximately 1 to 2 minutes each if defrosted completely or 5 to 6 minutes if frozen. Place on a warm plate, opening large end so that the tamale shows well. Spoon roasted tomato-garlic sauce (see recipe below) around the edge of the plate. Garnish with thin sliced green onions or chopped chives. MAKES 10 TAMALES.

## ROASTED TOMATO-GARLIC SAUCE

10 Roma Tomatoes, cut in halves
10 Cloves Of Garlic, left whole
1 Tablespoon Fresh Basil, julienned fine
2 Teaspoons Kosher Salt
Fresh Ground Pepper
¼ Cup Olive Oil

Place halved tomatoes, cut side up in small roasting pan. Place whole garlic cloves around tomatoes. Sprinkle basil, kosher salt, and fresh ground pepper over all. Sprinkle evenly with olive oil and place in 325°F oven. Roast, uncovered 30 to 45 minutes, stirring once or twice, until tomatoes and garlic are soft and slightly browned. Remove from oven and let cool. Process in food processor fitted with metal blade till slightly chunky. Refrigerate till ready to serve. Reheat to simmer to serve. SERVES 10.

# Grilled Steak Oriental

*Leftovers of this steak make an excellent salad!*

| | |
|---|---|
| ¼ Cup Sesame Seeds | 1 Tablespoon Brown Sugar, firmly packed |
| ¼ Cup Sliced Green Onions, including tops | 1 Tablespoon Fresh Ginger, minced |
| 1 Tablespoon Soy Sauce | 1 Teaspoon Dry Mustard |
| 1 Tablespoon Sesame Oil | 1 Teaspoon Worcestershire Sauce |
| 1 Tablespoon Vinegar | 1½ Pounds Flank Steak, well trimmed of fat |

MARINADE: Toast sesame seeds in a frying pan over medium heat until golden, shaking pan frequently. Crush seeds, and then place in a bowl and stir in onions, soy sauce, sesame oil, vinegar, sugar, ginger, garlic, mustard, and Worcestershire sauce.

Place steak in a 9 x 13-inch dish. Pour the marinade over the steak to coat. Cover and refrigerate for at least 4 hours or, preferably over night, turning several times.

Lift the steak from marinade and drain briefly, reserving marinade. Place steak on a lightly greased grill. Cook, turning once and basting several times with marinade, until medium rare – approximately 10 to 14 minutes.

To serve, let steak stand for 5 minutes, then cut across the grain into thin slanting slices. Serve topped with a little of the marinade heated to boiling. SERVES 4.

# Chicken Piccata Milanese

*This is a stellar chicken recipe – it is very important that the chicken breasts be pounded very thin!*

| | |
|---|---|
| 4 Whole Chicken Breasts | 1½ Tablespoons Capers, drained |
| ¾ Cup All-Purpose Flour, seasoned with salt & pepper | ½ Cup Shredded Parmesan |
| ½ Cup Butter | 6 Thin Lemon Slices |
| ½ Cup Lemon Juice | ¼ Cup Chopped Parsley |
| 1 Cup Dry White Wine | |

Pound each chicken breast between sheets of plastic wrap till ⅛-inch thick. Dredge in seasoned flour, shaking off the excess. Heat butter in a sauté pan until hot but not beginning to brown. Sauté chicken on each side about 2 minutes. Do not overcook! Place on warmed plate and tent loosely with foil.

Add lemon juice and white wine to sauté pan, deglazing bits from the pan. Add the capers and heat until just below a simmer. Pour over chicken, top with lemon slices and sprinkle with Parmesan and chopped parsley. Serve immediately. SERVES 4.

# Grilled Fillet Of Salmon

### (With A Roasted Red Pepper-Garlic Coulis)

*Salmon was the most popular fish at the Café – even in the middle of the Sonoran Desert.*
*This is a very refreshing sauce!*

4   Salmon Fillets, approximately 4 ounces each
2   Tablespoons Oil

Combine all ingredients and mix well.  Cover and store in refrigerator till ready to use.  Keeps 3 to 5 days.

Preheat broiler or grill.  Place oil in pie pan and turn filets on both sides to coat.  Place on grill and cook until firm to the touch, turning once.  Remove from the grill and top with approximately ¼ cup of Roasted Red Pepper-Garlic Coulis (see recipe on page 84), garnish with a sprig of fresh cilantro, and serve immediately.  SERVES 4.


# Grilled Swordfish Steaks

### (With An Herb Marinade & Fresh Tomato Salsa)

*I am not a lover of fish but this is delicious!*

2   Pounds Swordfish Steak, 1" thick
1   Cup Olive Oil
1   Tablespoon Dried Oregano, crumbled
2   Tablespoons Dried Basil, crumbled
2   Tablespoons Lemon Juice
4   Garlic Cloves, minced
1   Teaspoon Celery Salt
1   Teaspoon Coarse Black Pepper
½   Teaspoon Salt
Snipped Parsley

Cut fish into serving portions; rinse and pat dry.  Arrange single layer of fish in shallow dish.  Combine olive oil with remaining ingredients except parsley; pour over fish.  Marinate, covered, in refrigerator 1 hour, turning once.  Remove fish and reserve marinade.  Broil fish in well greased shallow pan keeping 4 inches from source of heat, or grill on well greased grill keeping 4 to 6 inches from medium hot coals.  Cook basting often with marinade, 6 to 7 minutes.  Turn carefully, baste often.  Cook until fish flakes easily with fork, 4 to 5 minutes.  Arrange swordfish steaks on heated platter; top with Karen's Fresh Tomato Salsa (see recipe on page 214).  SERVES 6.

# Orange Roughy In Parchment

## (With Fresh Tomato Sauce & Basil Butter)

*I love to cook in parchment and the aroma of this dish when opened is exceptional.*

6-8  Ounces Orange Roughy Fillets
6  Sheets Parchment, approximately 9" x 9"
3  Medium Size Romano Tomatoes, chopped to a medium dice
3  Green Onions, thinly sliced (including tops)
2  Garlic Cloves, finely minced
2  Tablespoons Fresh Parsley, finely chopped
Fresh Ground Black Pepper
Basil Butter (see recipe below)

Combine tomatoes, green onions, garlic, and parsley in a small bowl. Rinse fish fillets and pat dry. Lay sheet of parchment flat on counter and place fillet on ½ of it. Spoon approximately ⅙th of the mixture on top of the fillet, sprinkle with pepper, and fold the other half of the parchment over it. Be sure to arrange the fillet so that there is approximately a 1¼-inch border of parchment that is free to roll up to seal the packet. Roll the parchment border to form a good seal on the packet. If you have any trouble with this, use an egg white blended with 1 teaspoon of water to brush on the edges of the parchment to seal completely. Repeat with the other 5 fillets. NOTE: In order to have fish cook evenly it is a good idea to fold the thin end of the fillet under itself so that the thickness is approximately the same throughout. Bake in a preheated 400°F oven approximately 3 to 5 minutes per 1 inch of thickness. Remove from oven and, cutting a cross in the parchment, open the packet up. Spoon approximately 1 tablespoon of Basil Butter into opening and allow to melt as you are serving. Garnish with lemon and parsley. SERVES 6.

## BASIL BUTTER

1  Cup Basil Leaves, tightly packed & patted dry
1  Cube (8 tablespoons) Unsalted Butter

In a food processor fitted with a steel blade and using a pulsing on/off action, chop the basil until medium fine, not pureed. Add the cube of butter and combine well. Scrape into bowl and chill until ready to use.

Wine Recommendation:
Dry Rosé/Vin Gris (Bonny Doon)

# Chicken Breast Stuffed With Rice & Pine Nuts

## (With An Apricot-Marsala Sauce)

4 Chicken Breasts, with skin on

1 Package (4 servings) White & Wild Rice Mix

½ Cup Toasted Pine Nuts

1 8-Ounce Jar Apricot Preserves

1 Tablespoon Marsala Wine

Salt & Pepper, to taste

Preheat oven to 350°F. Prepare rice according to package directions; add pine nuts and mix. Mix apricot preserves with Marsala and heat in small saucepan till thick, stirring frequently. Divide rice into 4 parts. Place ¼ under skin side of each chicken breast. Place breasts in a greased baking dish and season with salt and pepper. Place in oven and roast approximately 45 minutes. Spread Apricot-Marsala Sauce on each chicken breast and return to oven. Bake approximately 15 minutes longer, or until thermometer registers 160°F in meatiest part of breast. Remove from oven and serve. SERVES 4.

# Grilled Flank Steak With Honey—Mustard Baste

1½ Pounds Flank Steak, trimmed of excess fat

¼ Cup Lemon Juice

¼ Cup Honey

2 Tablespoons Dijon Mustard

2 Tablespoons Soy Sauce

1 Clove Garlic, minced

¼ Teaspoon Pepper

Mix marinade (lemon juice, honey, mustard, soy sauce, garlic, and pepper). Lay flank steak in dish large enough to lie flat. Pour marinade over, cover, and refrigerate overnight, turning several times. Remove steak from marinade and drain well. Grill steak approximately 10 to 14 minutes for medium rare. Let stand 5 to 7 minutes before slicing. Slice on diagonal into strips. Pour marinade into small pan and boil till thickened. Serve with steak. SERVES 4-6.

# Pasta With Shrimp & Jalapeño—Orange Sauce

*Pasta With Shrimp & Jalapeño-Orange Sauce*

*We were always looking for new ways to serve pasta and this was one of the most interesting we found!*

6  Tablespoons Unsalted Butter (¾ stick)

24  Large Shrimp, peeled & deveined

2  Tablespoons Shallots, minced

1  Small Jalapeño Chile, seeded & thinly sliced

½  Cup Dry White Wine

1½  Cups Orange Juice

¾  Cup Heavy Cream

12  Ounces Linguine

Fresh Parsley, minced

Melt butter in heavy large skillet over medium-high heat. Add shrimp and cook until just pink, about 1 minute per side. Transfer shrimp to plate. Add shallots and jalapeño to skillet and sauté 1 minute. Add wine and bring to boil. Mix in orange juice and cream. Boil until reduced to thin sauce, stirring occasionally, about 10 minutes. Season to taste with salt and pepper. Cook pasta in large pot of boiling salted water until just tender but still firm to bite, stirring occasionally to prevent sticking. Drain. Bring sauce to simmer. Add shrimp and cook until heated through. Add pasta and toss well. Divide pasta among plates. Sprinkle with minced fresh parsley and serve. SERVES 4.

# Nut Crusted Mahi Mahi

*(In An Herbed Coconut Lime Puddle)*

*A little time is needed for preparation but it can be done in stages – well worth the effort.*

## SAUCE
### (Can be done 1 day ahead)

| | |
|---|---|
| 2 Cups Chicken Broth | 3 Sprigs Cilantro, finely chopped |
| ¼ Cup Limeade Concentrate, undiluted | Additional Cilantro Sprigs For Garnish |
| ¼ Cup Rice Vinegar | 1 Garlic Clove, finely minced |
| 1 Jalapeño Pepper, seeded & chopped fine | 1 Teaspoon Lemon Thyme |
| 2 Tablespoons Chives, chopped | 1 Can Coconut Milk |
| 1 Tablespoon Fresh Ginger, finely chopped | 1 Lime, sliced thin for garnish |

Place chicken broth, limeade, rice vinegar, jalapeño, chives, ginger, chopped cilantro, garlic, and thyme in a medium sized pot (2 quart) and place over high heat. Bring to a boil and boil rapidly until liquid is reduced by ½. Strain and measure (it should measure 1 cup). Add 1 can of coconut milk. Return to pan and bring to a boil again. Boil 5 minutes. This can be refrigerated at this point until ready to use. Before serving, bring back to a boil and keep hot till ready to serve.

## MAHI MAHI FILLETS — PREPARATION

4 Mahi Mahi Fillets, each about 4-6 ounces
½ Cup Flour, seasoned with ½ teaspoon salt & 2-3 grindings fresh pepper
1 Egg, beaten & placed in a pie pan
2 Cups Macadamia Nuts Or Cashews, finely chopped

Preheat oven to 350ºF. Pat fillets dry with paper toweling. Place flour and nuts each on a sheet of waxed paper. Dip each fillet in flour, then in egg, and finally in nuts (do this with both sides and pat nuts on firmly). Allow fillets to sit while heating peanut oil in a non-stick frying pan. When hot, place fillets in pan and brown slightly on both sides. Remove from frying pan and place on lightly greased sheet pan. Place in oven and bake an additional 10 to 15 minutes or until fillets are firm to the touch.

TO SERVE: Puddle 2 to 3 tablespoons of sauce on each of four plates. Remove fish from sheet pan and place in middle of the sauce. Top each fillet with 1 to 2 sprigs Cilantro and a thin slice of lime. Serve immediately. SERVES 4.

Wine Recommendation:
Australian Riesling (Clos Clare)
Austrian Gruner Veltliner or Reisling (Weingartner)

# Flank Steak With Whisky Sauce

¼ Cup Teriyaki Sauce Or Karen's® Soy-Ginger Vinaigrette

4 Cloves Garlic, finely chopped

2 Teaspoons Red Wine Vinegar

2 Teaspoons Worcestershire Sauce

1 Teaspoon Tabasco Sauce

15 Ounces Beef Flank Steak, trimmed of all visible fat

2 Teaspoons Cornstarch

1 Cup Beef Broth

4 Teaspoons Margarine

¼ Cup Onion, finely chopped

6 Tablespoons Whiskey

2 Teaspoons Dijon Mustard

2 Teaspoons Chopped Parsley

1 Teaspoon Pepper

Watercress, for garnish (optional)

Combine teriyaki sauce, 1½ teaspoons chopped garlic, vinegar, Worcestershire and Tabasco in a medium size non-aluminum bowl. Add steak and turn several times to coat. Cover with plastic wrap. Refrigerate at least 30 minutes or, preferably, overnight.

Preheat broiler. To prepare sauce, stir together cornstarch and broth in glass liquid measure until combined. Heat margarine in small saucepan over medium heat till bubbly. Add onion and remaining chopped garlic; cook 2 minutes or until onion begins to soften. Remove from heat. Carefully add whiskey and mustard; stir to combine. Return pan to heat and bring to boiling. Cook 3 to 4 minutes or until reduced by about half. Re-stir cornstarch mixture and add to saucepan along with parsley and pepper; stir to combine. Return to boiling. Reduce heat to low; simmer 4 to 5 minutes, stirring occasionally. Cover saucepan and keep warm while cooking beef.

Place steak on broiler rack; discard marinade. For rare beef, broil 5 inches from heat for about 8 minutes, turning heat halfway through. Let meat stand 5 minutes. Slice across grain. Serve with sauce and garnish with watercress.
MAKES 4 SERVINGS.

Wine Recommendation:
Chateauneuf du Pape (Vieux Telegraphe)
Madiran (Montus)

# Honey Jalapeño — Chile — Cheese Chicken

½  Cup Flour, seasoned with salt & pepper

4  Chicken Breasts, boneless & skinless

½  Cup Shredded Jack & Colby Cheese Mix

4  Whole Mild Green Chiles; cleaned, seeded & halved

1  Cup *Karen's® Honey-Jalapeño Sauce Or Your Favorite Hot Pepper Jelly

Preheat oven to 375⁰F.  Heat a non-stick skillet to medium high.  Dredge chicken breasts on both sides in seasoned flour.  Spray skillet with pan release spray and brown chicken on both sides.  Place browned breasts on a lightly greased sheet pan.  Place 1 slice cheese and 2 chile halves on each chicken breast.  Place in oven and bake till cheese is melted and bubbly.  Remove from oven and spread approximately ¼ cup Honey Jalapeño Sauce on each breast.  Return to oven and bake approximately 5 to 6 minutes more (till sauce is melted and bubbly).  Remove from oven and serve.  SERVES 4.

*Karen's® Honey Jalapeño Sauce *is available by mail order.  Contact Karen's Fine Foods by phone at 520-544-0986.*

*This is a very quick dish to prepare – great for those hurry-up dinners.*

*Honey Jalapeño-Chile-Cheese Chicken served with Potato Souffle*

*entrees*

# Gemelli Pasta With Italian Sausage & Roasted Red Pepper Sauce

4 Tablespoons Olive Oil
8 6-Ounce Italian Sausage Links, casings removed
8 Roasted Garlic Cloves
2 Cups Canned Tomatoes
1½ Cups Roasted Red Peppers
12 Leaves Of Fresh Basil, cut in fine julienne
1 Pound Gemelli Pasta
1 Cup Grated Mozzarella Cheese
4 Sprigs Of Fresh Basil

Sauté sausage in pan with olive oil till browned and cooked through. In food processor, chop till chunky the garlic, tomatoes, and peppers. Add julienned basil. Add this mixture to sausage and heat till simmering. If it looks dry, add ¼ to ½ cup of dry white wine.

Meanwhile, boil pasta in large amount of boiling water till al dente. Drain, toss with sausage mixture and divide into four equal portions. (I like to serve this pasta in flat pasta/soup bowls). Top with grated Mozzarella cheese and place under a broiler till bubbling and lightly browned. Remove from oven and place bowl on another plate as a liner. Garnish with basil sprig and serve immediately. SERVES 4.

# Grilled Fillet Mignon

## (With Gorgonzola Sauce)

4 Beef Tenderloin Fillets, 6-8 ounces each
¼ Teaspoon Each Of Kosher Salt & Freshly Ground Pepper
2 Cups Heavy Cream
½ Cup Gorgonzola Cheese, crumbled

Approximately 2 to 4 hours before grilling prep fillets by sprinkling with kosher salt and freshly ground pepper. Wrap individually in plastic wrap and refrigerate. Approximately 30 minutes before grilling remove steaks from refrigerator and allow to come to room temperature. During this time reduce the cream to 1 cup by boiling rapidly. Add cheese, mix well, cover, and keep warm. Spray grill with pan release spray and preheat approximately 10 minutes. Place steaks on grill and grill to desired degree of doneness. Serve by pooling sauce on plate and placing steak on top. Garnish with chopped chives. SERVES 4.

# Focaccia Bread

*A favorite and lots of ways to vary it.*

1½ Tablespoons Yeast
2 Cups Lukewarm Water
¼ Cup Plus 2 Tablespoons Of Olive Oil
7¾ Cups Plus 2 Tablespoons Of Bread Flour
¼ Cup Plus 2 Tablespoons Fresh Herbs, finely chopped
1½ Teaspoons Salt
1½ Cups Olive Oil
1½ Tablespoons Kosher Salt

In a large bowl, dissolve yeast in ½ cup of lukewarm water and proof for 10 minutes. Add olive oil, flour, herbs, 1½ teaspoon salt, and remaining water. Knead in mixer with dough hook until smooth and elastic; add flour to prevent sticking if necessary. Oil the same bowl and turn dough ball several times to coat well; cover and put in warm place until it doubles in size, 1½ to 2 hours.

Punch dough down and divide in 2 halves. Shape into balls and return to bowl. Coat with olive oil, cover, and allow to rise 20 to 30 minutes.

Preheat oven to 400°F. Flatten each ball with hands onto a baking sheet to form a large, flat circle ½-inch thick. Make 4 to 5 slashes on each circle with a sharp knife. Use fingers to spread slashes apart slightly. Sprinkle with kosher salt. Bake 20 minutes or, until golden brown. Brush lightly with oil and allow to cool on wire racks. MAKES 2 ROUND LOAVES.

# Cheesy — Corn Muffins

1½ Cups Yellow Cornmeal
½ Cup All-Purpose Flour
1 Tablespoon Baking Powder
2 Teaspoons Sugar
1 Teaspoon Salt
2 Large Eggs

1 Cup Sour Cream
¼ Cup Vegetable Oil
1 12-Ounce Can Mexican Style Corn, drained
1 Cup Shredded Cheddar Cheese
¼ Cup Canned Green Chiles, chopped

Preheat oven to 350°F. Grease muffin pan. In a large bowl, combine cornmeal, flour, baking powder, sugar, and salt. In medium bowl, whisk together eggs, sour cream, and oil until smooth. Add corn, cheese, and chiles. Add to dry ingredients and mix well. Spoon batter into muffin pan, dividing evenly. Bake 25 minutes. Let muffins cool in pan 5 to 10 minutes before removing. MAKES 6 MUFFINS.

# Grilled Vegetable Sandwich On Focaccia Bread

Grilled Vegetable Sandwich On Focaccia Bread

*Even if you are not a vegetarian, you would like this – it is the best combination we found.*

4-6  6" Squares Of Focaccia Bread, sliced horizontally (see recipe on page 138)
1  Cup Olive Oil
½  Cup Cider Vinegar
1  Teaspoon Oregano Or Mixed Italian Herbs
½  Teaspoon Salt
¼  Teaspoon Pepper
4-6  Red Onion Slices, ¼" thick
8-12  Pieces Of Roasted Red Bell Peppers
8-12  Slices Portabello Mushrooms
4-6  Slices Eggplant
8-12  Slices Zucchini
1½  Cups Feta Cheese, crumbled

Mix oil, vinegar, herbs, salt, and pepper and pour into a pie pan.

Place bread slices, cut side down, on a preheated griddle, or in a toaster, and toast lightly.

Dip each vegetable slice, on both sides, into the oil-vinegar mixture. (Do not allow vegetables to sit in the mixture too long.) Place on a preheated, greased griddle, grill, or grill pan, and grill until vegetables are done, slightly browned, or blackened, whichever you prefer.

Place Focaccia on plate, toasted side up. Place vegetables on ½ of the bread slices in this order; eggplant, onion, zucchini, mushrooms, and red peppers. Finish by sprinkling with feta cheese and top with second slice of bread and press down well. Slice diagonally and serve, garnished with fresh fruit. SERVES 4-6.

# Italian Roast Beef Sandwich With Onions & Hot —Sweet Mustard

1 Loaf Tomato-Basil Bread (see recipe on page 86)
12-18 Slices Italian-Style Roast Beef, thinly sliced
4-6 Roasted Red Bell Peppers, in thin strips
4-6 Slices Red Onion, ½" thick
2 Tablespoons Olive Oil
1 Jar Hot Sweet Mustard

Sauté onions in olive oil until limp and slightly caramelized. Place bread slices on a flat surface and spread with mustard. Top with peppers, onions, roast beef, and second slice of bread. Cut on the diagonal. Serve with pasta salad or potato salad. SERVES 4.

# Grilled Ham & Cheese Sandwich With Grilled Pineapple

8 Slices French Bread, thinly sliced
16 Slices Smoked Ham
8 Slices Emmenthal Cheese
4 Pineapple Slices, fresh & peeled, if possible
Mayonnaise
Pan Spray
Soy-Ginger Vinaigrette (see recipe on page 210)

Spread one side each piece of bread with mayonnaise.

Place pineapple slices on a broiler pan and brush Soy-Ginger Vinaigrette liberally over topside. Broil till bubbling. Turn over, brush other side with Soy-Ginger, and broil till this side is bubbly; remove and set aside. Heat a griddle until medium hot. On a flat work surface, place one ham slice topped with one cheese slice on each of four pieces of bread. Top with one cheese slice, then one ham slice, then one pineapple slice, and then top with second piece of bread. Spray each sandwich on both sides with pan spray. Place on griddle and cook until browned lightly on each side. Serve immediately. SERVES 4.

# Sweet Pepper Corn Bread

| | |
|---|---|
| ¾ Cup Sugar | 3 Teaspoons Baking Powder |
| ½ Cup Salad Oil | ⅛ Teaspoon Salt |
| 2 Eggs, beaten | 1½ Cups Yellow Corn Meal |
| 1½ Cups All-Purpose Flour | ½ Cup Red Pimientos, diced |

Grease and flour a 9-inch square pan and set aside.  Blend together sugar and oil.  Mix in eggs.  Stir in flour, baking powder, and salt.  Blend well, stir in cornmeal.  Slowly blend in milk.  Mix in diced red pimientos.  Pour into prepared pan.  Bake in a 400ºF oven for 30 minutes.  CUT INTO 12 SQUARES.

# Whole Wheat Nut Bread

| | |
|---|---|
| 1 Cup All-Purpose Flour | 1 Egg, beaten |
| 1 Cup Whole Wheat Flour | 1 6-Ounce Can Apricot Nectar |
| ½ Cup Packed Brown Sugar | 1 Teaspoon Lemon Zest, finely chopped |
| ¼ Cup Sugar | 2 Tablespoons Lemon Juice |
| ½ Teaspoon Baking Soda | 2 Tablespoons Vegetable Oil |
| ½ Teaspoon Salt | ½ Cup Chopped Walnuts |

Combine flours, sugars, soda, and salt.  Combine next 5 ingredients; add to dry ingredients; stirring just till moistened.  Stir in nuts.  Pour into greased 8 x 4 x 2-inch loaf pan.  Bake in 350ºF oven 50 to 60 minutes or till done.  Cool 10 minutes then remove from pan and place on wire rack to cool completely.  Wrap and store overnight before slicing.  MAKES 1 LOAF.

# Sal's Dutch Babies

*Our friends Sally and Joe Laidlaw served these for breakfast at their B&B on Galiano Island.*

3 Eggs
¾ Cup Milk
¾ Cup Flour Plus 1 Tablespoon Sugar

Add the eggs and milk to a blender and blend.  Add the flour-sugar mixture to the blender slowly while blending.

Preheat oven to 400ºF.  Place tabs of butter in 4 to 6 inch shallow oven proof pans and place in oven until butter begins to bubble.  Add batter and bake 20 to 25 minutes.  Serve sprinkled with powdered sugar and fresh fruit.  SERVES 2.

# Harvey Wallbanger Cake

*A really moist, tasty cake. People loved to try it and it was a great hit when served with orange ice cream.*

1 Yellow Cake Mix
1 4-Ounce Package Instant Vanilla Pudding
½ Cup Vegetable Oil
½ Cup Sugar
4 Eggs
¼ Cup Vodka
¼ Cup Galliano Liqueur
¾ Cup Orange Juice

**GLAZE**
1 Cup Powdered Sugar
1½ Tablespoons Vodka
1½ Tablespoons Galliano Liqueur
1½ Tablespoons Orange Juice

Preheat oven to 350⁰F. In a large bowl mix together cake mix, pudding mix, oil, sugar, eggs, vodka, Galliano, and orange juice. Beat well. Pour batter into a well-greased and floured 10-cup bundt pan. Bake for 45 to 50 minutes. Do not overcook! Allow cake to remain in pan for approximately 10 minutes before removing.

For glaze, combine powdered sugar, vodka, Galliano, and orange juice. Drizzle glaze over cooled cake. Serve with Orange Ice Cream (see recipe below), if desired. SERVES 12-15.

# Orange Ice Cream

1 Quart Ice Cream, softened
Zest Of 1 Orange
1 Tablespoon Triple Sec
1 Tablespoon Orange Juice

In the bowl of a food processor fitted with a steel blade, combine all ingredients. Process until well combined. Put in a freezer container and store in the freezer until ready to use. MAKES 1 QUART.

Wine Recommendation:
Muscat de Beaumes de Venise

# Crème Brulee

*The best!*

2½ Cups Whipping Cream
½ Cup Sugar
6 Egg Yolks
1 Teaspoon Vanilla
Sugar

Heat cream almost to the boiling point. In a bowl combine ½ cup of sugar with the egg yolks and whisk until the mixture is smooth. Pour the heated cream very slowly into the egg mixture, stirring constantly. Add the vanilla and stir until well combined. Pour the mixture into 8 ramekins. Place the ramekins in a pan of hot water and put in a 350°F oven for 45 minutes or, until set in the middle. Remove from oven and chill.

When ready to serve sprinkle sugar lightly over each dish and place under broiler until the sugar browns lightly and bubbles. To serve, garnish with fresh berries. SERVES 8.

# Chocolate Chip Cookies

*An old favorite – we have never found one that is any better!*

2¼ Cups All-Purpose Flour
1 Teaspoon Baking Soda
1 Teaspoon Salt
1 Cup Butter, softened
¾ Cup Granulated Sugar
¾ Cup Brown Sugar
1 Teaspoon Vanilla
2 Eggs
2 Cups (12-ounce package) Chocolate Chips
1 Cup Chopped Pecans

Combine dry ingredients in a small bowl and mix. In a larger bowl beat butter, the sugars, and vanilla together until light and fluffy. Beat in eggs, one at a time, until well combined. Gradually beat in dry ingredients from small bowl, then the chocolate chips and chopped pecans. Drop by rounded teaspoonfuls on a greased baking sheet. Bake in a preheated 350°F oven for approximately 10 minutes or, until golden brown. Allow to stand for 10 minutes after removing from oven before removing from baking sheet. Cool completely before packaging. MAKES APPROXI-MATELY 5 DOZEN.

# Kahlua – Bittersweet Chocolate Mousse

12  Large Eggs, separated
2  Pounds Dark Bittersweet Chocolate
1½  Cups Kahlua
4  Teaspoons Brown Sugar
6  Cups Whipping Cream
4  Teaspoons Vanilla

Separate eggs into separate bowls, keeping eggs at room temperature. Beat yolks until blended, wash beaters thoroughly and then beat whites until stiff. Melt Chocolate in a double boiler and set aside. Place Kahlua and brown sugar in small pan on medium heat and stir until sugar dissolves. DO NOT BOIL! Set aside. With a wooden spoon blend yolks into warm chocolate. Add Kahlua mixture and blend until shiny and smooth. Remove from heat. While chocolate is cooling, whip cream and vanilla together until stiff. When chocolate has cooled, gently fold in egg whites. Add whipped cream and fold together to blend well. Spoon into dessert glasses and chill at least 2 hours. Serve garnished with toasted almond slices. SERVES 6-8.

# Truffle Cakes

1  Package (18¼ ounces) Chocolate Cake Mix
1  Package (3½ ounces) Chocolate Pudding Mix
1  Cup Sour Cream
1  Cup Cream Cheese (8-ounce package)
4  Eggs
⅓  Cup Kahlua Liqueur
½  Cup Chocolate Chips

Place all ingredients except chocolate chips in mixer bowl and mix till well combined. Add chocolate chips and mix well by hand. Pour batter into mini bundt pans which have been sprayed with pan release. Bake in preheated 350°F oven approximately 20 to 25 minutes or till cakes test done. Cool on wire racks. Serve with a chocolate truffle and ice cream.

## CHOCOLATE TRUFFLES
½  Cup Chocolate Chips
2  Tablespoons Whipping Cream

Melt chocolate chips and whipping cream together. Chill. Serve with truffle cake by scooping a teaspoonful out (or use a very small scoop) and place at side of cake. Place a scoop of ice cream on top.
CAKE AND TRUFFLES MAKE 12 SERVINGS.

# Orange Chocolate Swirl Cheesecake

*Very, very pretty and impressive to serve. Orange and chocolate seem to be made for each other.*

*Orange Chocolate Swirl Cheesecake*

## CRUST

1½  Cups Vanilla Wafer Crumbs
¼  Cup Sugar
⅓  Cup Butter

## FILLING

5  8-Ounce Packages Cream Cheese, softened
1½  Cups Sugar
8  Eggs
3  Tablespoons Orange Juice
¾  Teaspoon Orange Peel, grated
6  Squares Bakers Semi-Sweet Chocolate, melted & cooled slightly

Preheat oven to 325°F.

CRUST:  Mix crumbs, sugar, and butter; press onto bottom and 1½ inches up the side of a 9-inch springform pan. Bake for 10 minutes.

FILLING: Beat cream cheese and sugar at medium speed with mixer until well blended.  Add eggs, 1 at a time, mixing at low speed after each egg, just until blended.  Blend in orange juice and peel.

Reserve 2 cups of the batter.  Pour remaining batter over crust.  Blend chocolate into reserved batter.  Add spoonfuls of the chocolate batter to the cream cheese batter in the crust.  Cut through the batters with a knife several times for marbled effect.  Bake 55 to 60 minutes or until center is almost set.  Remove from oven and cool on a wire rack.  Run knife or metal spatula around rim of pan to loosen cake; cool before removing rim.  Refrigerate 4 hours or overnight. SERVES 12.

# Frozen Boysenberry & White Chocolate Terrine

*You can substitute raspberries if you like – this is another very pretty dessert that can be made ahead of time.*

| | |
|---|---|
| 1 16-Ounce Bag Frozen Boysenberries | 1 Tablespoon Berry Flavored Liqueur, such as Chambord® |
| ¼ Cup Sugar | ½ Teaspoon Fresh Lemon Juice |
| | |
| ¾ Cup Sugar | 3 Ounces Imported White Chocolate, |
| ¼ Cup Water | such as Lindt, chopped & melted |
| 6 Large Egg Yolks | 2 Teaspoons Vanilla |
| | 1¾ Cups Whipping Cream |

## SAUCE

1 16-Ounce Bag Frozen Boysenberries Or Blackberries, thawed

¼ Cup Sugar

2 Tablespoons Berry Flavored Liqueur

Line a 9 x 5-inch loaf pan with plastic wrap. Puree 1 bag berries and ¼ cup sugar in blender just until smooth. Strain out seeds. Measure 1⅓ cups puree and place in a heavy small saucepan (reserve any remaining puree for sauce). Simmer the puree in saucepan over medium heat until reduced to a scant 1 cup, stirring occasionally, about 8 minutes. Transfer to a bowl and chill 30 minutes. Stir in liqueur and lemon juice. Refrigerate reduced puree until ready to use.

Combine ¾ cup sugar, water, and egg yolks in the top of a double boiler. Using double boiler set up, beat the yolk mixture with a hand held mixer until the mixture registers 140°F on a candy thermometer, occasionally scraping down side of bowl; about 5 minutes. Continue cooking 3 minutes, beating constantly. Remove from over water. Add warm melted chocolate, vanilla, and beat until cool.

Beat whipping cream in another bowl to form stiff peaks. Gently mix ¼ of whipped cream into chocolate mixture. Fold in remaining whipped cream.

Transfer 1¼ cups chocolate mixture to medium bowl. Fold in reduced berry puree. Fill prepared pan with ⅓ of remaining chocolate mixture. FREEZE EACH LAYER SLIGHTLY BEFORE ADDING NEXT! Cover with berry-chocolate mixture. Top with remaining chocolate mixture. Smooth. Freeze overnight.

FOR SAUCE: Puree berries, sugar, and liqueur until smooth, Strain out seeds. Add any puree left from above. Chill.

Unmold terrine and peel off plastic wrap. Slice into ½ to ¾-inch slices; drizzle with sauce, and garnish with mint. SERVES 12-15.

# Tiramisu

*This dessert freezes very well and lends itself well to dinner parties.*

1  Cup Sugar

½  Cup Marsala Wine

6  Large Egg Yolks

1  Pound Mascarpone Cheese, room temperature

1½  Cups Hot Water

5  Teaspoons Instant Espresso Powder Or Instant Coffee Powder

½  Cup Kahlua

1½  7½-Ounce Packages Champagne Biscuits

1  Ounce Semi-Sweet Chocolate, grated

Whisk first three ingredients in medium metal bowl.  Set bowl over saucepan of boiling water and whisk constantly until candy thermometer reaches 170°F, about 4 minutes.  Remove from over water.  Gradually whisk in mascarpone.  Combine 1½ hot water and espresso powder in medium bowl; stir to dissolve.  Mix in Kahlua.  Dip 1 biscuit BRIEFLY into espresso mixture.  Turn to coat.  Place flat side facing up in bottom of 9-inch diameter springform pan.  Repeat with enough biscuits to cover bottom of pan.  Pour half of mascarpone mixture over.  Dip more biscuits in espresso mixture and arrange atop mascarpone mixture in pan, covering completely.  Pour remaining mascarpone mixture over.  Sprinkle with chocolate.  Refrigerate until firm, at least 4 hours, or overnight.  Run small sharp knife around pan sides to loosen.  Release pan sides.  Cut tiramisu into wedges and serve.  SERVES 8.

# Margarita Pie

*Fun!*

### CRUST

½  Cup Vanilla Wafers, crushed          3  Tablespoons Granulated Sugar

½  Cup Salted Pretzels, crushed          ¼  Pound Butter, melted

Mix the vanilla wafer crumbs the pretzel crumbs, and the sugar together.  Add the melted butter and combine well.  Press onto the bottom and up the sides of a 9-inch pie pan and refrigerate.

### FILLING

1  Can Eagle Brand® Sweetened Condensed Milk          4  Tablespoons Golden Tequila

⅓  Cup Roses® Lime Juice          1½  Cups Heavy Whipping Cream

Fold together all ingredients, pour into pie pan and chill for at least 2 hours.  SERVES 6.

# Strawberry – Lemon Sorbet

3  Cups Pureed Strawberries, fresh or frozen
1  12-Ounce Can Frozen Lemonade, thawed slightly
2  Cups Simple Sugar Syrup (see recipe on page 205)
3  Cups Crushed Ice

Mix the cold sugar syrup, slightly thawed lemonade, and fruit puree in a food processor fitted with a steel blade.  Add crushed ice and continue to process until very smooth.  Pour into freezer container and store in freezer until ready to use.  MAKES ABOUT 2 QUARTS.

# Blueberry – Lemon Sorbet

Substitute blueberries for strawberries in the above recipe.

*The variations of this are numerous – experiment for your own special recipe!*

*Strawberry-Lemon Sorbet*

# Chocolate — Orange — Cinnamon Ice Cream

*This is, without doubt, the best ice cream we ever made!*

4  Cups Heavy Cream
Zest Of 3 Oranges, removed in strips using a zester
4  Cinnamon Sticks
½  Pound Semi-Sweet Chocolate Or Ghirardelli® Chocolate Chips
8  Large Egg Yolks
¾  Cup Sugar
1  Teaspoon Vanilla Extract

Heat the cream, zest, and cinnamon in a saucepan to boiling.  Remove from the heat and let steep for 2 hours.  Heat the chocolate in a small heavy saucepan over low heat until melted.  Continue cooking, stirring constantly, until it is "scorched" and thick, about 3 minutes.  DO NOT BURN.  Transfer to a large mixing bowl.  Strain the cream into another saucepan and reheat to boiling.  Whisk the egg yolks and ¼ cup sugar until combined.  Whisk about 1 cup of the hot cream into the yolks, then whisk into the remaining cream.  Add remaining sugar and cook, stirring constantly, over medium heat until thick enough to coat the back of a spoon, 3 to 5 minutes.  DO NOT BOIL.  Strain the custard into the chocolate and stir until smooth.  Strain again.  Place in a larger bowl, cover loosely with plastic wrap and chill well in refrigerator.  Freeze in an ice-cream maker according to manufacturer's instructions.  MAKES 1 QUART.

# Quick Chocolate — Orange — Cinnamon Ice Cream

*A shortened version but a real winner!*

1  Quart Chocolate Ice Cream, softened
¼  Cup Chocolate Syrup, preferably Ghirardelli's®

Grated Zest Of 1 Orange
1  Tablespoon Triple Sec (orange flavored liqueur)

Place all ingredients in bowl of food processor and process till smooth.  Pour into a freezer container and freeze until firm.  MAKES 1 QUART.

# Boysenberry Cream

1  Pint Sour Cream
¾  Cup Boysenberry Jam

Combine well.  Arrange fresh fruit and drizzle with sauce  MAKES 1½ CUPS.

*Many species of rare and specialty butterflies and birds migrate to Sonoita and surrounding areas from Central and South America in the summer.*

# Autumn

Autumn is the time of year when the light begins to change to a softer hue. The oaks begin to change color, the low areas in the rolling hills become vivid rivulets of bright yellow created by goldenrod and other wild flowers, the grass begins to turn back to straw color and the deer and javelina devour our pears and apples. We have decided that they must have an underground communication system to let their buddies know the fruit is ripe. It is a lovely time of year with gentle breezes, billowy white clouds in a beautiful blue sky. The mornings become crisp, the days comfortably cool and the nights colder. The stars after dark and before moonrise are absolutely brilliant. We had forgotten that there was a Milky Way when living in Tucson due to the light pollution. Sonoita presents the Milky Way, stars, planets and satellites in a bright, beautiful dazzling display.

# Goat Cheese & Sun Dried Tomato Canapés

*This is probably the simplest and best tasting appetizer I have ever used – great if you are in a hurry!*

¼ Pound Mild Goat Cheese, such as Montrachet
2 Tablespoons Sun-Dried Tomatoes, drained & minced, reserving 1 tablespoon of the oil
2 Tablespoons Fresh Parsley Leaves, minced
18 1½"-Rounds Whole-Wheat Bread, cut from slices & toasted lightly

In a small bowl stir together the cheese, the sun-dried tomatoes with the reserved oil, and the parsley until the mixture is combined well.  Spread 1 teaspoon of the mixture on each toast round, mounding it, and broil the canapés in a jelly-roll pan under a preheated broiler about 4 inches from the heat for 1 to 2 minutes, or until they are puffed and golden.  MAKES 18 CANAPES.

# Greek Spinach Filo Triangles

*Known by any other name as Spanakopita.  We learned to love these while we were in Greece!*

| | |
|---|---|
| 1 Pound Fresh Spinach | Salt, Pepper & Nutmeg |
| 6 Spring Onions, cleaned & sliced finely | 2 Eggs, beaten |
| 2 Tablespoons Olive Oil | 4 Ounces Feta Cheese, crumbled |
| 3 Tablespoons Dill, chopped | 4 Ounces Filo Pastry |
| 2 Tablespoons Parsley, chopped | Olive Oil, to brush |

Wash the spinach and cook in its own water for 3 to 4 minutes, then drain thoroughly and chop finely.

Sauté the spring onions in the olive oil until soft, about 4 to 5 minutes.  Stir in the spinach.  Cook gently for 5 minutes, then add the herbs.  Mix well, season with salt, pepper, and nutmeg, and set aside to cool.

Drain off any excess liquid from the spinach, then mix into the beaten eggs.  Finally fold in the crumbled cheese.

Cut the filo sheets in half lengthwise so that they measure 3½ inches by 12 inches.  Brush one sheet with olive oil, and then set another one on top.  Brush with oil again.  Spoon 1 tablespoon of the spinach mixture onto the top corner of the strip.  Bring the adjacent corner over the filling and press it onto the opposite side of the strip to make a diagonal fold.  Press the edges together to seal.  Fold over again and again until you reach the end of the pastry strip, finishing with a tight triangular package.  Brush the top with olive oil.  Make all the triangles in this way then place on a greased baking sheet.

Bake in a 375ºF oven for 25 to 25 minutes, or until golden-brown.  Set on a wire rack to cool slightly.  Serve warm.
MAKES 14.

# Smoked Salmon Over Angel Hair Pancakes

## (With Creamy Roasted Pepper Spread)

*Delicious! The variations are numerous – use your imagination!*

3 Eggs, beaten
3 Tablespoons Chives, finely chopped
4 Cups Angel Hair Pasta, cooked & drained, salt & pepper to taste

Mix all ingredients together well. Spray a non-stick crepe pan with pan release and heat until medium hot. Pour ⅓ cup of angel hair-egg mixture into pan and cook until set, flip and cook other side until slightly brown. Remove to a paper towel and continue until all the angel hair-egg mix is used up. Set aside, covered, while preparing the cream cheese mixture.

### ROASTED PEPPER-CREAM CHEESE MIXTURE

1  8-0unce Block Cream Cheese          1  Tablespoon Chopped Chives
3  Large Pieces Roasted Red Bell Pepper   Salt & Pepper, to taste

Combine all ingredients in the bowl of a food processor and process until well combined.

TO ASSEMBLE: Spread each pancake with 2 to 3 tablespoons of cream cheese mixture. Top with thin sliced smoked salmon and additional chives. Cut in wedges and serve immediately.

NOTE: Pancake can be made ahead and refrigerated. Warm slightly before spreading with cream cheese mixture and salmon. If you have left over cream cheese mixture it can be frozen for future use. MAKES 10-12 SERVINGS.

# Pesto Hots

½  Cup Fresh Basil Leaves, slivered
½  Cup Parmesan Cheese, grated
1  Garlic Clove, minced
6+/-  Tablespoons Mayonnaise
24+/-  Slices (¼" thick) French Bread Baguette

Stir together basil, cheese, garlic, and mayonnaise until well blended; add more mayonnaise, if necessary, to make a firm spreading consistency. Arrange bread slices in a single layer on a 12 x 15-inch baking sheet. Broil 4 to 6 inches below heat until toasted on topsides, about 1 minute. Remove from broiler, turn, and spread untoasted sides with a generous teaspoonful of mayonnaise mixture, spreading to edges. Return to broiler; cook until bubbly and lightly browned, 2 to 3 minutes. MAKES ABOUT 24 APPETIZERS.

# Butternut Squash Tartlets

2  Pie Crust Sticks

1¼  Pounds Butternut Squash

2  Tablespoons Fresh Rosemary Or Thyme

½  Pound Cream Cheese, softened

4  Eggs

½  Cup Heavy Cream

½  Teaspoon Grated Nutmeg

Salt & Pepper

½  Pound Cheddar Cheese, grated

Prepare piecrust according to directions.  Butter miniature muffin tins.  On a lightly floured work surface, roll out the dough to a ¼-inch thickness.  Using a pastry cutter, cut dough into circles slightly larger than the top opening of a miniature muffin tin (about 2½ inches) and fit into prepared tins. Chill for at least 20 minutes or overnight.

Heat oven to 425°F.  Bake pastry in preheated oven for 5 minutes.  Remove pastry dough from oven and press dough down if it has bubbled up.  Reduce heat to 350°F and continue cooking until pastry is browned and almost done, about 10 minutes.  Cool.  Pastry can be baked 2 days ahead and stored in airtight tins.

For filling, heat oven to 350°F.  Cut squash in half and scrape out seeds.  Make slashes in flesh and place on baking sheets, cut side down.  Bake in preheated oven until very soft, about 45 minutes.  Cool.  Scrape out flesh and puree in food processor until smooth.  Chop 1 tablespoon of the herbs.

In a bowl, cream the cream cheese, add pureed squash, and beat until smooth.  Beat in the eggs.  Add the heavy cream, nutmeg, and 1 tablespoon of chopped fresh herbs.  Season to taste with salt and pepper.  Filling can be made to this point 1 to 2 days ahead.

Grate cheddar cheese.  Put about ½ tablespoon of the grated cheese into each cooked pastry shell.  Chop remaining tablespoon of herbs.

COOKING AND SERVING:  Heat oven to 350°F.  Fill each tart shell with butternut squash mixture to within ¼ inch of the top.  Sprinkle all tarts with chopped herbs.  Bake in preheated oven until filling is puffy, about 10 minutes. Serve warm. MAKES ABOUT 60 TARTLETS.

# Polenta Cake With Red Pepper Coulis & Parmesan

1 Cup Chicken Broth
1 Cup Polenta
1 Cup Shredded Parmesan Cheese

Bring broth to boil, add Polenta. Cook, stirring constantly, until thick. Add Parmesan, mix well. Remove from heat and pour into ¾ cup muffin tins, well greased. Bake at 350°F for 10 minutes. Cool and remove from tins.

## RED PEPPER COULIS

2 Cups Roasted Red Bell Peppers
6 Garlic Cloves, roasted in olive oil for 20 minutes & drained (set aside ¾ cup of the oil)

## GARNISH

Fresh Basil Leaves      Shredded Parmesan Cheese

Place peppers and garlic in food processor and process until very fine. Add ¾ cup of oil, set aside from above, and process until well combined. Salt and pepper to taste.

When ready to serve; place Polenta cake on oiled grill for 6 minutes per side. Remove. Place approximately ¼ cup of Coulis on plate, place cake on top and garnish with fresh basil leaves and shredded Parmesan cheese. Serve immediately. SERVES 4.

# Apple – Cheese Omelet

1 Large Golden Delicious Apple
½ Cup Leeks, white part only, thinly sliced
2 Eggs
½ Cup 2% Milk
Pinch Salt & Pinch Pepper

2 Teaspoons Margarine
1 Cup Mushrooms, sliced
½ Cup Shredded Cheddar Cheese
2 Teaspoons Chopped Italian Parsley (for garnish)

Preheat oven to 400°F. Wrap handle of nonstick skillet with aluminum foil. Peel, core, and thinly slice apple. Rinse leeks in strainer or colander under running water to remove all sand. Beat together eggs, milk, salt, and pepper in small bowl till combined. Heat margarine in prepared skillet over medium heat. Add apples, leeks, and mushrooms; Cook 3 to 5 minutes or until tender-crisp. Evenly distribute vegetables in pan. Sprinkle on cheese. Reduce heat to medium-low. Stir egg mixture and pour into skillet, tilting pan and lifting edges of omelet to let egg run underneath. Cook 3 to 4 minutes or until omelet is almost set and bottom is lightly browned. Place skillet with omelet in pre-heated oven and bake for 5 minutes or until top of omelet is set. Invert onto serving platter. Cut in half. Garnish with parsley. Serve immediately. SERVES 4.

# French Vegetable Bouillon

*This is easy to make and so nice to have on hand!*

2 Leeks

4 Large Carrots

2 Medium Size Zucchini

¾ Pound Green Beans, ends trimmed

1 Large Tomato

2½ Quarts Chicken Broth

3 Large Stalks Celery, cut into thirds

1 Large Onion, quartered

¾ Cup Parsley Sprigs

1 Bay Leaf

½ Teaspoon Dry Thyme Leaves

½ Teaspoon Black Peppercorns

⅓ Cup Fresh Shelled Peas

Trim and discard root ends and tough, dark green tops from leeks. Thinly slice enough of the white part of leek crosswise to make ¼ cup; gently rinse and reserve for poaching later. Slice remaining leeks lengthwise and rinse thoroughly. Slice carrots and zucchini into 2-inch chunks; cut 1 chunk of each into match-stick-size pieces and reserve for poaching later. Cut 10 of the green beans in half and then lengthwise into thin slivers; set aside. Cut 2 thin outer slices with peel from tomato; cut each in half and then into triangles; set aside. (If not serving bouillon same day, cover and chill reserved vegetables for up to 3 days.) In a 6 to 8 quart pan over high heat, combine broth with remaining leeks, carrots, zucchini, beans, tomato, celery and leaves, onion, parsley, bay leaf, thyme, and pepper-corn; bring to a boil. Reduce heat, cover, and simmer gently for 4 hours, stir occasionally.

Line a colander with 2 or 3 thicknesses of dampened cheesecloth (pieces need to be large enough to hang over sides); place colander over a wide 4 to 5 quart pan. Pour bouillon through cheesecloth and, using the back of a large spoon, push vegetables against sides of colander, extracting as much liquid as possible. As bouillon cools, draw together corners of cheesecloth and twist tightly to squeeze out even more liquid; discard vegetables and remove colander from pan. At this point, you can cover and chill soup for up to 3 days.

If desired, clarify bouillon (directions follow). To continue, return bouillon to boiling. Reduce heat to low and add reserved leek, carrot, zucchini, beans, tomato, and peas. Cover and simmer gently until vegetables are barely tender when pierced, about 3 minutes. Ladle into bowls. SERVES 4-6.

To clarify, beat 4 egg whites until foamy. Bring bouillon to boil, whip in egg whites Return to full boil; remove from heat and let stand till slightly cooled. Line colander with cheesecloth as done above; place colander over 4 to 5-quart pan. Pour bouillon slowly through cheesecloth. Draw together corners and twist gently to extract as much liquid as possible; discard whites.

*appetizers, small dishes, soups*

# Zippy Potato Puffs

*A nifty little appetizer to add to your variety plate.*

2 Large Eggs
¼ Cup Vegetable Oil
3 Tablespoons Matzo Meal
1 Teaspoon Salt
½ Teaspoon Baking Powder
1 Small Onion
1¼ Pounds Potatoes
¼ Teaspoon Cayenne Pepper

Preheat oven to 400°F and grease muffin pan with 1¾ x 1-inch cups.

In a large bowl whisk together eggs, oil, matzo meal, salt, and baking powder. Grate onion on large holes of a 4-sided grater and whisk into egg mixture. Working quickly, in 2 batches, peel and quarter potatoes and in a food processor finely chop. Add finely chopped potatoes to egg mixture and stir until coated well.

Working quickly, spoon a rounded tablespoon of potato mixture into each muffin cup and bake in upper and lower thirds of oven, switching position of pans halfway through baking, until golden brown, about 30 minutes. MAKES 12-18 PIECES.

# Onion & Lentil Soup Gratiné

⅓ Cup Lentils, picked over & rinsed
½ Bay Leaf
2 Onions, halved lengthwise & sliced crosswise
2 Tablespoons Butter
2 Tablespoons Gin

2 Cups Beef Broth
1 Teaspoon Worcestershire Sauce
2 ½"-Slices Italian Bread, toasted lightly
⅔ Cup Gruyere Cheese, grated
Ground Paprika

In a saucepan combine the lentils and the bay leaf in enough water to cover the lentils by 3 inches, bring the water to a boil, and boil the lentils for 25 minutes, or until they are tender. While the lentils are boiling, in a kettle cook the onions in the butter over moderate heat, stirring occasionally, for 20 minutes, or until they are softened and golden. Add the gin, cook the mixture, stirring, until the gin is almost evaporated, and stir in the broth and the Worcestershire sauce. Drain the lentils in a sieve, discarding the bay leaf, rinse them briefly, and drain well. Add the lentils to the kettle, bring the soup to a boil, stirring, and simmer for 3 minutes. Divide the soup between 2 flameproof soup bowls, float the toasts in them, and sprinkle with the Gruyere. Broil the soups under a preheated broiler until the Gruyere is melted and bubbling and sprinkle them with the paprika. SERVES 2.

# Irish Potato — Cabbage Soup

*Being Callaghan, this soup is particularly delightful!*

1½ Tablespoons Butter
½ Cup Onions, chopped
½ Cup Potatoes, chopped
2 Cups Chicken Broth
1½ Cups Cabbage Leaves, chopped
¼ Cup Heavy Cream
Salt & Freshly Ground Pepper

Melt the butter in a heavy saucepan. When it foams, add the potatoes and onions and turn them in the butter until well coated. Sprinkle with salt and freshly ground pepper. Cover and sweat on a low heat for 10 minutes. Add the broth and boil until the potatoes are soft, then add the cabbage and cook with the lid off until the cabbage is cooked. Keep the lid off to retain the green color. Do not overcook or the vegetables will lose both their fresh flavor and color. Puree the soup with an immersion blender or a food processor and adjust seasoning. Add the cream before serving. SERVES 4.

# Ginger — Carrot Bisque

*These flavors pair extremely well.*

¼ Cup Plus 2 Tablespoons Unsalted Butter
2 Pounds Carrots, peeled & thinly sliced
2 Large Onions, chopped
1 Tablespoon Fresh Ginger, peeled & minced
2 Teaspoons Orange Peel, grated
½ Teaspoon Ground Coriander
5 Cups Chicken Broth
1 Cup Half & Half
½ Cup Fresh Parsley, minced

Melt butter in heavy large saucepan over medium heat. Add carrots and onions. Cover saucepan and cook until vegetables begin to soften, stirring occasionally, about 15 minutes. Mix in ginger, orange peel, and coriander. Add 2 cups stock. Reduce heat to medium-low. Cover pan and simmer soup until carrots are very tender, about 30 minutes. Puree soup with an immersion blender. Add remaining stock and half & half to soup. Season with salt and pepper. *(Can prepare 1 day ahead. Cover and refrigerate.)* Cook over medium heat to until warm. Ladle into bowls. Garnish with parsley. SERVES 10.

*Irish Potato-Cabbage Soup*

# Sweet Potato — Jalapeño Pepper Soup

*A really nice soup with Southwestern flavors.*

| | | | |
|---|---|---|---|
| 3 | Tablespoons Unsalted Butter | ¼ | Teaspoon Salt |
| 1 | Cup Onion, finely chopped | ¼ | Teaspoon Pepper |
| 3 | Sweet Potatoes (8 ounces each), pared & chopped | ½ | Cup Sour Cream |
| 6 | Cups Chicken Broth | 1½ | Teaspoons Fresh Lime Juice |
| 1 | Jalapeño Pepper, thinly sliced | ½ | Teaspoon Lemon Rind, grated |
| 1½ | Cups Fresh Or Frozen Corn Kernels | 3 | Tablespoons Fresh Cilantro, finely chopped |
| ½ | Cup Heavy Cream | | |

Melt butter in a 4-quart pot over medium heat. Add onion and cook, stirring occasionally, until onion begins to brown, about 5 minutes. Reduce heat to moderate-low, cover, and cook until onion is soft and nicely browned, about 10 minutes longer. Stir in sweet potatoes and chicken stock and bring to a boil. Lower heat and simmer, partially covered, for 25 minutes or until potatoes are tender. With an immersion blender, puree the soup until smooth. Stir in jalapeño and corn kernels. Cook 5 minutes longer or until pepper is crisp tender. Whisk in heavy cream, season with salt and pepper, and gently heat.

In a small bowl whisk together sour cream, lime juice, and lemon rind. Serve hot soup in individual bowls with a dollop of sour cream mixture and chopped cilantro. MAKES 8 SERVINGS.

# Leek, Potato & Sausage Soup

¼ Teaspoon Cumin Seed

¼ Teaspoon Caraway Seed

1 Medium Leek, white part only, washed & well dried, halved lengthwise & thinly sliced crosswise

1 Teaspoon Unsalted Butter

2 Cups Chicken Broth

1 Medium Potato, peeled & diced

¼ Pound Kielbasa (Polish sausage), cut crosswise & quartered

1 Tablespoon Heavy Cream

¼ Cup Spinach Leaves, thinly sliced fresh

Toast the cumin and caraway seeds in a heavy saucepan 2 to 3 minutes over moderate heat until fragrant. Transfer to a plate.

In same saucepan, melt butter and sauté the leek for 5 minutes or until very soft, stirring occasionally. Stir in chicken broth and potato; bring to a boil and simmer 10 minutes or, until potato is tender. Stir in toasted seeds, Kielbasa, and cream. Simmer for 5 minutes. Salt and pepper to taste. Just before serving stir in sliced spinach leaves. SERVES 4.

*appetizers, small dishes, soups*

# Roasted Red Pepper Soup

*This soup is wonderful with an off-dry white wine such as Fumé Blanc.*

Roasted Red Pepper Soup and Oatmeal Cornbread

6  Large Red Peppers, roasted
3  Carrots, peeled
4  Shallots, peeled
1  Pear, peeled
1  Clove Garlic, peeled
2  Tablespoons Olive Oil
4  Tablespoons Butter
4  Cups Chicken Broth
1  Teaspoon Crushed Dried
   Red Pepper
Pinch Of Cayenne Pepper
Salt & Pepper, to taste
Fresh Tarragon Or Parsley

Thinly slice 4 peppers , carrots, shallots, pear, and garlic.  Sauté the sliced vegetables and pear in the oil and butter until tender, about 10 minutes.  Add the stock, dried red pepper, cayenne pepper, and a dash of salt and black pepper.  Bring to a boil and simmer, covered, for 30 minutes.

Puree the soup in a blender or food processor, adding one of the roasted peppers.  Pour the pureed soup back into the pan and reheat.  Julienne the remaining roasted pepper and add to the soup.  Garnish with fresh tarragon or parsley.  SERVES 6.

Wine Recommendation:
Vouvray (Champalou)
Austrian Gruner Veltliner (Hirtzberger)

# Tomato — Herb Soup

3  Medium Onions, chopped

4  Medium Tomatoes, chopped

¼  Cup Olive Oil

3  Cloves Garlic, minced

1  Bay Leaf

1  Teaspoon Dried Thyme Leaves

¾  Teaspoon Dried Marjoram Leaves

¼  Teaspoon Black Pepper

8  Cups Water

½  Cup Grated Parmesan Cheese

Heat olive oil in a large, heavy soup pot over medium heat.  Add onions and sauté until lightly browned.  Add tomatoes and cook for 5 minutes more.  Raise heat to high and add garlic, bay leaf, thyme, marjoram, pepper, and water. Bring to a boil, reduce heat to medium, and cook for 15 minutes.  Puree soup in a food processor or with an immersion blender.  Return soup to pot, if a food processor was used, and reheat to a boil over high heat.

Ladle soup into bowls, top with parmesan crisp (see recipe on page 212) and garnish with chopped chives or herb sprig.  SERVES 4.

*Tomato-Herb Soup served with a Parmesan Crisp Chip*

*appetizers, small dishes, soups*

# Cream Of Broccoli & Stilton Soup

8 Ounces Stilton Cheese     ¼ Teaspoon White Pepper

7 Tablespoons Unsalted Butter     7 Cups Chicken Broth

1 Bunch Broccoli, trimmed, peeled & cut into 1" strips (4 cups)     2½ Tablespoons All-Purpose Flour

⅛ Cup Celery, diced     1¼ Cups Heavy Cream

1 Cup Onion, finely chopped

## VEGETABLE GARNISH

1 Medium-Size Leek (white part with 1 inch of green), julienned lengthwise

1 Celery Stalk, cut into fine julienne

1 Cup Tiny Broccoli Flowerets

Trim Stilton of its outer yellow-brown crust and use only center. You should have about 6 ounces. Crumble and set aside. Melt 4 tablespoons of butter in a 4-quart pot over medium heat. Add broccoli, celery, onion, and pepper. Simmer, partially covered, until just tender, about 5 minutes. Stir in chicken broth. Bring to a boil. Lower heat and simmer, covered, 30 to 35 minutes, or until vegetables are tender. Using an immersion blender, puree the soup in the pot until smooth.

In a saucepan, over medium heat, melt the remaining butter. Whisk in the flour and cook, whisking constantly, until mixture is hazelnut brown, about 2 minutes. (*BE CAREFUL NOT TO SCORCH FLOUR.*) Add slowly to pureed soup, whisking, until blended. Bring to a boil, lower heat, and simmer, whisking occasionally, 15 minutes.

Combine heavy cream and Stilton in a food processor. Whirl until smooth. Whisk cheese mixture into soup until well-blended and just heated through; DO NOT BOIL. Stir vegetable garnish into soup. Cook until just tender. Serve hot. MAKES 12 SERVINGS.

**ABOUT WHITE WINES:** *White wine offers far more latitude in food pairing than does red wine. Lighter whites, like German Kabinett Rieslings, are wonderful with all kinds of lighter fish preparations, many salads, light cheeses, soups, etc. Barrel-fermented Chardonnays are great with grilled swordfish, chicken, and pork, depending on the weight of the wine (white Burgundy best with grilled swordfish, for instance, and big California Chardonnay with pork). Alsatian whites cover almost all white wine possibilities - Rieslings with fish and lighter Asian-influenced food, Gewurtztraminer with rich, spicy Asian food, and Pinot Gris with rich and richer (read butter and fat) dishes. Some of the Alsatian and Austrian white wines have the requisite power and flavor intensity to match red meat dishes. Grilled sausages, lamb, or beef are definitely not out of the question with these wines. To best determine what your preferences are, try a sampler dinner at home (with take out - to make things easier on you) with several different wines, red and white, that represent a wide range of wine types and styles. And have some fun.*

Kent Callaghan, Wine Maker for Callaghan Vineyards

# Bogota Chicken Soup

8 Cups Chicken Broth (canned)

4 Medium Potatoes, pared & cut into 1" cubes

Bay Leaf

1½ Teaspoons Salt (or to taste)

¼ Teaspoon Freshly Ground Pepper

Spicy Coriander Sauce (see recipe on page 206)

2½ Cups Fresh Corn Kernels Or 1 10-Ounce Package Frozen

2 Cups Diced Cooked Chicken

½ Cup fresh coriander (cilantro) leaves

## GARNISHES

1 Ripe Avocado, pitted, peeled & diced

2 Hard-Cooked Eggs, peeled & chopped

2 Tablespoons Capers, drained

Tortilla Chips

Pour broth into large pan. Add potatoes, bay leaf, salt, and pepper; simmer uncovered until potatoes are tender, about 15 minutes. Meanwhile, make Spicy Coriander Sauce.

Using slotted spoon, remove about half the potatoes to mixing bowl and mash with potato masher or fork. Stir potatoes back into soup. Add corn, chicken, and coriander leaves; simmer 5 minutes. Serve soup hot, passing Coriander Sauce and garnishes. SERVES 6-8.

# Potato Lasagna

*This is so good. It can also be made in a large pan and cut into squares.*

1 Large Potato, peeled & very thinly sliced

2 Roasted Red Peppers, drained & sliced lengthwise

4 Portabello Mushrooms, thinly sliced

6-8 Button Mushrooms, thinly sliced

½ Cup Shredded Parmesan Cheese

½ Teaspoon Salt

2-3 Grindings Black Pepper

½ Cup Whipping Cream

1 Tablespoon Chives, chopped

Rinse potatoes under cold water and drain well. Put between pieces of paper toweling to dry well. Place all the ingredients in a bowl and toss to coat the potatoes well. Using two 2-inch baking rings, wrap them on the bottoms and up the sides (outside) with 2 thicknesses of aluminum foil. Place prepared rings on a baking sheet and spray rings well with pan release. Remove 2 to 3 slices of potato and place in each ring. Place 1 to 2 slices roasted pepper on top of potatoes in each ring, then 2 to 3 more slices of potato, then 1 to 2 pieces of mushroom. Continue layering in this manner until all potatoes, mushrooms, and roasted pepper are used up. Pour remaining cream, chives, and cheese evenly over each potato layer. Cover with aluminum foil and place in an oven preheated to 375°F. Bake 1 hour, remove aluminum foil and continue baking another 20 minutes or until potatoes are done. Remove from oven and allow to sit in rings approximately 20 to 30 minutes. Place a plate over the potato tower and invert quickly, allowing liquid to run over potato tower. Serve immediately. MAKES 2 SERVINGS.

*appetizers, small dishes, soups*

*Crystal clear water rushes down
from the majestic Santa Rita
Mountains spilling into moss
covered ravines and canyons.*

# Polenta

*There are lots of recipes for Polenta – we like this one the best*

3  Cups Chicken Broth
1  Cup Polenta
2  Tablespoons Butter
1  Green Onion, cleaned & sliced thin
1  Tablespoon Red Pepper, diced
½  Cup Shredded Parmesan Cheese

In a 4-quart stockpot, melt butter till bubbly, add onion, and sauté till slightly browned. Add broth, cover pot, and bring to a rapid boil. Add polenta slowly, whisking constantly, till smooth and thickened, add Parmesan cheese and whisk until blended. Remove from heat and pour into a well-greased loaf pan. Place in a preheated 350°F oven and bake for approximately 20 minutes. Remove from oven and let cool. Refrigerate until ready to use. Remove from refrigerator, allow to come to room temperature, invert on to a cutting board and slice into pieces ½-inch thick. Place on a greased baking sheet and heat in a 350°F oven until hot and slightly browned. SERVES 4-6.

# Tomato Tian

*We developed this recipe when we had an abundance of garden grown tomatoes – it has flavors similar to pizza and makes a good vegetarian dish.*

4  Garlic Cloves, finely chopped
1  Large Yellow Onion, finely chopped
4  Cups Roma Tomatoes, finely chopped
1  Tablespoon Dried Basil Leaves
2  Cups Fine Dry Bread Crumbs
6  Eggs, beaten
½  Cup Heavy Cream
1  Cup Shredded Parmesan Cheese
½  Cup Mozzarella Jack Cheese, grated
Salt & Pepper, to taste

Place 2 tablespoons of olive oil in a sauté pan over medium high heat. Heat until hot and add garlic, cook, and stir until golden, add onions, tomatoes and basil and cook until most of the liquid is evaporated. Remove from heat and cool. Add eggs, cream, breadcrumbs, Parmesan cheese, and salt and pepper. Pour into a well-greased 9-inch square pan and top with Mozzarella cheese. Place in a 350°F oven and bake 30 minutes or until cheese is melted and golden and Tian is set. Remove from oven and let set for 10 minutes. Cut in squares and serve. SERVES 9.

*vegetables, salads and grains*

# Mushrooms With Rice

| | |
|---|---|
| ½ Cup Olive Oil | 2½ Cups Chicken Broth |
| 2 Medium Onions, chopped | 1¼ Cups Dry White Wine |
| 1 Pound Mushrooms (any combination) | 1 Teaspoon Salt |
| 1 Cup Celery, chopped | ¼ Teaspoon Pepper |
| ½ Cup Parsley, chopped | 1 Cup Rice |

In a large saucepan heat the olive oil and sauté the onions until yellow. Add the mushrooms, mixing well, and simmer for 2 minutes. Add celery, parsley, chicken broth, wine, salt, and pepper and cook slowly for 20 minutes. Add the rice and cook on medium low heat until the rice is done and all liquid has been absorbed, about 20 minutes. Serve garnished with chopped parsley. SERVES 6-8.

# Fresh Corn Sauté With Green Onions

*You can substitute petite frozen corn for the fresh – it's very good!*

6 Large Ears Of Corn
½ Cup Green Onions, finely sliced, including some of the green tops
3 Tablespoons Unsalted Butter
½ Teaspoon Salt
¼ Teaspoon Freshly Ground White Pepper

Shuck corn, cut corn from cob with a sharp knife, then, using the dull side of the knife, scrape juice from the cob. In a sauté pan, heat butter, add corn. Stir in green onions. Sauté the vegetables in butter over high heat until the corn is tender and juices evaporate, about 5 minutes. Stir in salt and pepper. SERVES 6.

# Butternut Squash Puffs

1 Pound Butternut Squash, peeled, seeded & strings discarded
1 Tablespoon Butter
2 Tablespoons Brown Sugar, firmly packed
1 Large Egg

Cut flesh of cleaned and de-stringed squash into 1-inch pieces. Place squash with 1 tablespoon of water in a microwave dish, covered with plastic wrap. Place in microwave for 7 to 10 minutes, or until very tender. Transfer to mixer bowl and beat with mixer; add butter, 1 tablespoon of brown sugar, and beat until smooth. Beat in egg. Add salt and pepper to taste. Divide into 2 ramekins, sprinkle with remaining sugar, and bake in a 350°F oven until puffed and set. SERVES 2.

# Karen's Southwestern Chicken Salad

16 Ounces Mixed Greens

1½ Cups Cooked Rice

2 Cups Black Beans, cooked, rinsed & drained

2 Boneless & Skinless Chicken Breasts, grilled & chopped into small cubes

1 Cup Jicama, peeled & julienned into thin strips

1 Cup Red Bell Pepper, cleaned & julienned into thin strips

1 Cup Monterey Jack Cheese, finely shredded

Red Onions, thinly sliced

2 Roma Tomatoes, chopped into small dice

1 Cup Pumpkin Seeds

Arrange greens on 4 plates.  Mix rice and black beans together and mound ½ of mixture on each plate.  Place remaining ingredients on each plate in order given.  Dress with Chile Vinaigrette.  SERVES 4.

## CHILE VINAIGRETTE

1 Cup Canola Oil          1 Teaspoon Garlic Salt

½ Cup Cider Vinegar       1 Teaspoon Scallions, finely chopped

2 Teaspoons Crushed Red Chile Flakes

Whisk all ingredients together until well combined.  Refrigerate until ready to use.

*This recipe came to me one year as we were driving back from Canada. It is my favorite.*

*Karen's Southwestern Chicken Salad*

*vegetables, salads and grains*

# Karen's Grilled Polenta

4 Tablespoons Butter
1 Small Onion, finely chopped
4 Cups Water
1 Cup Polenta
½ Teaspoon Salt
½ Teaspoon Finely Ground Pepper
½ Cup Heavy Cream
¼ Pound Shredded Parmesan Cheese

Preheat oven to 350°F.  Generously grease an 8-inch square baking dish.  Melt butter in large saucepan; add onion and sauté till golden.  Add water and bring to boil.  Stirring vigorously, add polenta slowly (it spatters) and continue stirring and cooking till thick.  Stir in salt, pepper, and cream.  Remove from heat and add cheese, mixing well.  Pour into prepared pan and place in oven for 20 minutes or till firm.  Cover and refrigerate till ready to grill.

Heat grill, or French grill pan, add 2 tablespoons butter.  Cut polenta into 2-inch squares and grill till lightly browned. Serve immediately.  MAKES 9 SERVINGS.

# Italian Style Green Beans

1 Pound Fresh Green Beans, trimmed & cleaned
1½ Tablespoons Butter
1 Clove Garlic, finely chopped
½ Teaspoon Oregano Leaf, crumbled
2 Tablespoons Water
Pepper, to taste
8 Teaspoons Grated Parmesan Cheese
1 Lemon, cut into 8 wedges

Steam green beans till bright green and set aside.

In a large sauté pan over medium-high heat, melt butter, add garlic, and cook about 1 minute.  Add oregano, water, pepper, and green beans.  Cook until just heated through, tossing to coat.

Divide beans among dinner plates.  Top each with 1 teaspoon Parmesan cheese and a lemon wedge.
SERVES 6-8.

# Artichoke Potatoes

| | |
|---|---|
| 2 Tablespoons Butter | ½ Teaspoon Bouillon Granules |
| ½ Cup Onion, chopped | 1 Teaspoon Salt |
| 1 Garlic Clove | ¼ Teaspoon Pepper |
| 3 Russet Potatoes, peeled & thinly sliced | ¼ Teaspoon Thyme Leaves, crushed |
| 1 Cup Heavy Cream | 8 Ounces Marinated Artichoke Hearts, cut into quarters |
| ⅓ Cup Milk | 1 Lemon |

Butter sides and bottom of 8-inch baking dish. Sprinkle onion and garlic over bottom of dish. Layer in potatoes. In a separate bowl mix cream, milk, bouillon, salt, pepper, and thyme. Pour over potatoes. Place artichoke heart quarters over top and squeeze lemon juice over top. Bake in a 350°F oven approximately 1 hour or, until top is browned. SERVES 6.

# Pasta Spinach Salad

6 Ounces Rigatoni Or Cavatelli Pasta

2 Medium Tomatoes, peeled, seeded & chopped

½ Cup Crumbled Feta Cheese

¼ Cup Greek Salad Dressing (see recipe on page 124)

¼ Cup Green Onion, sliced

2 Tablespoons Pitted Olives, sliced

8 Cups Fresh Spinach, torn

¼ Cup Fresh Chives, chopped

Cook the rigatoni or cavatelli according to package directions; drain, rinse, and cool. In a bowl combine the cooked and drained pasta with the chopped tomatoes, crumbled feta cheese, salad dressing, sliced green onions, and sliced pitted olives. Toss gently to coat all of mixture with dressing. Cover and chill. To serve, arrange the spinach on one serving platter or on individual salad plates. Spoon on the pasta mixture; garnish with chopped fresh chives. MAKES 8 SERVINGS.

# Filet String Beans With Garlic

1 Pound Haricots Vert (slim French string beans)

2 Cloves Garlic, finely minced

1 Tablespoon Olive Oil

In a small saucepan heat olive oil on medium-high heat. Add garlic, and, tossing constantly, heat until golden brown. DO NOT OVERCOOK! Add string beans and toss until tender, approximately 5 minutes. Serve immediately. These are excellent sprinkled with sunflower seeds, chopped walnuts or, chopped cashews. SERVES 6.

*vegetables, salads and grains*

# Smoked Turkey & Potato Salad
## (With Mustard Dressing)

2 Red Potatoes
1¼ Pounds Smoked Turkey Breast
1 Red Onion
1 Head Bibb Or Boston Lettuce
¾ Cup Italian Parsley, minced

Cut the unpeeled potatoes into a ¾-inch dice. Put potatoes in a saucepan with cold, salted water to cover, and bring to a boil, covered. Uncover and continue cooking until tender, about 8 minutes. Drain potatoes and transfer to a large bowl. Whisk the dressing, pour ½ of it over warm potatoes, and toss gently. Set potatoes aside to cool. Cut turkey into ¾-inch dice. Peel and slice the onion. Wash and dry the lettuce. Mince the parsley. Add remaining dressing, turkey, onion, and parsley to the potatoes. Season to taste with salt and pepper and toss. To serve, put lettuce on plates and top with salad. SERVES 4.

**MUSTARD DRESSING**

1 Tablespoon White Wine Vinegar      Salt & Fresh Ground Pepper
⅓ Cup Whole-Grain Mustard      ½ Cup Corn Oil

In a small bowl whisk together the vinegar, mustard, ¼ teaspoon salt, and pepper to taste. Whisk in the oil, a little at a time.

# Sautéed Cabbage With Fennel Seeds

*This is a very interesting and tasty way to prepare cooked cabbage – a very popular vegetable at the Café.*

3 Cups Green Cabbage, coarsely shredded
1 Cup Purple Cabbage, coarsely shredded
1 Tablespoon Fennel Seeds
¼ Cup Rice Wine Vinegar
1 Teaspoon Herb Blend (such as Mrs. Dash® Original Blend)

ABOUT 2 HOURS BEFORE SERVING: Mix all ingredients in a bowl. Cover with plastic wrap and allow to sit at room temperature. Just before serving, heat 2 tablespoons of peanut oil in a large sauté pan. Add cabbage mixture and stir-fry till crisp tender. Serve immediately. SERVES 2.

VARIATION: Substitute Napa Cabbage for green cabbage and toasted sesame seeds for fennel seeds. Add 1 tablespoon soy sauce to mixture as you are sautéing.

# Karen's Wine Country Salad

*Marc came back from a day in Tucson and created this salad. Nice flavors and textures.*

4 Cups Mixed Fresh Salad Greens, washed, spun & trimmed

2 Apples (Fugi or Braeburn), halved, cored & thin sliced

1 Cup Havarti Cheese, cubed

1 Cup Smoky Gouda Cheese, cubed

1 Cup Emmenthal Cheese, cubed

½ Cup Dried Cranberries

½ Cup Dried Blueberries

1 Cup Candied Pecans (see recipe below)

Citrus Vinaigrette (see recipe below)

Arrange lettuce on 4 salad plates. Divide and arrange apple slices among the four plates. Divide and arrange the cheeses in center of each plate. Sprinkle cranberries and blueberries evenly over the plates. Sprinkle candied pecans over plates. Pass citrus vinaigrette or dress each plate with approximately 2 to 3 tablespoons per serving. Serves 4 as a side salad; 2 as a main course.

## CITRUS VINAIGRETTE

1 Cup Olive Oil ⅓ Cup Fresh Lemon Juice

½ Cup Rice Vinegar Salt & Pepper, to taste

Whisk all ingredients until well combined. Store, covered, in refrigerator till ready to use.

## CANDIED PECANS
*These are addictive!*

2 Cups Pecan Halves

1 Egg White

½ Cup Granulated Sugar

Preheat oven to 350°F. Whisk egg white and sugar together until sugar is dissolved. Add pecan halves and mix well. Spread on a parchment lined baking sheet. Bake for approximately 7 to 10 minutes or until egg whites are opaque and pecans are browned lightly. Remove from oven and cool completely. Break into individual halves and store in a ziploc bag in the refrigerator until ready to use. Will keep for 2 to 3 weeks.

<u>Wine Recommendation:</u>
German Riesling Spatlese

# Karen's Chicken Rolls With A Sherry Cream Sauce

## (Stuffed With Goat Cheese, Sun Dried Tomatoes & Spinach)

Start early in the day or one day ahead.

4 Half Chicken Breasts, pounded thin between 2 sheets of plastic wrap
10 Ounces Goat Cheese (Montrachet or Chevre)
¼ Cup Sun Dried Tomatoes, rehydrated in water & well drained
10 Spinach Leaves, blanched, patted dry & chopped in a coarse julienne
¼ Teaspoon Pepper

Mix together well in a large bowl the goat cheese, sun dried tomatoes, and julienned spinach leaves. Add pepper and form into 4 equal cylinders (logs).

Place chicken breasts on a flat surface. Place 1 cylinder of cheese mixture in the middle of each breast. Roll ends of breast over so that one end slightly overlaps the other. Put each rolled breast on a piece of plastic wrap, wrap tightly, place in a square pan, and put in refrigerator to chill 3 to 4 hours or overnight.

### SAUCE
½ Cup Sherry
½ Cup Dry White Wine
1½ Cups Heavy Cream
6 Tablespoons Sweet-Hot Mustard
Salt & Pepper, to taste
2 Tablespoons Butter
Flour

Heat sherry and wine in a small saucepan and, reduce by ½.

In a separate saucepan, reduce the 1½ cups of heavy cream to ¾ of a cup.

Combine wines and cream in a saucepan, add the mustard, and whisk until well blended. Season to taste with salt and pepper. Keep hot, not boiling, until ready to serve.

In a non-stick skillet, melt the butter. Remove plastic wrap from chicken rolls; dredge lightly in flour, and brown in skillet. Place in preheated 375°F oven until internal temperature is 160°F. Remove from oven, slice, and top with sauce. Serve immediately. SERVES 4.

# Sautéed Orange Roughy With Chardonnay Sauce

4-6  Orange Roughy Fillets
½  Cup Flour
4-6  Tablespoons Butter
1  Cup Chardonnay Wine
2-4  Tablespoons Chopped Shallots
1  Garlic Clove, finely chopped
¼  Cup Heavy Cream
½  Teaspoon Sugar
⅛  Teaspoon Salt
Pinch Of Cayenne
3-4  Tablespoons Butter

Dredge the fish in flour and shake off excess.  Sauté lightly in butter and place in a clean pan.  Place the pan in a Preheated 350°F oven.  Deglaze the skillet with the wine.  Add the shallots and garlic; cook until reduced by ½.  Add the cream, sugar, salt, cayenne, and simmer until thickened.  Whisk in the remaining butter 1 tablespoon at a time.  Remove fish from oven, spoon sauce over, and serve immediately.  SERVES 4-6.

# Oriental Poached Chicken Breasts

2  Tablespoons Mrs. Dash® Original
2  Tablespoons Soy Sauce
3  Cups Dry White Wine
2  Cups Seasoned Rice Vinegar
4  Skinless & Boneless Chicken Breast Halves
4  Spinach Leaves, washed & trimmed
4  Teaspoons Toasted Sesame Seeds

In a medium saucepan, combine first four ingredients.  Over high heat, bring to boil; reduce heat to low and cook 5 minutes.  Add chicken breasts and poach in simmering liquid 7 minutes; remove to plate and cover loosely.  Reserve liquid.

In large skillet over high heat, heat oil.  Stir fry spinach leaves in hot oil just till wilted.  Remove from heat and toss with 1 tablespoon poaching liquid.  To serve, arrange spinach on 4 plates.  Slice breasts into ½-inch slices.  Fan slices of each breast on top of spinach on each plate.  Drizzle with 1 teaspoon poaching liquid over each plate.  Sprinkle lightly with toasted sesame seeds.  Serve immediately.  SERVES 4.

# Sautéed Italian Sausage

### (With Peppers, Onions & Garlic)

12 Italian Sausages, Sweet, Hot, Or A Combination Of Both

1 Each Red, Green & Yellow Bell Peppers

1 Large Yellow Onion, peeled & thinly sliced

4 Garlic Cloves, finely minced

1 Tablespoon Olive Oil

1 Cup Dry White Wine

2 Tablespoons Dijon Mustard

1 Teaspoon Instant Chicken Bouillon Granules

¼ Cup Fresh Basil, cut in fine ribbons

Fresh Ground Black Pepper, to taste

In a large frying pan heat olive oil, add sausages and garlic and cook until browned on both sides. Add onions and cook until limp. Add bell peppers and cook until limp. Add wine, mustard, and bouillon, cover and cook until sauce is thickened, stirring constantly, about 10 minutes. Uncover; add basil leaves and stir just until wilted. Serve at once garnished with minced Italian parsley. SERVES 6.

*Simple, delicious, and attractive – great with polenta or pasta.*

*Sautéed Italian Sausage served with Polenta and Tomato Tien*

# Roast Pork Loin

## (With A Red Onion & Fennel Mustard Sauce)

4 Pounds Boneless Pork Loin
½ Teaspoon Fennel Seed, crushed
½ Teaspoon Dried Rosemary
¼ Teaspoon Freshly Ground Black Pepper
Olive Oil

One day ahead puree the 3 herbs and olive oil into a paste, coat the loin with it, wrap it with plastic wrap, and let it marinate overnight in the refrigerator. Preheat oven to 400°F. Position the loin on a rack in a pan just large enough to hold it. Insert meat thermometer into thickest part of center of loin. Roast at 400°F for 10 minutes, then reduce heat to 325°F for 1½ hours, or until the internal temperature of the loin registers 160°F. Throughout the cooking time, baste the loin at 15-minute intervals with the olive oil. Allow the loin to rest 5 to 10 minutes before slicing. Slice in ¼-inch slices, place on warm plates, spoon the Red Onion & Fennel Mustard Sauce (see recipe below) over, and serve.

## RED ONION & FENNEL MUSTARD SAUCE

3 Teaspoons Olive Oil
1¼ Pounds Red Onions, thinly sliced
3 Garlic Cloves, crushed
1½ Tablespoons Fennel Seed Crushed
1½ Tablespoons Dried Rosemary
1 Teaspoon Freshly Ground Black Pepper
¾ Cup Chardonnay Wine (dry)
2 Teaspoons Balsamic Vinegar
3 Cups Chicken Broth
2 Teaspoons Dijon Mustard

In a saucepan, over medium heat, heat the olive oil, add the onions, garlic, fennel, rosemary, and pepper, cover and cook until the onions are tender and lightly browned, about 15 minutes. Add the wine and vinegar and simmer until the liquid is reduced to approximately ¼ cup. Add the chicken broth and simmer for 15 minutes. Remove from heat and puree in a food processor. Strain the sauce through a fine sieve, add the mustard, and blend well. If needed, adjust to taste with additional mustard or salt. The sauce may be made ahead of time and refrigerated (Re-heat, BUT DO NOT BOIL, before serving). Spoon sauce over pork loin. SERVES 6-8.

Wine Recommendation:
Cote Rotie (Villard)

# Beef Roulade Stuffed With Barley

## (Served With A Red Wine Reduction Sauce)

*Pretty to serve for a dinner party.  Barley adds an interesting flavor and texture.*

1  2-Pound Top Round Steak, pounded to ¼" thickness
2  Cups Barley, prepared according to package directions

### TO  BARLEY  ADD:

½  Cup Scallions, thinly sliced
1  Teaspoon Rosemary
½  Teaspoon Thyme

Mix well with barley.

Place beef on a flat surface and cover to ½-inch of edges with barley mixture.  Roll up jellyroll fashion and tie at 2-inch intervals with string.  Wrap tightly with plastic wrap and refrigerate overnight.  To roast, preheat oven to 350°F, remove plastic wrap, and place beef roll on a sheet pan.  Place in oven and roast till meat thermometer registers 140°F.  Let stand 20 minutes before serving.  Slice into ½-inch slices.  SERVES 4-6.

### RED  WINE  REDUCTION  SAUCE

¼  Cup Butter          4  Cups Beef Broth
4  Shallots, finely chopped          ½  Cup Heavy Cream
1  Cup Red Wine

Sauté shallots in butter till browned.  Add red wine and reduce by ½.  Add beef broth and reduce by ½ again.  Add cream and heat thoroughly.  Serve over slices of Beef Roulade.

# Chicken Normandy

4  Chicken Breasts; boneless & skinless          2  Tablespoons Brown Sugar
¾  Cup Flour, seasoned with salt & pepper          ¼  Cup Sherry
2  Apples, peeled, cored & sliced into ¼" rings          1  Cup Heavy Cream
4  Tablespoons Butter

Dredge chicken breasts in seasoned flour.  Melt 2 tablespoons butter in sauté pan till bubbly; add breasts and sauté till browned and cooked through.  Remove from pan, place on a plate, and cover tightly.  Melt remaining butter and add apple rings.  Sauté till crisp tender and sprinkle with brown sugar.  Remove to plate with chicken, placing equal amounts on each breast.  Deglaze pan with sherry and reduce to ½.  Add cream and cook till thickened to a creamy thickness.  Divide equally among breasts and serve.  SERVES 4.

*Beef Roulade Stuffed With Barley served with*
*Roasted Tomatoes and Sizzling Carrots*

# Basque Chicken

*A real café style dish.  Simple to prepare and serve.*
*It is especially good with garlicky mashed potatoes.*

4  Small Serrano Chiles
1  Chicken (3-4 pounds), well rinsed, patted dry, cut into 8 serving pieces & at room temperature
Salt & Freshly Ground Pepper
5  Tablespoons Vegetable Oil
12  Large Garlic Cloves, sliced into thin pieces
2  Pounds Red Bell Peppers, cored, seeded & thickly sliced
4  Thick Slices Prosciutto, cubed
2  Large Onions, coarsely chopped
1  28-Ounce Can Imported Plum Tomatoes

Wear rubber gloves to prepare chiles.  Core and seed the chiles.  Slice into 1-inch strips; set aside.  Season the chicken liberally with salt and pepper.  In a nonreactive, deep-sided 12-inch skillet, heat 3 tablespoons of the oil over high heat.  When the oil is hot but not smoking, add the chicken and brown on one side until the skin turns an even, golden brown, about 5 minutes.  Be careful to avoid scorching the skin.  Turn the pieces over and brown them on the other side, for an additional 5 minutes.  Work in batches if necessary.

Return all of the chicken to the skillet (it's okay to crowd them in).  Add the garlic, bell pepper, chiles and Prosciutto, burying the ingredients amidst the chicken pieces.  Cook, covered, over medium heat, until the chicken is cooked through and the peppers are meltingly soft, about 45 minutes to 1 hour.  The pan will make a lot of crackling noises as the peppers give off much of their liquid.  Turn the mixture from time to time, and adjust heat to avoid scorching.  You want a tender sauce.

Meanwhile, in another large skillet, heat the remaining 2 tablespoons of oil over high heat until hot but not smoking.  Add the onions.  Reduce the heat to medium-low and cook until very soft, about 5 minutes.  Add the tomatoes and continue cooking for another 30 minutes.  The mixture should be soft and well blended.  Season to taste with salt.  (The dish can be easily prepared ahead of time up to this point and refrigerated.  Reheat both mixtures separately.)

To serve, layer the tomato and onion mixture on a preheated platter.  Cover with the chicken mixture, and serve immediately, with white rice or mashed potatoes.  SERVES 4-6.

Wine Recommendation:
Rosé (Chateau de Trinquevedel)

# Peppered Beef Tenderloin

## (With A Tomato Mushroom Wine Sauce)

1 Whole Beef Tenderloin (2-3 pounds), trimmed
¼ Cup Freshly Cracked Peppercorns
2 Teaspoons Kosher Salt
¼ Cup Olive Oil

Early in the day and at least 2 hours before roasting prepare, the tenderloin. Place a piece of plastic wrap flat on a work surface (it should be large enough to enclose the roast plus an overlap of 3 to 4 inches). Mix the peppercorns, salt, and olive oil in a small bowl. Place roast on the plastic wrap and smear with the pepper/oil mixture and rub firmly. Wrap roast tightly in plastic wrap, place in a pan, and refrigerate 2 to 6 hours.

About 1½ hours before serving preheat oven to 425°F. Place a roasting rack inside the pan you will roast the tenderloin in. Remove the plastic wrap and place the roast on the rack. Place a meat thermometer in center of the roast. Place roast in oven and roast for 15 minutes. Turn oven down to 375°F and continue roasting until the desired degree of doneness is reached (130°F to 135°F for rare; 150°F to 160°F for well done).

Remove from oven, place on a carving board, and allow to rest for 15 to 20 minutes before carving. To serve cut across grain in ¼ to ½-inch slices. Place 2 to 3 slices on warmed serving plates, ladle Tomato Mushroom Wine Sauce (see recipe below) over slices, and garnish with fresh sprigs of Thyme or Rosemary. SERVES 8.

## TOMATO MUSHROOM WINE SAUCE

1 Cup Dry White Wine
½ Cup Dry Sherry
3 Cups Beef Stock
4 Cups Tomato Juice
½ Cup Onion, sliced
2 Sprigs Parsley
2 Stalks Celery, chopped
1 Tablespoon Honey
½ Teaspoon Pepper
2 Cloves
1 Cup Button Mushrooms, thinly sliced

Combine all ingredients except mushrooms in a saucepan and bring to a boil. Reduce heat, cover, and cook slowly for 20 minutes. Strain sauce and return to saucepan. Add mushrooms. Adjust seasoning. Heat thoroughly and serve.

# Roasted Pork Loin

## (With Sautéed Apple Rings, Sherry Cream Sauce & Herbed Walnuts)

*The most popular pork dish we prepared. The presentation was very nice.*

Roasted Pork Loin, Sage Glazed Carrots and Acorn Squash Rings

1 Pork Loin (5 pounds), tied
Kosher Salt & Pepper
1 Tablespoon Olive Oil
2 Granny Smith Apples, peeled, cored & sliced in ¼" thick slices
3 Tablespoons Butter
¼-½ Cup Brown Sugar
2 Cups Walnuts, chopped
2 Tablespoons Olive Oil
¼ Teaspoon Salt
1 Teaspoon Pepper
¼ Teaspoon Sugar
1 Teaspoon Ground Sage

Up to 3 Hours before serving : Pat 1 tablespoon Kosher salt and 1 teaspoon freshly ground pepper over the surface of the pork loin. Wrap tightly in plastic wrap, place in a flat pan, and refrigerate. About 1 hour before cooking remove from refrigerator and allow to sit at room temperature.

1½-2 Hours Before Serving: Heat oven to 350ºF. Heat 1 tablespoon olive oil in a large skillet till almost smoking. Sear roast on all sides and place on a meat rack in a roasting pan. Insert a meat thermometer into middle of roast and place in oven. Roast until thermometer reaches 155ºF to 160ºF. Remove from oven and tent with foil for approximately 10 to 20 minutes. Slice in ¼-inch thick slices allowing 3 slices per serving. Place 2 to 3 sautéed apple rings (see below) on each serving, ladle Sherry Cream Sauce (see below) over, and sprinkle with walnuts. Serve, garnished with fresh sage. SERVES 6-8.

SAUTÉED APPLE RINGS: While roast is cooking, melt 3 tablespoon butter in a sauté pan. Add brown sugar and stir till combined. Add apple rings in single layers until all are sautéed limp. Place on a plate and cover till ready to serve.

HERBED WALNUTS: Mix chopped walnuts with olive oil, salt, pepper, sugar, and ground sage till well combined. Spread on sheet pan and roast in 350ºF oven approximately 10 to 15 minutes or until lightly browned. Remove from oven, cool, and place in an airtight container until ready to use.

### SHERRY CREAM SAUCE
1 Cup Dry Sherry      2 Cups Whipping Cream

In medium size saucepan, reduce sherry by ½. In another saucepan reduce cream by ½. Combine the sherry and cream and keep warm till ready to serve.

# Pork Chops Braised With Cider & Sautéed Apples

| | |
|---|---|
| 4 ¾"-Center Cut Pork Chops | 1 Small Tart Apple, cored & thinly sliced |
| 1 Tablespoon Vegetable Oil | ½ Cup Apple Cider |
| 2 Tablespoons Butter (¼ stick) | 1½ Tablespoons Apple Cider Vinegar |
| 1 Large Onion, thinly sliced | 1 Bay Leaf |

Season pork chops generously with salt and pepper. Heat oil in heavy large skillet over medium heat. Add pork to skillet and cook until brown and cooked through, about 5 minutes per side. Transfer pork to platter. Tent with foil to keep warm. Drain off all but 1 tablespoon drippings from skillet. Add butter to skillet and melt over medium heat. Add onion and apple to skillet and sauté until onion is almost soft, about 5 minutes. Mix in cider, vinegar, and bay leaf. Add any accumulated juices from pork chop platter to skillet. Increase heat and cook until sauce thickens slightly, about 3 minutes. Spoon sauce over pork chops and serve. SERVES 4.

# Italian Sausage & Meatballs With Mushroom —Sherry Cream Sauce

4 Tablespoons Butter

4 Tablespoons Flour

1 Teaspoon Onion Powder

½ Teaspoon Salt

½ Teaspoon Freshly Ground Pepper

1 Cup Half & Half

2 Tablespoons Sherry

1 Egg Yolk, beaten

1 Cup Romano Cheese, grated

1 Cup Button Mushrooms, cleaned & thinly sliced

16 Meatballs (small to medium size), cooked thoroughly

2 Italian Sausages, cooked & thinly sliced

In a heavy saucepan, melt butter, add flour, and stir until well combined. Add seasonings. Add cream slowly, whisking constantly, until smooth and thickened. Add sherry. Turn heat to low and slowly add egg yolk, whisking constantly. Add cheese, mushrooms, meatballs, and Italian sausage. Simmer for approximately 15 to 20 minutes. DO NOT OVERHEAT. If sauce becomes too thick, add additional half & half. Serve over red pepper pasta or pasta of your choice. Sprinkle with shredded Parmesan cheese and serve. SERVES 4.

# Sesame Chicken

### (With Napa Cabbage & Vegetables In Broth)

*If you like oriental flavors you will love this!*

2 Boneless Skinless Chicken Breasts
½ Cup Flour, seasoned with salt & pepper
1 Egg White, whisked slightly
½ Cup Toasted Sesame Seeds
¼ Cup Karen's® Soy-Ginger Vinaigrette (or use recipe on page 210)
4 Cups Napa Cabbage, shredded
½ Cup Carrots, finely julienned
1 Green Onion, cleaned & sliced on the diagonal
½ Red Bell Pepper, cleaned & julienned into thin strips

Preheat oven to 375°F. Spray a small baking sheet with butter flavored pan spray. Dredge chicken breasts on both sides in seasoned flour. Dip in egg white on both sides then in sesame seeds on both sides (add more seeds if necessary). Place prepared breasts on baking sheet and spray lightly, but evenly, with pan spray. Place in oven and bake approximately 20 minutes, or until internal temperature reaches 160°F in the meatiest part of the breast.

About 10 minutes before the chicken is done heat the Soy-Ginger Vinaigrette in a large sauté pan. Add green onions and stir fry 1 minute. Add carrots and stir fry 1 minute. Add shredded cabbage and bell pepper and stir fry 1 minute. Serve immediately in flat-bottomed bowls with vegetables and broth on bottom and the chicken breast on top.

TIP: Heat bowls while chicken is baking so the dish stays hot while serving. SERVES 2.

# Chicken Dijonnaise

*This was a favorite at Huguette's. It works really well for a buffet.*

6 Tablespoons Milk
4 Tablespoons Dijon Mustard
4 Chicken Breasts
½ Cup Bread Crumbs
2 Tablespoons Tarragon Leaves, crushed

Whisk milk and mustard together. Dip chicken in mixture, then coat with mixture of breadcrumbs and tarragon.

Place in a shallow baking dish and bake at 375°F for 30 minutes, covered; and then 15 minutes, uncovered. SERVES 4.

*A wide variety of unique and colorful lizards can often be seen sunbathing on the rocks, especially during the cooler parts of the day as they try to keep their body at an ideal temperature.*

# Pumpkin Muffins

*This batter can be stored in the refrigerator for one week. This my favorite muffin recipe.*

1⅔ Cups Flour

1⅛ Cups Sugar

¼ Teaspoon Baking Powder

1 Teaspoon Baking Soda

1 Teaspoon Salt

1 Teaspoon Cinnamon

¼ Teaspoon Ginger

⅓ Cup Butter, softened

1 Cup Pumpkin, cooked & mashed

⅛ Cup Water

1 Egg

⅔ Cup Raisins

⅛ Cup Walnuts Or Pecans, chopped

Sift dry ingredients into a bowl. Add butter, pumpkin, water, and beat until ingredients are well mixed. Add egg and beat two more minutes. Stir in raisins and nuts. Pour into muffin pan with medium sized muffin cups that have been well greased. Bake at 350°F for approximately 25 minutes. MAKES ABOUT 1 DOZEN.

# Anadama Bread

*The Callaghan family favorite. It makes great toast and grilled cheese sandwiches!*

| | |
|---|---|
| 3 Cups Milk | 2 Teaspoons Salt |
| ¾ Cup Yellow Cornmeal | 2 Tablespoons Yeast |
| ¾ Cup Molasses | ¾ Cup Warm Water |
| 2 Tablespoons Butter | 8 Cups Bread Flour |

Heat milk to scalding and add cornmeal, stirring to prevent lumping. Stir in molasses, butter and salt. Cool to luke-warm. Soften yeast in ¾ cup of warm water. Add to cornmeal mixture. In mixer, with dough hook, mix in enough flour to make a smooth and resilient ball. Place in greased bowl and cover with plastic wrap. Let rise until doubled. Form into loaves and place in well-greased loaf pans. Let rise again until doubled. Place in a preheated 350°F oven until the loaves are browned and hollow sounding when taped with finger, approximately 30 minutes. Turn out onto wire rack and cool completely. MAKES 3 LOAVES.

# Maple Pecan Sticky Buns

1 Package White Bread Mix For Bread Machine
1 Egg

Prepare bread dough according to package directions EXCEPT: add one egg and, using a mixer fitted with a dough hook, mix until a soft dough is formed (that will clean the sides of the mixer bowl). Add a small amount of bread flour, if necessary. When finished mixing, spray a large bowl with pan release spray and place dough in it turning to grease top. Cover with plastic wrap and allow to rise till doubled.

## MEANWHILE COMBINE:
½ Cup Butter
¼ Cup Biscuit Mix
¼ Cup Sugar
2 Tablespoons Cinnamon

Mix well, cover, and set aside until ready to roll dough out.

When dough is about doubled prepare 1 cup muffin tins (about 10 places or cups) in the following manner.

## IN EACH CUP PLACE:
1 Tablespoon Butter
2 Tablespoons Pure Maple Syrup
2 Teaspoons Pecans, coarsely chopped

Spray sides of muffin cups with pan release.

ASSEMBLE STICKY BUNS: When dough has doubled, lightly flour a board about 12 inches by 15 inches. Roll dough out to about ½-inch thickness. Spread cinnamon-sugar-butter mixture over entire surface of dough, pressing down with the flat of your hand. Roll dough up, jellyroll fashion. Roll and press back and forth 2 or 3 times to eliminate air pockets. Slice dough into 1-inch slices (about 10) and place in prepared muffin pans. Allow to rise, uncovered, till almost doubled.

Preheat oven to 350°F. Put muffin tin(s) on baking sheet, place in oven, and bake approximately 25 to 30 minutes or until browned on top. (Do not underbake as they will be gummy.) Remove from oven and invert immediately. Remove muffin pan and scrape any syrup or nuts out of cups. Allow to cool and place on plates. SERVES 8-10.

# Karen's Coffee Can Batter Bread

*This recipe was given to me years ago by my friend, Ardith. It lends itself to many variations.*
*Make it uniquely yours!*

| | | | |
|---|---|---|---|
| 1 | Package Active Dry Yeast | 2 | Tablespoons Vegetable Oil |
| ½ | Cup Warm Water | 2½ | Cups All-Purpose Flour |
| ¼ | Teaspoon Ground Ginger | 2 | Cups Whole-Wheat Flour |
| 3 | Tablespoons Sugar | ¼ | Cup Toasted Sesame Seeds |
| 1½ | Cups Milk | ¼ | Cup Cracked Wheat |
| 1 | Teaspoon Salt | ¼ | Sunflower Seeds |

In a large mixer bowl, sprinkle yeast over warm water; blend in ginger and 1 tablespoon of the sugar. Let stand until bubbly, about 5 minutes. Stir in remaining 2 tablespoons sugar, milk, salt, and oil. With a heavy-duty mixer, equipped with a dough hook, beat in 3 cups of the flours, the sesame seeds, cracked wheat, and sunflower seeds until the dough begins to pull from sides of the bowl. Beat in about 1½ cups more flour, ½ cup at a time, until dough almost pulls cleanly from sides of bowl.

Divide batter in half and place 1 portion in each of 2 well-greased 1-pound coffee cans, or spoon all batter into 1 well-greased 2-pound coffee can. Cover with well greased plastic lids. Let covered cans stand in warm place until batter rises and pops off plastic lids, 45 to 55 minutes for 1-pound cans, 55 to 60 minutes for 2-pound can. Remove plastic lids.

Set cans on lowest rack of a 350°F oven. Bake uncovered, until crust is very brown, about 45 minutes for 1-pound cans, about 60 minutes for 2-pound can. Brush tops lightly with butter. Let cans cool on a wire rack for about 5 to 10 minutes; then loosen loaves around edges of can with a thin knife, slide bread out from cans, and let cool in upright position on rack. NOTE: The easiest way to remove bread from can is to cut the bottom out of the can with a can opener and push out the loaf. This makes the cans unusable again. MAKES 1-2 LOAVES.

# Farm Corn Muffins

| | | | |
|---|---|---|---|
| 1 | Cup Yellow Cornmeal | 1 | Egg |
| 1 | Cup All-Purpose Flour | 1 | 8½-Ounce Can Cream-Style Corn |
| 1 | Tablespoon Plus 2 Teaspoons Baking Powder | 8 | Ounces Sour Cream |
| ¼ | Teaspoon Salt | 2 | Tablespoons Vegetable Oil |

Combine first 6 ingredients in a large bowl; make a well in the center of the mixture. Combine remaining ingredients; add to dry ingredients, stirring just until moistened. Spoon into greased muffin pans. Bake at 400°F for 12 to 15 minutes or until golden brown. MAKES 2 DOZEN.

# Smoked Chicken Sandwich With Fontina Cheese, Cranberry Pesto & Fresh Apples

1   Loaf Pistachio Wheat Bread (see recipe on page 44), sliced into ½" slices
8-12   Slices Smoked Breast Of Chicken
4-6   Slices Fontina Cheese
8-12   Fresh Apple Rings
Cranberry Pesto (see recipe on page 207)

Spread slices of bread, one side only, with Cranberry Pesto.  Place chicken slices, folded to fit, on bread (2 per sandwich).  Place cheese slice on top and place half of each sandwich (with cheese) under broiler and broil until cheese is melted and bubbly.  Remove from broiler, top with apple slices, and second bread slice.  Serve with fresh cabbage or potato salad.  SERVES 4-6.

*Smoked Chicken Sandwich With Fontina Cheese,
Cranberry Pesto & Fresh Apples*

# Turkey, Ham & Cheese Sandwich With Basil—Walnut Pesto

*A best seller at Karen's Wine Country Café.*

1  Loaf Vienna Bread (see recipe on page 90), sliced in ½" thick slices
4-6  Slices Ham
4-6  Slices Smoked Turkey Breast
4-6  Slices Jarlsberg Or Emmenthal Cheese
8-12  Slices Tomato
Basil-Walnut Pesto (see recipe below)

Spread one slice of each piece of bread with pesto sauce. Place bread slices, plain side down in a sauté or grill pan, which has been sprayed with pan release. Place 1 slice each of ham, turkey, and cheese on the pesto side of half the bread slices and then place 2 to 3 tomato slices on top. Then place second piece of bread, pesto side down, on top. When bottom slice of bread is browned slightly, flip the sandwich over and grill remaining side until browned slightly.
MAKES 4-6 SANDWICHES.

## BASIL-WALNUT PESTO
¼  Cup Walnuts
3  Garlic Cloves
2  Cups Packed Basil Leaves, rinsed & dried
⅓  Cup Extra-Virgin Olive Oil
3  Tablespoons Freshly Grated Parmesan Cheese
½  Teaspoon Salt
½  Teaspoon Freshly Ground Pepper

In a food processor, mince the garlic. Add the basil and nuts and process until minced. With the machine on, add the oil in a thin stream and process until well blended. Add the Parmesan and the salt and pepper and process to mix.
MAKES 1 CUP.

# Cinnamon – Raisin Graham Bread

2-2½ Cups All-Purpose Flour

1 Package Active Dry Yeast

2 Teaspoons Ground Cinnamon

¼ Cup Brown Sugar

1 Cup 2% Milk

¼ Cup Dark Molasses

¾ Cup Water

3 Tablespoons Butter

½ Teaspoon Salt

3 Cups Whole Wheat Flour

1 Cup Raisins

In large mixer bowl combine 2 cups flour, yeast and spices. Heat and stir milk, molasses, butter, ¾ cup water and ½ teaspoon salt till warm and butter is almost melted. Add to flour mixture. Beat with mixer equipped with dough hook on low speed ½ minute, scraping bowl. Beat 3 minutes on high speed. Mix in whole-wheat flour and raisins. Mix in remaining all-purpose flour till dough cleans sides of bowl. Place dough in greased bowl, turning to coat; cover lightly and let rise till doubled. Punch down; divide in half and shape into 2 round loaves on greased baking sheet. Flatten to 6-inch diameter. Cover; let rise till doubled. Bake in 375ºF oven 25 to 30 minutes. Cool. MAKES 2 LOAVES.

# Sal's Bran Muffins

5½ Cups Flour

2½ Cups Sugar

3 Cups Natural Bran

2 Cups All-Bran Cereal

3 Tablespoons Baking Soda

1 Quart Buttermilk

4 Eggs, beaten

½ Cup Molasses

2 Cups Raisins

Mix the dry ingredients together in a large bowl. Whisk the buttermilk, eggs, and molasses in a separate bowl. Make a well in the center of dry ingredients and pour in liquid. Mix well. Stir in raisins. (At this point the batter can be stored in a sealed plastic container if the refrigerator for up to 6 weeks.) Preheat oven to 375ºF. Grease muffin tin. Fill with batter to ⅔ of cup. Place in oven and bake for 20 minutes. MAKES LOTS!

# Apple Dumplings

### (Served With Cinnamon Sauce)

*We had customers who would place a special request for these when they made their reservations.*

| | |
|---|---|
| 1   Package Frozen Puff Pastry Sheets | 2   Tablespoons Cinnamon |
| 12   Granny Smith Apples | ¼   Cup Butter, cut into ¼" slices |
| 1½   Cups Sugar | |

Thaw 2 pastry sheets on a cutting board large enough to accommodate a 12 x 12-inch pastry sheet. Roll 1 pastry sheet at a time to this size. Cut each sheet into 6- 4 x 6-inch pieces.

Meanwhile peel and core apples. Place one apple in the middle of each 4 x 6-inch piece. Push a piece of butter into the empty core of each apple and sprinkle 1 tablespoon, of a mixture of the sugar and cinnamon, over the top of each apple. Bring 2 corners of each pastry piece up to top of apple and press together well. Bring the opposite 2 corners up and over top of apple and press all together firmly. Place on ungreased baking sheet and put in preheated 350⁰F oven. Bake until moderately browned on top and sides. DO NOT OVERCOOK. Remove from oven and allow to cool completely. Place on a plate and cover with plastic wrap. When ready to serve, remove plastic wrap, heat in a 350⁰F oven for approximately 10 minutes, and serve with Cinnamon Sauce (see recipe below) and vanilla ice cream. SERVES 12.

## CINNAMON SAUCE

| | |
|---|---|
| 1   Cup Sugar | 3   Cups Cold Water |
| 2   Tablespoons Cinnamon | ¼   Cup Brandy |
| 1   Tablespoon Cornstarch | ¼   Cup Butter |

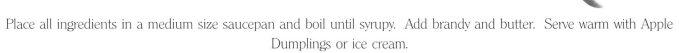

Place all ingredients in a medium size saucepan and boil until syrupy. Add brandy and butter. Serve warm with Apple Dumplings or ice cream.

# Brownie Swirl Cheesecake

| | |
|---|---|
| 1   Package Brownie Mix | 1   Teaspoon Vanilla |
| 2   Packages (8 ounces each) Cream Cheese, softened | 2   Eggs |
| ½   Cup Sugar | 1   Cup Ghirardelli® Chocolate Chips |

Heat oven to 350⁰F. Prepare brownie mix as directed on package. Pour ½ evenly into greased 9-inch springform pan. Bake 15 minutes or until set. Pour other ½ into a 9-inch square pan and bake as brownies to be served as brownies. Beat cream cheese, sugar, and vanilla until well blended. Add eggs, one at a time, mixing well after each addition. Pour ½ of the filling over the brownie layer in the springform pan. Melt the chocolate chips and combine with the other ½ of the cream cheese mixture and drop, by spoonfuls, on the cheese mixture in the springform pan. Swirl with a knife. Bake 35 minutes, or until well set. Cool before removing rim of springform pan. Refrigerate. SERVES 12.

# Coconut Cream Tarts

### (With Macadamia Nut Crusts)

*These were the desserts chosen by a Sonoita couple for their golden wedding anniversary celebration.*

Coconut Cream Tarts

⅓ Cup All-Purpose Flour
¾ Cup Sugar
4 Large Eggs
2 Cups Milk
1 Tablespoon Vanilla
1½ Cups Flaked Coconut, divided
2½ Cups All-Purpose Flour
¾ Cup Butter, cold & cut up
2 Tablespoons Water
1½ Cups Macadamia Nuts, chopped
1 Cup Whipping Cream
3 Tablespoons Sugar

Combine ⅓ cup flour and ¾ cup sugar, stirring well; stir in eggs. Cook milk in saucepan over medium heat until hot. Gradually stir about one-fourth of hot milk into egg mixture; add to remaining hot milk, stirring constantly. Cook over medium-high heat, stirring constantly, 5 to 6 minutes or until thickened. Remove from heat; stir in vanilla and 1 cup of coconut. Cover and chill 3 hours.

Bake remaining coconut in shallow pan at 350°F, stirring occasionally, 5 to 6 minutes or until toasted; set aside.

Pulse 2½ cups flour and butter in a food processor until crumbly. Add 2 tablespoons water and pulse 30 seconds or until dough forms a ball. Turn out onto a lightly floured surface; knead in nuts. Divide dough into 12 equal portions; press each portion into a 3 to 4-inch tart pan. Prick bottoms with a fork, and place on a 15 x 10-inch jellyroll pan. Cover and freeze 30 minutes.

Bake on jellyroll pan at 375°F for 15 to 20 minutes or until golden. Cool tarts in pans 5 minutes; remove from pans and cool completely on a wire rack. Spoon coconut mixture into tart shells.

Beat whipping cream and 3 tablespoons of sugar until soft peaks form; dollop or pipe onto tarts. Sprinkle the tops with toasted coconut and then chill. MAKES 12.

# Chocolate Raspberry Cheesecake

| | |
|---|---|
| 1½ Cups Vanilla Wafer Crumbs, crushed | ½ Cup Cold Water |
| ⅓ Cup Cocoa | ½ Cup Boiling Water |
| ⅓ Cup Powdered Sugar | 2 8-Ounce Packages Cream Cheese, softened |
| ⅓ Cup Butter, melted | ½ Cup Granulated Sugar |
| 1 10-Ounce Package Frozen Raspberries, defrosted | 1 Teaspoon Vanilla |
| 1 Envelope Unflavored Gelatin | 3 Tablespoons Seedless Red Raspberry Preserves |

Heat oven to 350°F. In a mixing bowl stir together crumbs, cocoa, and powdered sugar. Stir in melted butter and combine well. Press mixture onto bottom and 1½ inches up side of a 9-inch springform pan. Bake 10 minutes; remove and cool completely. Puree and strain raspberries, set aside. In a small bowl sprinkle gelatin over cold water, let stand several minutes to soften. Add boiling water; stir until gelatin dissolves completely and mixture is clear. In a large mixer bowl beat cream cheese, granulated sugar, and vanilla, blending well. Gradually add raspberry puree and gelatin, mixing thoroughly. Pour into prepared crust. Refrigerate several hours or overnight. Remove rim of pan. Spread preserves over top. Serve slices garnished with chocolate whipped cream (see recipe below). SERVES 10-12.

## CHOCOLATE WHIPPED CREAM
*This can be used with almost any chocolate dessert.*

| | |
|---|---|
| ½ Cup Powdered Sugar | 1 Cup Whipping Cream, chilled |
| ¼ Cup Cocoa | 1 Teaspoon Vanilla |

In a small mixer bowl stir together powdered sugar and cocoa, combine well. Add chilled whipping cream and vanilla; beat until stiff. Keep refrigerated.

# Banana Brittle

*These are delicious as a snack too. If they become less brittle, simply pop them in the oven for a few minutes.*

| | |
|---|---|
| 2 Tablespoons Unsalted Butter | 3 Semi-Ripe Medium Bananas, very thinly sliced crosswise |
| 1 Tablespoon Vegetable Oil | ¾ Teaspoon Cinnamon |
| 5 Tablespoons Sugar | ¼ Cup Unsalted Peanuts, minced |

Preheat oven to 350°F. On a large baking sheet, melt the butter in the oil. Spread to coat the pan evenly and sprinkle with 3 tablespoons of the sugar. Cover with the banana slices in a slightly overlapping layer. Sprinkle with the remaining 2 tablespoons of sugar, the cinnamon, and peanuts. Bakes for approximately 20 minutes, or until the slices around the edges are crisp and golden. Let cool slightly so they firm up. Transfer the browned slices to a plate and bake the rest for about 3 minutes or until browned. The brittle can be wrapped in wax paper and kept in an airtight container for up to five days. Serve over ice cream, cereal, or fresh fruit. MAKES ABOUT 4 CUPS.

# Lemon Poundcake With Strawberry Sauce

1   8-Ounce Package Cream Cheese, softened
4   Eggs
1   Package Yellow Cake Mix
¾   Cup Milk
2   Tablespoons Lemon Peel

Preheat oven to 350°F.  Grease and flour a 9-inch tube pan, set aside.  Beat cream cheese until light and fluffy.  Scrape beaters.  Add eggs, one at a time, beating well after each addition.  At low speed, beat in the cake mix (⅓ at a time), alternately with the milk (two additions).  Beat just until well combined.  Blend in lemon peel.  Pour batter into prepared pan and bake in the middle of the preheated oven for 55 minutes or until the cake springs back when touched lightly in middle of top.  Remove from oven and let cake stand on wire rack for 15 minutes.  Remove from pan and allow to cool completely.  This is best if made the day before.  Before serving, glaze with Lemon Glaze (see recipe below), slice, place on dessert plate, top with Strawberry Sauce (see recipe below) and garnish with additional whole strawberries.  SERVES 8.

## LEMON GLAZE

1½   Cups Powdered Sugar
½   Cup Fresh Squeezed Lemon Juice
1   Teaspoon Lemon Peel, finely grated

Combine well in a food processor.  Pour over cake while still warm, if possible.

## STRAWBERRY SAUCE

2   Cups Strawberries
1   Cup Granulated Sugar
2   Tablespoons Fresh Squeezed Lemon Juice

Puree strawberries in a food processor fitted with a steel blade.  Add sugar and lemon juice and combine well.  Serve over slices of Lemon Poundcake.

# Bailey's® White Chocolate Mousse

2   Packages White Chocolate (squares)     4   Egg Yolks
1   Cup Bailey's® Irish Cream              4   Cups Heavy Cream

Melt chocolate in top of double boiler.  Combine Bailey's and egg yolks, whisk well, add to chocolate, and combine well.

Whip cream until stiff peaks are formed when beaters are removed.  Gradually fold in the chocolate mixture and continue folding in until well combined.  Pour into individual serving dishes and chill well.  SERVES 8.

# Tarte Tatin

*We made this often as our apples ripened in the fall – it was really good with a mix of tart apples!*

## PASTRY
1   Cup All-Purpose Flour
1   Tablespoon Sugar
Pinch  Salt
¼   Cup Butter, cut up
1   Egg Yolk
2   Teaspoons Water

## FILLING
½   Cup Sugar
7   Granny Smith Apples,
      peeled, cored & thinly sliced
4   Tablespoons Butter, cut up

PASTRY:  In a medium bowl combine flour, sugar, and salt.  With pastry blender or 2 knives, cut in butter until mixture resembles coarse crumbs.*  In cup combine egg yolks and water.  Sprinkle over pastry, tossing with a fork until pastry holds together.  Shape into a ball.  Wrap in plastic wrap and refrigerate at least 30 minutes.  Meanwhile preheat  oven to  350⁰F.

In skillet combine ½ cup sugar and 4 tablespoons butter; cook over medium heat, stirring, until sugar dissolves.  Continue cooking until syrup is a deep caramel color.  Place apples on syrup in skillet and cook until liquid from apples has evaporated. While cooking, roll out piecrust into circle large enough to cover skillet.  Place over skillet after liquid has evaporated, trim off excess crust, and place in oven.  Bake approximately 50 to 55 minutes, or until crust is browned and apples are tender.  Cool on wire rack.  Carefully invert onto a serving plate.  MAKES 6-8 SERVINGS.

*Alternatively, process in a food processor fitted with a steel blade.*

# Karen's Vermouth Cake

1 French Vanilla Cake Mix, prepared according to directions & baked in round layers
1 Small Package Vanilla Instant Pudding Mix, prepared to instructions, substituting heavy cream in place of milk.
1 Cup Raspberry Jam, strained to eliminate seeds
¼ Cup Sweet Vermouth
1 Dark Chocolate Frosting Mix, ready to spread or Quick Chocolate Ganache*

Split cake layers in half. Sprinkle each layer with 1 tablespoon of sweet vermouth. Place bottom layer on plate. Spread thinly with strained raspberry jam. Spread thinly with chilled pudding mix (except for top layer). Repeat until all layers are filled and placed one on top of the other (top layer will be frosted). Frost cake with ready to spread frosting and refrigerate until ready to serve and refrigerate any unused portion. SERVES 12.

## *QUICK CHOCOLATE GANACHE
3 Cups Chocolate Chips
2 Cups Whipping Cream

Melt together, Beat well. If too stiff, add additional cream. Store in refrigerator but bring to room temperature before using.

*A variation of a recipe we got from a Tucson restaurant years ago. A real favorite!*

Karen's Vermouth Cake

# Sal's Lemon Pudding

| | |
|---|---|
| 3 Tablespoons Butter | 2 Tablespoons Lemon Zest |
| 1 Cup Sugar | ¼ Cup Salt |
| 4 Egg Yolks | 1 Cup Milk |
| 3 Tablespoons Flour | ¼ Cup Toasted Almond Slices |
| ⅓ Cup Lemon Juice | 4 Egg Whites |

Preheat oven to 350°F. Cream butter and sugar; add egg yolks and beat well. Add flour, lemon juice, lemon zest, and salt, mix well. Stir in milk. Blend in almonds. Beat egg whites until form stiff peaks and fold into mixture. Pour into a 9-inch square baking dish sprayed with pan release. Place baking dish in a pan and fill with hot water half way up the side of baking dish. Place in oven and bake at 350°F for 20 minutes. Lower temperature to 325°F and bake an additional 20 minutes. Serve immediately. SERVES 8-10.

# Blackberry Tart

1 Package Pie Crust Mix

¾ Cup (1½ sticks) Butter

3 Extra Large Eggs

1 Cup Sugar

5 Tablespoons Flour

1 Teaspoon Vanilla Extract

5 Tablespoons Red Currant Or Grape Jelly

4 Cups Fresh Blackberries Or Frozen Unsweetened Blackberries, thawed & drained well

Whipping Cream

Prepare piecrust mix according to directions, roll out to a ⅛-inch thickness, and fit into a 9-inch tart pan with removable bottom. Place in refrigerator while preparing filling. Preheat oven to 350°F.

FILLING: Cook butter in heavy small saucepan over medium heat until melted and golden brown. Blend eggs and sugar in large bowl. Add flour and vanilla and whisk just until combined. Whisk in butter. Set tart shell on a heavy baking sheet. Pour filling into tart shell. Bake until pastry and filling are golden brown, 30 to 35 minutes. Transfer tart to wire rack and cool completely. Melt jelly in heavy small saucepan over low heat. Brush 2 tablespoons jelly over filling in tart shell. Set blackberries atop tart, covering filling completely. Brush remaining jelly over berries. Let stand until jelly sets. Serve with whipped cream. SERVES 8-10.

Wine Recommendation:
Ruby Port (Graham's Six Grapes)
U.S. Black Muscat dessert wine (Quady Elysium)

# Cranberry Ice Milk With Raspberry Sauce

2  Cups Unsweetened Apple Juice

1  12-Ounce Bag Fresh Cranberries, rinsed & sorted

½  Cup Sugar

1  Cinnamon Stick

1  Cup Milk

Combine first 4 ingredients in heavy saucepan over low heat and simmer until cranberries pop and mixture thickens slightly, stirring occasionally, about 10 to 15 minutes.  Cool slightly; remove cinnamon stick.  Strain mixture through sieve into bowl, pressing to extract as much pulp as possible.  Cool completely.  Cover and refrigerate until well chilled.  (Can be prepared 1 day ahead.)  Stir milk into cranberry puree.  Transfer to ice-cream maker and freeze according to manufacturer's directions.  Scoop ice milk into airtight container.  Freeze at least 3 hours or overnight.  Spoon Raspberry Sauce (see recipe on page 208) into dessert bowls.  Top with scoops of ice milk and serve.  MAKES 6 SERVINGS.

# Cheesecake Tartlets

1  Cup Graham Cracker Crumbs (8 Graham Crackers, crushed)

5  Tablespoons Butter, softened

Combine and place in 6 individual tart pans that have been coated with pan release spray.  Press down firmly on bottom and up sides of each pan.  Place on a cookie sheet and chill well.

Preheat oven to 375ºF.

### IN A FOOD PROCESSOR COMBINE:

1  8-Ounce Package Cream Cheese

⅓  Cup Sugar

1  Egg

2  Tablespoons Flour

2  Teaspoons Lemon Juice

½  Teaspoon Vanilla

Blend until thoroughly combined, pour into the 6 tart shells (should fill each about ¾ full).  Place in oven and bake approximately 10 minutes, or until puffed.  Do not overcook!  Place in refrigerator and chill about 3 hours.  Using a thin bladed knife, loosen edges of each tart and slide onto individual plates.  Before serving, spread with your choice of Lemon Curd, Peach or Apricot Preserves, Fresh Raspberries or, thin sliced Strawberries.  SERVES 6.

HARSHAW TOWNSITE
CORONADO NATIONAL FOREST
ELEVATION 4850

*Miscellaneous*

# Tomato Sorbet

3½  Cups Tomato Puree
2¼  Cups Simple Sugar Syrup (see recipe on page 205)
Juice Of 2 Lemons, or to taste
Dash Of Tabasco
Salt

Puree tomato in food processor (not too much or it will become milky).  Press puree through sieve and discard solids.  Mix puree, syrup, lemon juice, and Tabasco together and season with salt to taste.  Cover, freeze partially, remove from freezer, beat, and return to freezer.  When ready to serve, use small ice cream scoop to make small rounds, 2 to 3, and serve garnished with mint.  MAKES 1½ QUARTS.

# Fruit Sorbets

3¼  Cups Fruit Puree
1½  Cups Simple Sugar Syrup (see recipe on page 205)

Combine, mix thoroughly, freeze partially, remove and beat, and return to freezer.  Serve in small rounds garnished with mint.  MAKES 1 QUART.

# Iced Cappuccino

3  Cups Strong Coffee
2  Cups Half & Half
2  Tablespoons Sugar
3  Tablespoons Chocolate Syrup

Mix well and refrigerate.  Serve over crushed ice.  Should re-mix before serving as chocolate has a tendency to settle out.  MAKES 5 CUPS.

# Cranberry Butter

¾  Cups Cranberries      2  Teaspoons Lemon Zest
6  Tablespoons Powdered Sugar      1  Cup Unsalted Butter (2 sticks)

Coarsely chop cranberries with sugar and lemon zest in food processor using pulsing action (on/off).  Add butter and blend until mixture is combined but slightly chunky.  MAKES 2 CUPS.

*miscellaneous*

# Tomato Pear Chutney

2 Pounds Tomatoes, coarsely chopped in food processor
2 Pounds Firm Ripe Pears, cored & coarsely chopped in food processor
2 Large Green Or Red Bell Peppers, seeded & chopped in food processor
2 Cups Brown Sugar, firmly packed
1 Cup White Vinegar
2 Teaspoons Salt
1 Teaspoon Ground Ginger
1 Teaspoon Dry Mustard
¼ Teaspoon Cayenne
¾ Cup Crystallized Ginger, coarsely chopped
¼ Cup Pimento Or Additional Red Bell Pepper, diced

Tomatoes and pears should equal 8 cups. Place in a 5-quart pot with peppers, sugar, vinegar, salt, mustard, and cayenne. Bring to boil over high heat. Reduce heat and boil gently until thickened slightly, stirring often, about 1 hour. Stir in ginger and boil gently, stirring often till thickened, about 15 minutes. Ladle into clean canning jars, wiping lip before applying lids. Tighten lid and process for 20 minutes. After cooling make, sure each jar has a secure vacuum seal. MAKES 12 CUPS.

# Maple Whipped Cream

1 Cup Chilled Whipping Cream    3 Tablespoons Pure Maple Syrup

Whip cream with syrup in a large bowl until soft peaks form. MAKES 2 CUPS.

# Bourbon Cranberry Sauce

1 Pound Cranberries (about 4 cups)    ¼ Teaspoon Ground Cinnamon
2 Cups Sugar    ¼ Cup Bourbon

Preheat oven to 350⁰F. Combine first 3 ingredients in a 9 x 13-inch baking dish. Cover tightly with foil and bake until cranberries are tender and sugar is dissolved, stirring once, about 1 hour. Remove from oven and stir in bourbon. Refrigerate cranberry sauce until well chilled. *(Can be prepared 5-7 days ahead.)* Transfer to bowl and serve. MAKES 4½ CUPS.

# Simple Sugar Syrup

1 Cup Sugar    ½ Cup Water

Bring to a boil and boil until sugar is dissolved (syrupy). Cool slightly and pour into a clean jar, cover, label with contents and date, and refrigerate until ready to use. MAKES 1 CUP.

# Spicy Coriander Sauce

⅓ Cup Olive Oil

3 Tablespoons White Wine Vinegar

½ Teaspoon Salt

¼ Teaspoon Freshly Ground Pepper

½ Cup Fresh Coriander (cilantro) Leaves, chopped

¼ Cup Onion, minced

1 Teaspoon Dried Red Pepper Flakes

Whisk, oil, vinegar, salt, and pepper together in a small bowl. Stir in coriander leaves, onion, and pepper flakes. Let stand until ready to serve (at least 1 hour). MAKES APPROXIMATELY 1 CUP.

# Scottish Marmalade

1 Large Grapefruit

1 Large Orange

3 Lemons

6 Cups Water

6 Cups Sugar

Using vegetable peeler, remove peel (colored part only) in strips from grapefruit, orange, and lemons. Cut strips into small pieces. Cut off white pith from all fruit. Cut fruit into ¼-inch thick slices. Combine chopped peel, fruit, and water in a heavy large pot. Bring to a boil, stirring frequently. Reduce heat, cover, and simmer until fruit mixture is very soft, stirring frequently, about 50 minutes. Add sugar and stir to dissolve. Increase heat and boil until candy thermometer registers 220°F, stirring frequently, about 45 minutes.

Spoon marmalade into clean hot canning jars to within ¼-inch of the top. Immediately wipe rim clean using towel dipped into hot water. Place lid on jar; seal tightly. Repeat with remaining marmalade and jars. Arrange jars in large pot. Cover with boiling water with at least 1½ inches above top of lids. Cover pot and boil for 15 minutes. Remove jars from water bath. Place upside down and allow to cool. Press center of each lid down, should not flex or spring back. If it does not flex or spring back, store in cool dry place for up to a year. If lid flexes and/or springs back, refrigerate. Refrigerate marmalade after opening. MAKES 4 CUPS.

# Vanilla

In a clean bottle (approximately 1½ cups) place 2 vanilla beans. Fill bottle with brandy (does not have to be expensive brandy) and allow to steep at least 1 month, 3 to 4 months are preferable. Keep 2 to 3 bottles going and refill with brandy as vanilla is used up.

# Spiced Cranberry — Orange Sauce

1½  Cups Dried Cherries
1½  Cups Dried Cranberries
2  Cups Fresh Cranberries
2  Cups Sugar
½  Cup Crystallized Ginger, coarsely chopped
1¼  Cups Fresh Orange Juice
2  Tablespoons Lemon Zest, finely grated
2  Large Cinnamon Sticks
⅔  Cup Red Wine

In a heavy, large, non-reactive pan, combine all ingredients and bring to a boil over moderately high heat.  Reduce heat to moderate and cook, stirring occasionally, until cranberries pop.  Transfer to a refrigerator container and let cool. Cover and refrigerate.  Remove cinnamon sticks before beginning to serve.  MAKES 6 CUPS.

# Roasted Red Pepper — Tomato Sauce

3  Cups Roasted Red Peppers, ½ pureed & ½ chopped finely
2  Cups Tomato Sauce
4  Cloves Garlic, pureed with roasted peppers
1  Tablespoon Onion Powder
1  Teaspoon Crushed Red Pepper Flakes
Salt & Freshly Ground Pepper, to taste

Blend all ingredients together in a medium saucepan and heat to boiling.  Reduce heat to low and simmer 10 minutes. If sauce becomes to thick, add dry vermouth to reach desired consistency.  MAKES 4 CUPS.

# Cranberry Pesto

2  Cloves Garlic, peeled
1  Teaspoon Salt
1  Cup Basil Leaves, tightly packed
1  Cup Dried Cranberries
2  Tablespoons Chopped Walnuts
½  Cup Olive Oil
½  Cup Grated Parmesan Cheese
3  Tablespoons Butter, softened

Place the first five ingredients in the work bowl of a food processor.  With metal blade, pulse until very finely and evenly chopped.  Add olive oil, Parmesan cheese, and butter and pulse to the consistency of a paste.  Store in a covered container in refrigerator.  MAKES 2 CUPS.

# Strawberry Sauce

1  12-Ounce Package Frozen Unsweetened Strawberries, thawed
3  Tablespoons Sugar
1  Tablespoon Fresh Lemon Juice

Puree berries with sugar and juice in processor.  Strain through sieve to eliminate seeds, pressing to extract as much pulp as possible.  Cover and refrigerate until well chilled.  (*Can be prepared 2 days ahead.*)  MAKES ABOUT 1½ CUPS.

# Raspberry Sauce

1  12-Ounce Package Frozen Unsweetened Raspberries, thawed
½  Cup Water
3  Tablespoons Sugar
1  Tablespoon Fresh Lemon Juice

Puree raspberries with remaining ingredients in processor.  Strain through sieve into bowl to eliminate seeds, pressing to extract as much pulp as possible.  Cover and refrigerate until chilled.  (*Can be prepared 2 days ahead.*)  MAKES ABOUT 1¼ CUPS.

# Tomato Vinaigrette

⅔  Cup Canola Oil
⅓  Cup Cider Vinegar
1  Clove Garlic, peeled & finely chopped
½  Onion, finely minced
3  Roma Tomatoes, chopped fine in food processor
2  Tablespoons Fresh Basil, finely chopped
Salt & Pepper, to taste

Mix all ingredients together well and store in refrigerator.  MAKES 2 CUPS.

# Balsamic — Mustard Seed Vinaigrette

⅓  Cup Balsamic Vinegar
1  Tablespoon Yellow Mustard Seeds
¾  Cup Olive Oil

Stir together the vinegar and mustard seeds in a small bowl.  Let stand about 45 minutes.  Whisk in the oil.  Store in a covered container in refrigerator for up to 1 week.  MAKES 1¼ CUPS.

# Chile Vinaigrette

1 Cup Canola Oil
½ Cup Cider Vinegar
2 Teaspoons Crushed Red Chile Flakes
1 Teaspoon Garlic Salt
1 Teaspoon Scallions, finely chopped

Whisk all ingredients together until well combined. Refrigerate until ready to use. MAKES 1½ CUPS.

# Jalapeño — Tomato Vinaigrette

4 Tomatoes
2 Cloves Garlic
1 Small Red Onion
2 Jalapeño Peppers
1 Cup Fresh Mint Leaves, minced
1 Cup Fresh Cilantro Leaves, minced
2 Tablespoons Red Wine Vinegar
2 Tablespoons Olive Oil
Salt & Fresh Ground Pepper

Peel, seed, and coarsely chop the tomatoes and put into a large bowl. Peel and mince the garlic and onion. Stem, seed, and mince the jalapeños. Mince the mint and cilantro. Add the garlic, onions, jalapeños, mint, and cilantro to the bowl with the tomatoes. Stir in vinegar, oil, and 1½ teaspoons salt and let stand at room temperature, stirring once or twice, for at least 45 minutes. Store covered, in refrigerator for 1 day. MAKES 1¼ CUPS.

# Citrus Vinaigrette

1 Cup Olive Oil
¼ Cup Rice Vinegar
2 Tablespoons Lemon Juice
Salt & Pepper

In a food processor work bowl, combine olive oil, rice vinegar, and lemon juice. Blend in processor until completely combined. Salt and pepper to taste. Cover and refrigerate until ready to use. MAKES 1¼ CUPS.

# Oregano Dressing

½  Cup Fresh Oregano Leaves Or Marjoram Leaves

2  Cloves Garlic

1  Egg

3  Tablespoons Red Wine Vinegar

Salt & Fresh Ground Pepper

1  Cup Olive Oil

Stem oregano to make ½ cup leaves.  In the bowl of a food processor, combine the oregano, garlic, egg, vinegar, 1 teaspoon salt, and ¼ teaspoon pepper and process until smooth, about I minute.  With the motor still running, add the oil in a slow thin stream.  Adjust seasoning to taste and refrigerate.  MAKES 1½ CUPS.

# Mustard Dressing

1  Tablespoon White Wine Vinegar

⅓  Cup Whole-Grain Mustard

Salt & Fresh Ground Pepper

½  Cup Corn Oil

In a small bowl whisk together the vinegar, mustard, and ¼ teaspoon salt.  Whisk in the oil, a little at a time.  MAKES APPROXIMATELY 1 CUP.

# Soy – Ginger Vinaigrette

¼ Cup Sesame Seeds, toasted

2 Tablespoons Soy Sauce

1 Tablespoon Sesame Oil

¼ Seasoned Rice Wine Vinegar

1 Tablespoon Fresh Ginger, minced finely

1 Teaspoon Dry Mustard

1 Teaspoon Worcestershire

1 Cup Canola Oil

Place all ingredients in a jar with a tight lid. Shake well and refrigerate until ready to use. Shake well before serving. MAKES 1½ CUPS.

# Garam Masala

*(A spice blend used in Northern India)*

1 Tablespoon Whole Cumin Seeds
1 Tablespoon Whole Coriander Seeds
1 Tablespoon Whole Cardamom Seeds
½ Cinnamon Stick
1½ Tablespoons Black Peppercorns
½ Teaspoon Whole Cloves

Put the spices in a non-stick skillet and toast until fragrant and lightly colored, about 3 minutes. Cool and grind in a coffee grinder or with a mortar and pestle. Transfer to a jar with an airtight lid. (Can store up to 3 months.) MAKES ¼ CUP.

# Lemon Curd

Zest Of 2 Lemons
¾ Cup Lemon Juice, freshly squeezed
⅞ Cup Sugar
¾ Cup Butter
5 Egg Yolks
½ Teaspoon Vanilla
¼ Cup Water

Put all ingredients into the top of a double boiler. The water should be just simmering so that you do not overcook the eggs. Stirring constantly, cook until the mixture thickens. This will take 20 to 25 minutes. Ladle into hot jars, clean rims, and seal with hot lids. MAKES 4 HALF-PINT JARS.

# Chardonnay Sauce

½ Cup Chardonnay Wine
¾ Cup Heavy Cream
1 Tablespoon Hot Mustard
1 Tablespoon Dijon Mustard
Salt & Fresh Ground Pepper

Heat wine in small pan over high heat 1 to 2 minutes to burn off alcohol. In a second pan, over medium high heat, reduce cream by ½. Add wine and mustards to cream and whisk until well blended. Season to taste with salt and pepper. MAKES ¾ CUP.

# Parsley Cream Sauce

| | |
|---|---|
| 1 Cup Chicken Broth | ¾ Stick Unsalted Butter |
| ¼ Cup Whipping Cream | 1 Tablespoon Fresh Parsley, minced |

In heavy small saucepan boil broth and cream until reduced to ⅓ cup, 15 minutes.  Gradually whisk in the butter.  Stir in parsley.  Season with salt and pepper.  MAKES ¾ CUP.

# Parmesan Crisps (Chips)

*These make great garnishes for salads, soups or just for snacking.*

Line a flat baking sheet with parchment.  Place approximately 2 tablespoons shredded Parmesan cheese in mounds at even intervals on the sheet.  Flatten with your hand making sure none overlap.  Bake at 350ºF until melted and lightly browned around edges.  Allow to cool completely before removing.  Store in an airtight container.  MAKES 12-15.

# Compound Butter

1 Cup Butter (2 cubes), at room temperature
¼ Fresh Thyme Leaves, stripped from stems
(Can substitute parsley, basil, tarragon, oregano or a combination of herbs.
For Chile Butter Substitute 1 Tablespoon Chile Powder)
6 Garlic Cloves, peeled
½ Teaspoon Each Of Salt & Pepper

Place the butter in a food processor fitted with a steel blade.  Add the thyme, garlic, salt, and pepper; process until well combined.  Place a sheet of plastic wrap on a work surface.  Scrape contents of work bowl onto plastic wrap.  Wrap long ends over and rolling at the same time, shape into a log approximately 1 inch in diameter.  Wrap completely in plastic wrap, label, and store in the refrigerator until ready to use.  MAKES 1¼ CUPS.

# Roasted Garlic/Garlic Oil

20-30 Cloves Fresh Garlic, peeled, trimmed, rinsed with fresh water & drained

Dry garlic thoroughly.  Place in a 13 x 9-inch flat roasting pan.  Pout in enough olive oil to submerge garlic completely.  Place in a 350ºF oven and roast, uncovered, till cloves float and are slightly browned.  Remove from oven and allow to cool.

Pour oil through a strainer into a measuring cup.  Put garlic in a bowl, cover with plastic wrap, and refrigerate till ready to use.  Pour into an airtight bottle or jar and refrigerate for use as needed.  MAKES 6-8 CUPS OIL.

# Cinnamon Whipped Cream

1½ Cups Whipping Cream
¼ Cup Sugar
1 Teaspoon Cinnamon

Using a mixer equipped with a deep mixing bowl and a whisk attachment beat the cream on high speed till soft peaks form. Combine sugar and cinnamon and add, while beating, to whipped cream; continue beating until stiff peaks form. Place in a smaller container, cover tightly, and store till ready to use. MAKES 3 CUPS.

# Herbed Butter

1 Cube (3 tablespoons) Unsalted Butter
1 Tablespoon Chives, chopped
1 Tablespoon Thyme, chopped
1 Tablespoon Parsley, chopped
1 Teaspoon Cracked Black Peppercorns

Bring butter to room temperature. Place in bowl of food processor along with chopped herbs. Process by pulsing till butter and herbs are well combined. MAKES 6 SERVINGS FOR STEAKS OR FISH.

# Capered Salsa

*For Grilled Fish Or Sautéed Chicken*

6 Roma Tomatoes, diced in ¼" dice
1 Small Red Onion, diced in ¼" dice
2 Tablespoons Capers
½ Teaspoon Garlic Salt, or to taste
⅛ Teaspoon Fresh Ground Pepper
¼ Cup Lemon Juice
¼ Cup Olive Oil

Mix well. Store in refrigerator. MAKES 1½ CUPS.

# Tomato Roses

*Beautiful as garnishes, especially with a sprig of fresh basil.*

Wash tomato.  Using a sharp, thin bladed knife, beginning at the bottom of tomato, cut a thin slice across bottom, being careful not to cut completely through.  Begin slicing skin away from tomato in a circular motion, rotating tomato, until reaching top.  Rewind skin to make a "rose."

# Pico De Gallo

10  Large Tomatoes, diced to ¼" dice
10  Canned Green Chiles, diced to ¼"
3  Large Red Onions, diced to ¼"
1¼  Teaspoon Garlic Salt
⅔  Teaspoon Red Pepper Flakes
10  Limes, juice only
1¼  Cup Olive Oil

Combine all ingredients and mix well.  Cover and store in refrigerator till ready to use.  Keeps 3 to 5 days.
MAKES 2½ QUARTS.

# Karen's Fresh Tomato Salsa

3  Medium Ripe Tomatoes, quartered & drained
1  Clove Garlic, quartered
1  Jalapeño Pepper, seeded & quartered
1  Small Can Green Chiles, diced
½  Red Onion, quartered
1  Tablespoon Cilantro
2  Tablespoons Lime Juice, freshly squeezed
2  Tablespoons Balsamic Vinegar
½  Teaspoon Salt
¼  Teaspoon Pepper

Using a food processor equipped with a metal blade, place onions, and garlic in work bowl and pulse 2 to 3 times for 10 to 15 seconds each until you have a medium/fine chop.  Add tomatoes and jalapeño; pulse 2 to 3 times until coarsely chopped.  Add cilantro and green chiles and pulse 2 to 3 times until finely chopped.  Remove from work bowl to large mixing bowl, add remaining ingredients, and mix well.  The flavor will meld together if the salsa is stored in the refrigerator overnight before using.  MAKES 1½ CUPS.

*Index*

*Karen's Fine Foods are available by mail order from:*

KAREN'S FINE FOODS
584 E. Squirrel Tail Drive
Tucson, AZ 85704
Phone: 520.544.0986
E-mail: tkcallagha@aol.com

*Karen's Fine Foods are also available at these locations:*

TABLE TALK
2936 E. Broadway
Tucson, AZ 85716
520.881.3322

TABLE TALK
7001 N. Oracle Rd.
Tucson, AZ 85704
520.297.5658

KAREN'S WINE COUNTRY CAFE
P.O. Box 1299
Sonoita, AZ 85637
520.455.5282

TABLE TALK
6842 E. Tanque Verde Rd.
Tucson, AZ 85715
520.886.8433

MARIPOSA BOOKS & MORE
307 McKeown Ave.
Patagonia, AZ 85624
520.394.9186

## A GREAT GIFT IDEA:

# *Sonoita Seasons*
### *Recipes from Karen's Wine Country Café in Sonoita, Arizona*

If you'd like to order a copy of SONOITA SEASONS, please send a check for $34.95 ($29.95 plus $5.00 shipping/handling) to SONOITA SEASONS, P.O. Box 530, Sonoita, AZ 85637. Be sure to include your return address with the check. If this is a gift, please specify name and mailing address of recipient, and we'll send a SONOITA SEASONS Cook Book directly to them with a gift card. Please indicate what message you would like placed with the card.